CHRISTIANITY, ISLAM, AND ATHEISM

William Kilpatrick

CHRISTIANITY, ISLAM, AND ATHEISM

The Struggle for the Soul of the West

IGNATIUS PRESS   SAN FRANCISCO

Except where noted, all quotes from the Koran are from
the translation by N.J. Dawood
published in 2000 by Penguin Books, London
© 2000 by N.J. Dawood
Used with permission

Unless otherwise noted, Scripture quotations (except those within citations) have
been taken from the Revised Standard Version of the Holy Bible, Second Catholic
Edition, © 2006. The Revised Standard Version of the Holy Bible: the Old
Testament, © 1952, 2006; the Apocrypha, © 1957, 2006; the New Testament,
© 1946, 2006; the Catholic Edition of the Old Testament, incorporating the
Apocrypha, © 1966, 2006, the Catholic Edition of the New Testament, © 1965,
2006 by the Division of Christian Education of the National Council of the
Churches of Christ in the United States of America.
All rights reserved

Cover photograph:
"God is Great" on minaret, Kurdistan, Iraq
© iStockphoto

Cover design by Roxanne Mei Lum

Published 2012 by Ignatius Press, San Francisco
© 2012 by William Kilpatrick
All rights reserved
ISBN 978-1-58617-696-9
Library of Congress Control Number 2012936911
Printed in the United States of America ∞

CONTENTS

INTRODUCTION

Christians in the Muslim world face daily persecution. In some places they are threatened with extinction. Will Christians in Europe and America someday find themselves in the same precarious position that Christians in Egypt, Pakistan, and Iraq now occupy? That will depend on whether they wake up and defend their freedom while they still can.

Muslim persecution of Christians has increased dramatically in recent years. One of the main reasons for this is that, in failing to understand Islam, Western countries have helped to unleash the antagonism toward non-Muslims that lies at the heart of the Islamic faith. For the better part of the twentieth century, secular, despotic governments in the Middle East and in other Muslim regions acted as a restraining force on the more violent manifestations of Islam. Then, starting with the ouster of the shah of Iran in 1979, the situation began to change. Secular strongmen were pushed aside or eliminated, and traditional Islam was able to reassert itself. Western nations played a large part in this transformation. They encouraged, supported, and sometimes actively participated in the overthrow of autocratic rulers with the naïve confidence that democracy would usher in an "Arab Spring", that is, a blossoming of human rights and liberties. But the overthrow of the shah in Iran, of Hussein in Iraq, of Mubarak in Egypt, and of Gadhafi in Libya didn't have the expected result—neither did free elections in Gaza, Lebanon, and Turkey. Many Muslims in the Middle East, North Africa, and parts of Asia have become more radicalized and more dangerous, with the result that the future of the non-Muslim population in those areas hangs by a thread. Christians in many predominately Muslim regions now live in a nightmare world of beatings, abductions, rape, imprisonment, torture, looting of shops, and burning of churches.

"My people are destroyed for lack of knowledge", said the prophet Hosea (Hos 4:6). Western lack of knowledge about Islam is not the only reason Christians in the East are being destroyed, but it is a contributing factor. A basic knowledge of Islam would include the fact that it requires the ultimate subjugation of other religions. Moreover, even a cursory glance at Islam's founding document, the Koran, reveals a pronounced disdain for non-Muslims. One of the main reasons for Western ignorance of these facts is that they conflict with one of the most cherished of contemporary Western beliefs: the belief in the benefits of cultural diversity. Paradoxically, this belief rests on a deeper conviction that differences between peoples are in reality only surface phenomena—that although cultures and religions appear to be diverse, they are actually very much the same. Although Islam appears to be different, it must, according to this view, be just like other religions. What appear to be differences are only misunderstandings, and facts that don't support this claim are routinely ignored or suppressed. For this reason, most of the atrocities committed against Christians by Muslims receive very little media attention. When the facts can't be ignored, they are often misrepresented. Thus, attacks on Christians by Muslims are described by the media as "sectarian strife" or as "clashes" between Christians and Muslims.

A carefully guarded ignorance about Islam is widespread in the Western world, and if Western citizens choose to remain in the dark, the problems faced by Christians in Muslim lands could soon become our problems. Europe is already well along the road to Islamization, due in part to immigration and high Muslim birthrates, but also due to strictly enforced speech rules. In several European countries, telling the truth about Islam is a crime. Although further behind, America is on the same road as Europe. The extent of Islamic penetration of our institutions is far greater than most Americans realize, but the mainstream media, along with courts, universities, and various politicians, have been quite willing to obscure this reality.

In some cases this suppression of the facts is conscious and deliberate, but in many cases it's the result of garden-variety group think. Journalists, for example, tend to come from similar backgrounds and attend the same schools of journalism. They belong to a circle of like-minded people among whom certain thoughts are automatically affirmed, while others are automatically excluded. Many of the information gatekeepers sincerely believe the propaganda generated by Islamic apologists because it fits comfortably into their pre-existing thought world. When it comes to covering Islam, they are club reporters, not cub reporters. As Rifqa Bary said to a group of reporters covering her story, "You guys don't understand." She might more accurately have said, "You won't understand."

Who is Rifqa Bary? That her story received only grudging coverage might serve as an illustration of how effectively negative information about Islam is controlled. Bary, a Muslim girl living with her parents in Ohio, had secretly converted to Christianity at the age of fifteen. When her parents discovered the truth two years later, Bary, fearing for her life, fled to Florida, to the home of a Christian pastor and his wife with whom she had been in communication. A court battle ensued and eventually resulted in her return to Ohio, but not to her parents. Rather, she was put under the protection of Ohio social services until she reached eighteen, the age of legal emancipation.

Much of the court battle revolved around the question of whether Bary was in any danger from her parents. Her defense argued that Islamic law requires the death penalty for apostates and that her parents would be expected to carry out the execution in order to cleanse their honor. This is what Bary tearfully told Florida reporters:

> I don't know if you know about honor killing. . . . You guys don't understand. Islam is very different than you guys think. They have to kill me. My blood is now *halal*, which means that because I am now a Christian, I'm from a Muslim background, it's an honor. If they love God more than me, they have to do this. And I'm fighting for my life, you guys don't understand. You don't understand.[1]

Most of the media coverage, however, suggested that Bary was the one who had misunderstood her religion, that what she asserted couldn't possibly be the case. Her claim flew in the face of the established narrative that Islam was a religion of peace and justice. The murder of apostates simply didn't fit into the narrative.

If the reporters covering the case had done their homework, they would have discovered that there is an almost universal consensus among Muslim scholars that male apostates must be killed, although many Muslim authorities hold that female apostates need only be imprisoned until they repent and reconvert. Bary was aware of the lesser punishment, but she also knew that Islamic law allows Muslim men to take matters into their own hands when it comes to their wayward daughters. "Either they do that [kill me]," she said, "or they send me back to Sri Lanka. There is an asylum there where they put people like me."[2]

Even though the killing or imprisoning of Muslim converts to Christianity has become more and more common in Muslim communities, the plight of Rifqa Bary didn't fit into the prevailing consensus about Islam, so the majority of reporters decided to frame the story in terms with which they were more familiar. Thus, after the story was processed through the media's mental sorting machine, Rifqa Bary was cast as an over-excitable American teenager who had a squabble with her parents and ran away from home. Multiply the misreporting of Bary's story a thousand times, and you'll have a rough idea of the amount of distortion and misinformation that surrounds one of the main issues of our time.

This book is intended, in part, as a wake-up call. That in itself is revealing. It's amazing that eleven years after 9/11 and eighteen thousand terrorist attacks later, wake-up calls are still needed. Yet the majority of people in the West still do not seem to have grasped the supremacist nature of Islam, let alone the threat it poses to them.

What is it that has served to delay that awakening? As I've said, part of the responsibility lies with the Western faith in cultural equivalence. Any evidence that Islam is markedly warlike and intolerant would undermine the doctrine that all cultures and religions are roughly equal. Consequently, Western societies have ignored and even suppressed the facts about Islam and the important differences between it and Christianity.

Unfortunately, many Christians have also fallen into the habit of ignoring the differences. The Islamic faith is founded on a blunt rejection of basic Christian beliefs, but you would hardly know it from reading official Church statements or from listening to leading prelates. Instead of informing their flocks that Islam rejects Christ and requires its faithful to work toward the eventual subjugation of Christians, many Christian leaders have been more intent on emphasizing the common ground that Christians and Muslims share. For example, the Second Vatican Council's declaration *Nostra Aetate* focuses almost exclusively on the similarities between Muslims and Christians. That approach was in keeping with the spirit of change and openness that marked the Council; moreover, it seemed to fit with the prevailing circumstances in the Muslim world at the time. The search for shared beliefs and values arose at a time when the militant side of Islam was kept firmly in check by secular rulers. But it now seems that the Islamic world the Council Fathers were familiar with was an aberration—a brief departure from the path laid out by Muhammad when he called for Muslims to make the whole world submit to Allah.

During the 1960s, Westernized and secularized Egyptians could laugh along with President Nasser when, speaking before a large assembly, he related how, years earlier, a Muslim Brotherhood leader had demanded that he enforce the wearing of the hijab, the head scarf traditionally worn by Muslim women. Nasser replied, "Sir ... you cannot make one girl, your own daughter, wear it, and yet you want me to go and make ten million women wear it?"[3] Nasser's remarks brought a burst of applause and laughter from the audience; but, as is now evident, the wearing of the hijab is no longer a laughing matter in Egypt, and the Muslim Brotherhood, the butt of Nasser's joke, is now the dominant political force there.

Many Christians still hope that Muslims and Christians can unite in a common front against atheism and aggressive secularism, but that spirit of cooperation and mutual respect is not shared by many of Islam's religious leaders. The situation that prevailed in the Muslim world at the time of the Second Vatican Council is rapidly disappearing. The face of Islam that now presents itself very much resembles the supremacist religion that once threatened Christendom. In light of this development, it now seems that the common-ground thesis is overdue for a reexamination.

Tolerance needs to be balanced with justice, and justice seems to require that Christians be provided with a fuller account of Islam—if for no other reason than that their survival may depend on that knowledge. Although there is some common ground between Christianity and Islam—as there is some common ground among all religions—it might be wise to start looking at some of the profound differences between the two faiths. For example, because jihad is not an interior spiritual struggle as many have been led to believe, but rather a serious obligation to subdue non-Muslims, a lot of Western Christians are going to be woefully unprepared for the kinds of things that are already happening to Christians in Egypt, Iraq, Iran, Pakistan, Malaysia, Indonesia, Nigeria, and Sudan.

Being prepared is contingent on being informed, and many Western Christians are no better informed about Islamic beliefs than the pundits and politicians who, in the early months of 2011, predicted that an Arab spring was just around the corner. But finding a fuller account of Islam can be challenging for Christians because many authoritative Church sources are brief and incomplete. Take the *Catechism of the Catholic Church*, for example. Its statement about Muslims (it says nothing of Islam *per se*) is forty-four words in length, which is about eighty words less than the warning label on a bottle of Tylenol, and it contains no warnings, only the comforting assurance that "together with us they adore the one, merciful God." Well, yes, the Koran refers to God as "merciful", but Islam seems to have its own unique understanding of that word. For example, textbooks for tenth graders in Saudi Arabia instruct them on how to cut off the hand and foot of a thief (illustrations included) as prescribed in the Koran (5:33, 5:38).[4] It would be nice to think that this is only for the purpose of giving students a feel for the way things were done in Muhammad's day; but as a matter of fact, amputations (along with beheadings) are conducted on a weekly basis in public squares in Saudi Arabia. When the Saudis apply a procrustean solution to the misfits in their society, they do so in the literal sense of the term.

Christians have a procrustean problem of their own in regard to Islam. They have developed a habit of trying to force Islamic beliefs to fit into a bed of familiar and comfortable Christian assumptions. Thus, on the rare occasions when Christians hear anything about Islam, they are likely to hear that Muslims worship one God (just like us), that they hold to an Abrahamic faith (just like us), that they revere Jesus (just like us), honor Mary (just like us), and value the moral life (just like us). But trying to fit Islam into a preconceived Catholic/Christian format makes for a very rough fit, as I hope to make clear in the following pages.

An excessive emphasis on tolerance and sensitivity has resulted in a dangerous knowledge gap for Christians. Moreover, when Christians put tolerance above justice, they harm not only themselves, but Muslims as well. Christians need to ask whether the current conciliatory approach to Islam is just toward all those Muslims who suffer under the barbarities of sharia law. As has often been noted, the main victims of Islam are Muslims. Should Christians be more worried about offending the sensibilities of some Muslims, or should they be concerned about the men, women, and children who are oppressed by Islamic laws? Tolerance is fine up to a point, but as Thomas Mann observed, "Tolerance becomes a crime when applied to evil."

One thing seems clear. It is well past time for Christians to throw off their complacency and begin instead to think more deeply about what Islam is and what is at stake if we allow it to take root in our societies. And if Christians need to readjust their thinking, so too do

Muslims. It is ironic that our society, which believes so strongly in change, nevertheless insists on the unchangeability of other people's beliefs. It is one of the legacies of multiculturalism that we have come to believe that our own culture is infinitely malleable, while believing that non-Western cultures are immutable. Because we think Muslim beliefs can never be changed, we never suggest that they ought to be changed.

It seems time to chart a different course. Any adequate response to the threat from Islam will require us to push Muslims to rethink their faith on the most basic level. In this regard, critics of Islam tend to avoid the main question in favor of secondary questions. The secondary questions are: Is Islam a religion of peace? Is Islam compatible with modern values? Are women treated fairly under sharia law? The main question is: Did Muhammad actually receive a revelation from God? That is really the heart of the matter. As long as Muslims believe that Muhammad received his marching orders from God, the Islamic jihad will continue. But take away the divine mandate to subjugate everyone, and you take away the rationale for Islam's war against the world.

Because the driving force behind Islamic aggression is Islamic theology, we can no longer afford to treat Islamic theology as a protected species. Paradoxically, the best way to secure peace and, at the same time, to show our love for Muslims is to instill doubts about Islam in the minds of Muslims. At the same time, of course, we must make sure that we have something better to offer in its place.

Muhammad said that he came as a "warner". The pages ahead are a warning about the threat from the religion he founded. But this book is intended to serve as more than a wake-up call. Many others have discussed the dangers posed by Islam, but not many say what can be done about it. In addition to analyzing the threat, this book lays out the practical steps that both Christians and non-Christians can take to push back against the spread of Islam. At the same time, it offers guidelines for countering the efforts of Islam's many enablers in the West.

PART I

THE ISLAMIC THREAT

I

The Crisis of Faith

Among the banners that can be seen in various Muslim demonstrations in Europe is one that reads, "Islam—our religion today, your religion tomorrow". For anyone who follows the pronouncements of Islamic religious authorities around the world, there can be little doubt that this is their goal. In the seventh and eighth centuries, Islamic warriors subdued approximately half of the Christian world. Today, many Muslims consider that a job only half-done. The subordination of all people to Muslim rule is an objective that lies at the heart of traditional Islam.

How do Islamists hope to achieve this goal? One way is through violent jihad—the use of force against non-Muslims until they submit to Allah. The widespread persecution of Christians and Jews in Muslim lands is a glaring example of this form of jihad. Another tactic is stealth jihad—the incremental spread of Islamic law in Western societies through agitation and intimidation. How has the West responded? Murders of Christians in the thousands and even tens of thousands in Asia and Africa have been met with indifference, while the slightest insults to Islam—a mild cartoon, a misnamed teddy bear—have produced abject apologies and immediate concessions.

To add to the irony, the accelerating Islamic threat to non-Islamic religions has resulted not in a defense of those religions by Western elites, but in a stepped-up assault against them. After 9/11, celebrity atheists, with a good deal of media assist, launched an extensive propaganda war against religion in general and Christianity in particular. In recent years dozens of books have attacked Christianity not only as narrow-minded and intolerant, but also as a positive threat—maybe the biggest threat—to our society. A common theme of these attack books is that, if Christians aren't reined in, they will take over our society as the Taliban took over Afghanistan, and with much the same results.

Instead of taking the rise of fundamentalist Islam as an opportunity to rally behind Western values, critics of Christianity have taken it as an occasion to attack what is at the very core of their own civilization. They fail to understand that, if Christianity is pulled down, all the taken-for-granted values that are inextricably linked to Christianity will be pulled down with it. Freedom of speech and religion, equality for women, and even freedom from slavery—all these achievements can turn out to be temporary phenomena without the Christian soil that nourishes them.

With attacks on their faith coming from two fronts, one might expect to find Christians gearing up to defend themselves: a little more Scripture study here, a little more public engagement there, a bit more spirited response everywhere. But many Christians in America haven't faced up to the threat. Like many of their fellow citizens, they have been subjected to years of indoctrination in the fashionable ideology of multiculturalism. They are more afraid of breaking with politically correct protocols than of Muslim aggressiveness. Like many Americans, Christians haven't adjusted to the fact that we live in a new era—one governed by a new set of realities that can't be addressed or even understood within the already outdated framework of multiculturalism.

At every level of society, we continue to hear the same exhausted platitudes—about diversity's being our strength, about Islam as a religion of peace, about the shameful heritage of Christianity and the West. This apologetic attitude carries a steep price, because, as Islam expert Robert Spencer points out, "People who are ashamed of their own culture will not defend it." [1] And Christianity, more than anything else, is at the center of our culture's defense.

For proof, look at Europe, where Christianity has been disintegrating and taking European culture along with it. In Europe, Islam is the fastest-growing religion, and the rapid population shift in favor of Muslims has caused many Europeans to adopt an attitude of appeasement and even capitulation. After a Muslim radical murdered filmmaker Theo van Gogh, Dutch schoolchildren were forbidden to wear Dutch flags on their backpacks, lest Muslims find them provocative. [2] In Birmingham, England, Christian evangelists were warned by police that distributing Gospel leaflets in a Muslim area of the city would be considered a hate crime. [3] In Cheshire, England, two students were punished by their teacher for refusing to pray to Allah as part of their religious-education class. [4] According to a France 2 television documentary, all of the slaughterhouses in the greater Paris area now produce all of their meat in accordance with Islamic sharia law. The ritually slaughtered meat is not labeled as such and is being sold in French grocery stores and served in school cafeterias to an unwitting non-Muslim population.[5] These and countless other incidents of self-censorship and self-abasement bespeak not only a loss of cultural confidence but also a loss of population.

Over the last few decades, native Europeans have suffered a population decline of a magnitude that hasn't been seen since the Black Death wiped out a third of the continent's inhabitants. Muslims will eventually become dominant in Europe by the simple expedient of having more children than anyone else. And this Islamization won't take as long as some demographers think, because the population shifts already underway will be accelerated by emigration once it dawns on Harry that he might feel more comfortable in Brisbane than in Birmingham, or once Hendrik decides that he prefers the safety of Curacao to the scenery of Amsterdam. It's not necessary for Muslims to become a majority or anywhere near a majority in order for them to transform the face of Europe. All the evidence suggests that the tipping point comes long before that. Several European countries with less than a 5-percent Muslim population have already begun to cede control of their culture to Islam.

What is happening in Europe is due in large part to the abandonment of Christianity. This rejection was made explicit in 2003 when the European Union refused to acknowledge Europe's Christian roots in the preamble to the European Constitution, but it had been going on for years prior to that event. Church attendance in some countries has dropped to 5 percent; polls in Denmark reveal that only 9 percent of Danes say that religion is very important in their lives; in England, cathedrals have been converted into nightclubs; in Sweden, a Christian pastor was jailed for reiterating Christian teaching from the pulpit; in many parts of Europe, Christianity is the butt of crude caricatures and cartoons. Instead of resisting these trends, many European Christians became converts to a belief in the primacy of pleasure and convenience. As historian Bruce Thornton points out in *Decline and Fall*, Europe's spiritual decline is neatly captured in the opening of *La Dolce Vita*, Federico Fellini's aptly named film about postwar Italian decadence. The scene shows a helicopter carrying a dangling statue of Christ away from the modern residential district of Rome.[6]

The adoption of this *la dolce vita* mindset is one reason for Europe's precipitous drop in population. As Europeans started to lose their faith, they stopped having babies. They stopped having babies because they had nothing meaningful to pass on to the next generation—and also because babies get in the way of self-gratification. The decline of Christianity in Europe created a population vacuum and a spiritual vacuum, both of which Islam soon began to fill. If Christian faith had been more robust in Europe, it is unlikely that radical Islam would have advanced so far, so fast.

Will Americans learn the lesson of Europe? And will we learn it in time? It will be a close thing. That's because in a secular society, it's not easy to grasp the importance of the spiritual. Failing to grasp it, many Americans—even those who keep up with the news from across the Atlantic—assume that Islamization can't happen here. They have faith that, if nothing else, America's military might will protect us. But the internal problem facing us is not one that can be solved by the military. England and France have advanced military capabilities, but that hasn't slowed the growing power of Islam in those countries. The US army dwarfs that of Saudi Arabia, but the Saudi government has nonetheless been enormously successful in shaping our perceptions of Islam by lavishly funding Middle East studies programs in American universities and Islam-friendly curriculums in our grammar and high schools.[7] The success of the Saudi effort may be gauged by the fact that when public schools in Michigan and New Jersey staged mock terrorism drills, the terrorists turned out to be Christian homeschoolers.[8]

In short, the present crisis can't be solved by troops and air strikes alone. Our ability to defend ourselves depends in large measure on the conviction that we have something worth defending. Many in Europe have lost that conviction. Thus, they find it hard to resist when Muslims demand that the Holocaust or the Crusades be dropped from the school curriculum. Why make a fuss? And if a Muslim family in Britain wants to force a teenage daughter into marriage with a cousin back in Pakistan, why make a fuss about that? When author Oriana Fallaci was ordered by an Italian judge to stand trial for defaming Islam, few Europeans came to her defense; and when Ayaan Hirsi Ali had to flee Holland because of her defense of abused Muslim women, many Dutchmen were relieved by her departure. When your vision of life doesn't extend much beyond your next vacation or your next pension check, you're not inclined to put up a fight over principles, especially against people willing to use violence against you. Europe is the birthplace of Enlightenment values; but, as it turns out, Enlightenment values, when divorced from the Christian beliefs that made them possible, don't have much kick—as Fallaci and Hirsi Ali found out the hard way.

So, inch by inch and by daily capitulations—some small, some large—Europe, once the heart of Christendom, is being slowly brought into the sphere of Muslim influence. How about America? Can't happen here? But in many ways, it already is happening. Take some examples from American universities. A student at Pace University in New York was charged with a felony "hate crime" for putting a Koran in a toilet. Meanwhile, Muslim students on other college campuses chant, "Death to the Jews!", and there are no repercussions for them.[9] Many American universities have banned or attempted to ban Christian student organizations from campus; at the same time, other universities are installing ritual footbaths in washrooms at the behest of Muslim student groups. On some American campuses, the sound of the muezzin's call to prayer can be heard from ivy-covered towers, although college administrators would never dream of allowing the *Angelus* to chime from the same buildings. The demands made by Muslim students are examples of what Rabbi Aryeh Spero calls "soft jihad", and so far Americans have not been able to muster much resistance to it. Spero writes:

> How distressing it is that so few are willing to accept, and engage in, the confrontation necessary to preserve our culture, and that so many have become so soft that they make excuses for their cowardice. How alarming it is that so many in high places here no longer believe in our own heritage, seeing in it only evil and racism while imputing to all other cultures, and Islam, nobility only.
>
> People give respect and gravitate to those things in society that society venerates. In the past, it was Christianity and the American civilization. If, because of political correctness, we raise the Koran above the Bible, as Pace University has done, cherish Moslem sensibilities over Jewish life, as San Francisco State has done, then our children will look to Islam for those things transcendent.[10]

We are beginning to find out that one's view of "things transcendent" makes quite a difference. Patrick believes that by praying and making sacrifices for others he may someday enjoy the company of

God and the saints. Ahmed believes that by fighting infidels for Allah he will someday enjoy the company of seventy-two "high-bosomed" beauties. No small difference. And these differing views of things transcendent carry very different worldly implications. When Patrick is tempted to think of women as mere pleasure objects, something in his conscience reminds him that women are his equals in dignity and worth. When Ahmed has the same thoughts, he knows that such thinking has the divine seal of approval, because, after all, sexual pleasure is the essence of the Islamic afterlife, and if women are destined to serve men in paradise, it isn't difficult to figure out their role on earth. Muslim women may be forbidden to Ahmed before marriage, but afterward his wife and daughters are his to command. No matter how decent any individual Muslim man may be, his thoughts will tend to be colored by Islam's condescending attitude toward women.

Much of this book is concerned with comparing Islam and Christianity—not only on the issue of peace, which is uppermost in many people's minds, but also on other matters. Unfortunately, any close examination of Islam is offensive to devout Muslims and leads to the charge that one is defaming Islam and committing a hate crime. It goes without saying that offending people's faith simply for the sake of being provocative is proof of bad manners and a childish outlook. But it is a kind of folly to refuse to look at the differences between two religions when one of those religions is promising to bury the other. It may be a matter of survival to understand Islam more fully and what its triumph over non-Muslims entails. We often hear that the true Islam is a religion of peace that has been hijacked by a minority of violent extremists. If that's so, why not open the books on Islam? Why do so many Islamic leaders resist the kind of in-depth examination that would prove the peaceful version to be the true one? It's one thing to resent a hasty judgment about your deeply held faith; it's another thing to put your faith beyond discussion.

Because critics of Christianity continue to lump it together with Islam as just another backward superstition, it's important to set the record straight. Because criticism of Islam is fast becoming a punishable offense, the window of opportunity for making comparisons may soon close—all the more reason for inquiring minds to start inquiring. Robert Spencer is one of those minds. He deserves a lot of credit for beginning the process of spelling out the differences. In his book *Religion of Peace?: Why Christianity Is and Islam Isn't*, Spencer examines the moral-equivalence argument and observes that, contrary to what some atheists assert, the imitation of Christ and the imitation of Muhammad lead a person in very different directions.[11] That's a main contention of this book as well: even a poor imitation of Christ (which is all that most Christians can muster) is preferable to an excellent imitation of Muhammad.

These are things we are not supposed to say or even to think. But sometimes cultural survival trumps politically correct taboos. Any number of previous societies have invited disaster because they were ruled by equivalent taboos. The Aztec superstition about the return of a white-skinned god played a role in Montezuma's hesitation to resist the Spanish conquerors. The inability to break out of a dated military mindset led the French to rely on the irrelevant Maginot Line against the Nazi blitzkrieg. And, somewhat apropos of modern Europe, the once-thriving Shaker communities in America died out as a result of a decision to reject childbearing.

What's the crippling superstition that rules Western societies today? It's the dogma that all cultures and religions are the same. We need to overcome this taboo because, as syndicated columnist Dennis Prager points out, "Only good religion can counter bad religion."[12] In a Christian culture the natural response to a threat is to draw strength from one's faith; but under dogmatic relativism society's natural immune responses are suppressed, leaving nothing to fall back on but shallow secular nostrums. A secular society, however, can't fight a spiritual war—at least not very successfully. It simply can't come up with the virtues necessary to sustain itself—such as perseverance and courage, not to mention faith and hope. Indeed, a purely secular society eventually turns suicidal and begins to collude in its own downfall. This happens because its citizens discover they have nothing to live for or even to care deeply about. Much of the behavior we now see in Western Europe and, to a lesser degree, in America can be understood only as suicidal: schools that celebrate Ramadan but ban Christmas; judges who bar Christian symbols from the public square but increasingly accommodate Islamic law; politicians and activists who object to every anti-terrorist measure in the name of civil liberties; politically correct military leaders who turn a blind eye to terrorists within the ranks.

Contrary to multiculturalist doctrine, there are things worth defending in our culture, and Christianity is chief among them. Why? Because *cultus*, or religion, is at the heart of culture. And, also contrary to multiculturalist doctrine, religions are not all the same. They differ enormously, and these differences lead to significant cultural differences.

Think of it this way. Imagine you are conversing with a young, educated Pakistani man. He is charming, a good conversationalist, up to date on the news and the latest electronic accessories, concerned about global warming, and perhaps even familiar with the ins and outs of American political campaigns. Then imagine that the conversation takes a turn to, say, the subject of Israel. You are shocked to find that the amiable young man considers Jews to be subhuman, the descendants of pigs and monkeys. He sincerely believes that the extermination of the Jews would make the world a better place. He is not ranting or raving, just speaking matter-of-factly about something he takes for granted. Or suppose that the subject of honor killing comes up. He informs you that although he loves his sister, and although it would be regrettable, he or his father would, of course, have to kill her if she in some way besmirched the family honor.

Whatever similar interests may have united the two of you, there is now a deep gulf between you. What accounts for it? Culture—culture shaped by religion. Even if you do not practice any particular faith, you are still the heir of a culture that was shaped by Christian beliefs— beliefs about charity, forgiveness, and the divine image in every person. You may have neglected or rejected your religion, but you still know the Gospel story of Jesus and the woman caught in adultery. You know that Jesus challenged the Pharisees for their duplicity. Christian or not, you understand that a human life is more important than a man's pride.

All cultures the same? A moment's reflection will tell you they're not. Whatever they may say about the equality of cultures, most people in the United States and Western Europe don't want to live in Pakistan or Iran or Saudi Arabia. Cultures aren't the same because religions aren't the same. Some religions are more rational, more compassionate, more forgiving, and more peaceful than others. The concern that Western societies have for human dignity, rights, and freedoms is an outgrowth of Christianity. There has been no similar, lasting development in Islamic societies.

Still, the attempt to tar Christianity with the same brush that's applied to the Taliban in Afghanistan or the virtue police in Saudi Arabia has had its effect. A 2007 Barna Group study concludes that a negative perception of Christianity is on the rise. A review of the study reports, "Young Americans today are more skeptical and resistant to Christianity than were people of the same age just a decade ago." Only 16 percent of non-Christians ages sixteen to twenty-nine said they have a "good impression" of Christianity, whereas ten years ago, the majority in this group had a favorable impression of Christianity. And the non-Christian segment is growing: "Each new generation has a larger share of people who are not Christians, which includes atheists, agnostics, people with no faith orientation, or people associated with another faith." Now here's the telling detail: negative attitudes toward Christianity were increasing among Christians themselves—particularly young Christians. "Half of young churchgoers said they perceive Christianity to be judgmental, hypocritical and too political." Half of the senior pastors who were polled said that "ministry is more difficult than ever before because people are increasingly hostile and negative toward Christianity." [13]

If you wonder where all this hostility is coming from, you might take a trip to your local bookstore, where you will find titles such as *The God Delusion, God Is Not Great, The End of Faith, God: The Failed Hypothesis, Atheist Manifesto, Breaking the Spell, Atheist Universe, American Theocracy, Religion Gone Bad, American Fascists: The Christian Right and The War on America, Papal Sins,* and *Hitler's Pope.*

And that's just in the nonfiction section. Over in fiction you can find *The Da Vinci Code* and other "hidden Jesus" speculations, and in the children's section there's Philip Pullman's *His Dark Materials* trilogy—which might be described as *The Da Vinci Code* for kids, except that it's better written and more determinedly anti-Christian. The first book of the trilogy, *The Golden Compass,* was made into a film with brand partners such as Coca-Cola and Burger King lending their support. It's only one of the more recent in a long line of Hollywood films with anti-Christian themes or elements. Add to this the multiculturalist educational campaign to discredit the Christian/Western heritage in the eyes of students, and it's not hard to see why the hostility toward Christianity has been intensifying.

These deliberate attempts to weaken Christianity come at a time when a strong Christianity is most needed. The various pseudo-religions that we in the West have invented as substitutes for Christianity can't stand up to Islam. Having pushed Christianity out of the public square, we are now finding that the secular substitutes are no match for a fervently held credo of conquest and in fact serve only to hasten its victory. In Europe, comfort, convenience, and pleasure are the new gods, but they don't serve very well: once material pleasures become the highest goods, people will give up honor, conscience, and freedom to preserve them. In the long run—if you care about the long run—it's a poor survival strategy. This willingness to appease is duly noted by the jihadists, and it reinforces their belief that Europeans are their spiritual inferiors and so deserve to be subordinated to Islam. Thus, Eutopia gradually—or not so gradually—becomes Eurabia.

As Christianity goes, so goes the culture. And Christianity isn't faring well in the West. Even in America, where church attendance is high, Christian belief is often mixed up with and compromised by multiculturalist assumptions—particularly the assumption that all differences should be celebrated. For some Christians, multicultural relativism serves as a replacement religion—one that confers a sense of morality without any need for moral effort. It offers the spiritual uplift of feeling tolerant without the bother of developing any personal virtues. And, by displacing sin onto the backs of long-dead imperialists, it ensures that the only sins people need apologize for are those committed by their ancestors. But multiculturalism is proving to be another in a long list of gods that failed. In particular, it fails to prepare the faithful for the realities of a resurgent Islam. Cultural relativism, as Bruce Thornton observes, "makes it impossible to pass judgments on dysfunctional cultures and to stand up for the unique good of one's own when it is under attack." [14] Yes, or even to notice when one's culture is under attack.

Multiculturalism, materialism, rigid secularism—these anti-Christian ideologies function like a fifth column or Trojan horse for Islamists. Except that Islam didn't put them in place; we installed them of our own accord. In many cases, this was done with the best of intentions by those who genuinely believe that Christianity is bad for society; in other cases, it represents the death wish of those who no longer believe in anything.

We seem to be at one of those strange junctures in history when societies fight against their own interests because they are no longer able to understand their best interests. In the sixteenth and seventeenth centuries, Muslim Turks came close to seizing the whole European continent because European Christians were too busy fighting among themselves to mount an effective defense. Similarly, secularists and Christians have been so busy fighting a cultural war against each other that they fail to see the war that has been declared on both of them by Islamists.

No intelligent secularist ought to take comfort in the situation, because for secularists it's a win/lose battle. If they win—if they convince Western people to disarm themselves spiritually—they lose the Christian culture that gave them their liberty. For a while the culture can limp along—as Europe has—on the built-up momentum Christianity provided. After that? Well, the rushing sound they'll hear won't be the sound of secular victory. It will be the sound of a spiritual vacuum being filled by a new and different kind of spirit. If, in the chapters that follow, I talk as much about militant secularism as militant Islam, there's a good reason. The two are intimately connected. Our ability to resist the one depends on our ability to resist the other. The extent to which atheists and secularists manage to convince enough people that all we are is our mortal bodies is the same extent to which people will adopt the live-for-the-moment mentality that is fatal to our society's survival. Under the present circumstances, those who live for the moment, without any thought for the gathering storm that is Islam, will find it to be a very brief moment.

The good news is that militant Islam is not an irresistible force. It can be stopped, and it can be rolled back. And, with some luck, the defeat of the Islamists can be accomplished without the use of military force. But to do the job, the West must find the will to engage Muslim triumphalists in a war of ideas. Intellectually and theologically, Islam is a house of cards. The whole edifice rests on the testimony of one man. Its founding document—claimed to be the verbatim word of God—is an incoherent patchwork of borrowed beliefs and repeated curses. In short, Islam can't stand up to a close examination.

Yet, in one of those strange ironies that history occasionally serves up, Islam is winning the war of ideas. The Islamist version of events is the version the media often adopts. Islam's ability to rally much of the world behind its hatred of Israel is only one example of its propaganda skills. The propaganda war is going in favor of Islam precisely because the West doesn't realize it is supposed to be fighting a propaganda war.

That has to change. During the Second World War, we didn't hesitate to wage a propaganda war against the claims of Nazism; during the Cold War, we didn't shrink from pointing out the false tenets of communism. Although it is plain that we are at war with al-Qaeda and the Taliban, many in the West can't bring themselves to admit that we are engaged in a cold war with Islamism—a war that Muhammad long ago declared on unbelievers. Given that contemporary Muslim warriors have picked up Muhammad's mantle, it stands to reason that we should do our best to undermine what they claim is their motivation—namely, the words and example of Muhammad. In other words, we should want Muslims to lose faith in Islam just as Germans lost faith in Nazism and Soviet Communists lost faith in communism. Instead of making excuses for Islam—which is pretty much what we have been doing up to now—we should be devoting our energies to exposing its hollowness.

A propaganda war, it should be noted, does not require spreading falsehoods. For example, the Radio Free Europe broadcasts to countries behind the Iron Curtain were simply aimed at spreading the truth about the failures and injustices of the Soviet system. Think of it as an information campaign. A similar campaign is now needed to awaken the world to the truth about Islam.

One of the best weapons in the West's informational arsenal is the unique nature of our own beliefs and values—most of which derive from the Judeo-Christian tradition. A side-by-side examination of Islamic beliefs and Christian beliefs would help to accomplish two things. First, it would begin to restore confidence to confused Christians. One thing you find in examining the Koran is that there are striking differences between it and the New Testament. That's something Christians need to learn or relearn, because it serves as an antidote to the enervating multiculturalist message that Islam and Christianity are roughly equivalent and, therefore, as Robert Spencer puts it, "essentially the same—in their values and in their capacity to inspire both violence and peace".[15] Second, such an examination might begin to sow doubts in the minds of some Muslims. We know that just prior to its recent revival, Islam had begun to lose its hold on the minds of many Muslims. Indeed, the reemergence of supremacist Islam was in large part a reaction to that loss of faith. There are signs now that those doubts can be reawakened.

The more you study the two faiths, the more apparent it is that the rational/factual case for Christianity is far more compelling than the one for Islam. Knowing this is important because success in resisting Islamization depends a lot on what Mark Steyn calls "civilizational confidence", which is a justifiable belief that you have truth and good-ness on your side. It may sound unsophisticated to put it that way, but that's the way it is. Without the confidence, you lose the civilization.

There is a test of resolve coming. When Christians are put to that test, they had better know what they believe, why they believe it, and why it is worth defending. It would also help if they understood what sort of dangers they are up against—the topic of the next chapter.

2

The Islamization of the World

It is not often in history that we get the chance to see an ominous future playing out before our eyes, nor is it often that we are afforded time to do something about it before it is too late.

Imagine if, long before the Holocaust, the Jews of Europe had a clear picture of the fate in store for them and had taken action to save themselves. Or imagine if the Germans who cast their ballots for the Nazis in the early thirties could have foreseen, before they voted, the horrific future consequences of their choice—their armies destroyed, their cities turned to rubble. Or again, just focusing on the situation of Europe in the thirties, imagine if the French and British leaders could have foreseen the results of appeasement and had chosen instead to take preemptive action against Hitler when their armies still outmatched his.

We are in a similar situation today, except that we have the advantage of hindsight. The scenario that is unfolding now in Europe bears a striking resemblance to the rise of Nazism in the 1930s. And the response to Islamic intimidation and anti-Semitism seems to follow a familiar script: silent acquiescence, appeasement, small and large capitulations, and even collaboration. What is happening in Europe is clear—almost as clear as anything can be. Islam has arisen from a long slumber, and its warriors are bent on repeating its ancient history of conquests. Islamic leaders—many, many Islamic leaders—have declared openly that Muslims have a duty to bring the non-Muslim world under their heel.[1]

Just because all this is clear doesn't mean that everyone sees it. Many are blind to the danger or vastly underestimate the threat. The Western world has been slow to wake up to the war that has been declared upon it; many of its citizens prefer instead to agonize over secondary issues such as recession or more remote dangers such as global warming; and many more simply amuse themselves to death with an endless parade of sideshow attractions: Will Lindsay Lohan go back to jail? Will Tiger Woods get back his game? What happened to Kim Kardashian's marriage? And other momentous issues of the day.

It's human nature to avoid facing harsh realities and difficult choices. But in the case of Western societies, all the usual excuses for denying plain facts have been bolstered by the ideology of multiculturalism. Karl Marx thought religion was the opiate of the people, but that was because he never got the chance to see what a good dose of multiculturalism could do.

By now everyone knows the multiculturalist creed: all cultures are equally good, except Western culture, which is at the root of the world's evils; all differences should be not only tolerated, but celebrated. If anyone anywhere is unhappy, it must be the fault of Europeans or Americans; if you are Caucasian or Christian, you should be deferential and apologetic; and, if there is any violence emanating from the Muslim community, it can't possibly have anything to do with Islam.

Thus, shortly after two failed bombing attempts by Muslim terrorists, British Prime Minister Gordon Brown banned the word *Muslim* in connection with terrorism, and in a display of multiculturalist pique, the home secretary lashed out against "any attempt to identify a murderous ideology with a great faith such as Islam".[2] Somewhat later, and with a nice Orwellian touch, the British government renamed *Islamic terrorism* as *anti-Islamic activity*. Meanwhile in the United States, the military's top authority on Islamic war doctrine, Maj. Stephen Coughlin, was fired from his Pentagon post after a high-level Muslim official objected to a report submitted by Coughlin that drew a connection between Islamic law and violence.[3] Over at Homeland Security, the word *jihad* was simply dropped from the agency lexicon, creating, in effect, the first Department of Homeland Security and Sensitivity.

Young people supposedly rebel against what they're taught in school, but this has not been the case with multiculturalist education. Suzy and Jimmy in the United States and their peers in Canada, England, Germany, and France have simply accepted it with unquestioning docility. Not since the Cultural Revolution swept through China under Mao has there been a more successful, large-scale campaign of indoctrination. Unless you count the thoroughgoing indoctrination of Muslim children under way in mosques and madrassas all over the world—a phenomenon that Alex Alexiev calls "the largest worldwide propaganda campaign ever mounted". Ahmed and Aisha don't know much about diversity, but they know all about jihad and the so-called Jewish conspiracy.

So on the one hand, you have a generation or two of Westerners trained in such a way that when they should be seeing wolves at the door, they can see only lambs; and on the other hand, you have a generation or two of Muslims conditioned to believe that the world is divided into two camps: Muslims over here; infidels, who are no better than pigs and dogs, over there. On one side, you have a loose cohort held together by allegiance to a mushy form of tolerance, whose greatest fear is offending against sensibilities; on the other side, you have a band of brothers whose greatest fear is missing out on the jihad. Who seems more likely to prevail?

Like the elephant in the living room, the Islamic threat is so big and so uncomfortably close that many would prefer to avert their gaze and contemplate more manageable problems. But the problem can't be wished away. Here are some examples of what we face.

The Nuclear Threat

Most people think of Iran as being the major Islamic nuclear threat. But that threat is still in the future. One Islamic country, however, already has nuclear weapons. Pakistan has had the bomb for almost twenty years. In Iran, the leaders dream of apocalyptic destruction, and the masses yearn for normalcy. In Pakistan, the situation is the opposite. The leadership is moderate by Islamic standards, but the general public is steeped in Islamic fundamentalism; and despite purported government efforts, Pakistan is a haven for Islamic radicals. The adage "uneasy lies the head that wears the crown" seems tailor-made for Pakistani leaders. Former President Musharraf survived five assassination attempts; his political rival and former prime minister, Benazir Bhutto, was not so lucky. Her widower, Asif Ali Zardari, is now president, but his hold on power is generally conceded to be shaky. The nuclear weapons in Pakistan could easily fall into the hands of militant extremists.

Even without the bomb, Iran has been throwing its weight around as though it already possessed it. It has threatened Israel with extinction, created a proxy army in Lebanon, supported Hamas terrorists in

Palestine, funded a worldwide network of Hezbollah terrorist cells, and taken hostages with impunity. Even more worrisome, several of the top leaders in Iran, including President Ahmadinejad and Supreme Leader Ayatollah Khamenei, subscribe to a messianic belief in the return of the Mahdi, or Twelfth Imam. When he returns in the end times, the Twelfth Imam will usher in a reign of righteousness, but he can be woken from his trance state only by cataclysmic events—events that key leaders within the Iranian government say they desire to precipitate.

How far off is the Iranian bomb? Estimates range from one to three years. Some observers warn it is imminent. It is well to remember, however, that the technology for producing nuclear weapons is well understood. It's also instructive to recall that the United States was able to produce two atom bombs starting from scratch within a three-year period almost seventy years ago. Saudi Arabia and Egypt have signaled that if Iran develops nuclear weapons, they will be forced to do likewise. The Saudis would not even need to go to the trouble of developing such weapons, since they could easily afford to purchase them.

The Cold War is over, but Russia is still a nuclear power; and Russia has a growing Muslim population. Two and a half million Muslims—one-quarter of the city's population—now live in Moscow. According to some estimates, Muslims will make up a majority of Russia's army by 2015.[4] In addition, some of the former Soviet republics are Muslim-majority countries. Most of them probably possess the technology and the materials for producing suitcase nuclear bombs.

France has the largest Muslim population of any country in Europe. England has the most radicalized Muslims—most of Pakistani origin. Both countries are nuclear powers with advanced delivery systems. Given the current drift in these nations, it is not inconceivable that these weapons could someday fall into the hands of Islamic radicals living in Europe.

The Military Threat

Nuclear weapons are not the only thing to worry about. Even in terms of conventional military power, the picture is changing. Turkey has the eighth-largest army in the world, and the second-largest in NATO (larger than those in France, Germany, and England combined). Since 1924, Turkey has been a moderate, secular state, solidly aligned with the West. But under the leadership of Prime Minister Recep Tayyip Erdogan, Turkey has taken a sharp turn toward Islamic fundamentalism. Supported by Iran, Muslim groups that seek to replace the secular government with one based on Islamic law are on the rise. Moreover, there are signs that Turkey is intent on regaining its former status as the leading power in the Muslim world.

A similar shift of power is taking place all over the Middle East and North Africa. Gaza is controlled by Hamas; Lebanon has fallen under the control of Hezbollah; and, in Egypt the Muslim Brotherhood is fast becoming the dominant force. Yemen, Libya, Tunisia, Morocco, Bahrain, Jordan, Syria, Algeria, even Saudi Arabia—all are in the midst of upheavals that could put them in the hands of jihadists. Some hopeful news analysts see this trend as an "Arab Spring"—a democratization, even a liberalization, of the Muslim world—but as the movement unfolds, it appears to be in reality a case of re-Islamization. Moreover, despite our decade-long military intervention, Iraq will likely fall under the sway of Iran, and Afghanistan will go back to the Taliban. The overall direction of the Muslim world appears to be one not favorable to the West.

The Population Advantage

"Israelis might have nuclear bombs but we have the children bomb and these human bombs must continue until liberation." [5] Thus said the supposedly moderate imam Yusuf al-Qaradawi. Even without the nuclear bomb, Muslims still have the advantage of a population bomb. The world as a whole is not experiencing a population explosion. Quite the opposite; the world's population is in decline. For example, no country in Europe, with the exception of Muslim Albania, has a birthrate sufficient to replace its population. The average fertility rate in Europe is 1.4, well below the 2.1 babies per woman required to keep the population from sinking. In the Muslim world, however, it's a different story. The fertility rates in North Africa and the Middle East average 3.2.[6] But that's just an average. Pakistan's is 5.08; Afghanistan's is 6.69; and Yemen's is 6.58, which, according to one estimate, will give it a larger population than Russia by mid-century.[7]

Where does all that surplus population go? Much of it migrates to Europe, to places such as merry England, which hasn't had to worry about its own surplus population since the time of Dickens. In British towns such as Bradford and Leicester, for example, the Muslim population will soon outnumber everybody else. Similar population shifts are occurring all over Europe and in Russia, as was already noted. In Rotterdam, the Muslim population now stands at 40 percent. In Marseilles, it is 30 percent. And in all European countries, the Muslim fertility rate far exceeds the fertility rate for indigenous Europeans. The most popular boys name in Belgium is Muhammad (often spelled in Europe as Mohammed). In Malmo, Sweden, it's Muhammad. In Amsterdam, Muhammad.[8] Muhammad is now the most popular boy's name in Great Britain. Moreover, those Muhammads are a statistically younger group than the Harrys, Pierres, and Helmuts whose names now seem more suggestive of Europe's past than its future. As Mark Steyn points out, the Muslim population of France is about 10 percent, but Muslims make up 30 percent of the population under age twenty and about 45 percent of the under-twenties in some major urban centers.[9] It was just such exuberant youths who staged riots in over one hundred French cities for three weeks in the fall of 2005.

If you're middle-aged or older and feeling a bit arthritic, your natural tendency when faced with boisterous young people is to try to placate them and hope that eventually they will become old and cautious like yourself. This is pretty much what has been happening in Europe, where various forms of appeasement, rather than assimilation, have become the order of the day. After the French riots, for example, French officials called for the building of more mosques and madrassas. In parts of France, non-Muslim women have taken to wearing head scarves so they won't attract the wrong kind of attention from Muslim youth. Likewise, Swedish girls in a Stockholm suburb have taken to dying their blond hair black to avoid sexual harassment or worse. In 2004 Jens Orback, the Swedish minister for integration and gender equality, argued, "We must be open and tolerant towards Islam and Muslims because when we become a minority, they will be so towards us."[10] But if tolerance isn't displayed by Muslims in Sweden while they're still a minority, why expect it when they become the majority? And why make the assumption that a numerical majority is the key factor?

In view of the fact that the majority in Europe is already acting like a minority, it might not be wise to fixate on numbers alone when discussing Europe's future. Based on current birthrates, it would take a long time for Europe to become a Muslim-majority continent, but

Muslims could become the dominant force in Europe long before they reach majority status. Analysts at a social-networks research center at Rensselaer Polytechnic Institute have concluded that "when just 10 percent of the population holds an unshakable belief, their belief will always be adopted by the majority of the society".[11] At this point, Muslim beliefs seem considerably more unshakable than European beliefs. Moreover, Muslims in European countries tend to vote as a bloc, and some European politicians have begun to cater to those blocs, thus magnifying the Muslim influence. In the recent French election, the victory margin for President Francois Hollande—a Socialist and a strong proponent of Muslim immigration—was provided by Muslim voters. The other problem with focusing on birthrates alone is that three other factors must be taken into account when projecting Muslim population expansion: immigration, emigration, and conversions to Islam.

Immigration

The growth of Europe's Muslim population is a direct result of its birth dearth. With an aging population and a cradle-to-grave welfare system, European nations discovered that there weren't enough young workers to run the factories and fund public programs with their income taxes. Increased immigration seemed the obvious answer to the problem. A steady stream of immigrant workers, it was supposed, would keep the economy and the social-welfare turbine humming. But Europe is surrounded by Muslim countries. When the gates were opened, it was not the young Canadians who showed up, but the young Turks— along with the young Moroccans, Algerians, and Somalis. And they are still coming.

In the mid-twentieth century, there were practically no Muslims in Western Europe.[12] By the mid-1990s there were tens of millions— most of them immigrants from Turkey, North Africa, Pakistan, and Bangladesh. About five hundred thousand new immigrants, mostly Muslims, move to Britain every year.[13] In Europe as a whole, net immigration is 1.7 million per year. One and a half million of Sweden's population of nine million are either immigrants or children of immigrants.[14] In many large European cities, the Muslim population ranges between 25 and 40 percent. Cities such as Strasbourg, Marseille, Brussels, Amsterdam, Duisburg, Cologne, Dusseldorf, and the Berlin neighborhoods of Kreuzberg and Neukölln have begun to acquire a distinctly Muslim character.[15]

Despite much talk of restricting immigration, the numbers continue to grow. According to a recent Pew survey, the number of Muslims in Europe has grown from 29.6 million in 1990 to 44.1 million in 2010 and is projected to exceed 58 million by 2030.[16] Spain's foreign-born population is increasing by 21 percent per year.[17] The Muslim population of Britain is forecast to double in twenty years,[18] and in Germany the number will double in the next decade.[19] Because many Muslim immigrants come to Europe illegally, these numbers underestimate the scope of the problem. According to research conducted by the London School of Economics, there may be more than six hundred thousand illegal immigrants living in Britain.[20] In 2005 Spain's prime minister, José Luis Zapatero, granted amnesty to seven hundred thousand illegal immigrants.[21]

Muslim immigrants not only come in greater numbers than other groups do, but also are more resistant to integration. According to a recent Pew poll, the majority of Europeans believe that Muslims in their countries do not want to integrate.[22] An Ipsos poll of nine European countries found that more than half of all Europeans believe that immigration is having a negative effect on their lives.[23] In Germany, an opinion poll conducted by the University of Munster shows that the majority of Germans disagree with the statement that Islam "belongs in Germany".[24] In other words, the grand strategy did not work out as planned. The European policy makers assumed that Muslim immigrants would notice the superiority of Europe's enlightened culture and advanced economy and that either they or their children would gladly assimilate or else return to their countries of origin. Some assimilation has taken place, but many Muslims have looked down upon what they see as a secular and soulless culture. When he visited Cologne in February 2008, Turkish Prime Minister Recep Tayyip Erdogan told a crowd of twenty thousand Turkish immigrants that "assimilation is a crime against humanity."[25]

Many European Muslims have been unwilling to assimilate to what Sayyid Qutb, the leading Islamic theorist of the twentieth century, described as a "people drowning in dirt and mud".[26] Contrary to expectations, many Muslims in Europe—especially second- and third-generation Muslims—have acquired not a sense of gratitude and deference, but a sense of arrogant self-confidence. These are not the huddled masses "yearning to breathe free" but the aggrieved masses yearning to breathe fire. Why assimilate when you believe that you have the superior culture and the superior religion and that you will soon be in control? As one frequently displayed demonstration poster puts it, "Europe is the cancer, Islam is the answer", which at least has the merit of being less pointed than "Europe, you will pay. Your extermination is on its way!" And both of these have the merit of being more poetic than "Slay those who insult Islam", "Butcher those who insult Islam", and "Massacre those who insult Islam."

You might think that some boisterous European youth would come up with their own counter slogans—something like, "We think Europe is just swell. Islamists you can go to —." Well, you get the idea. But most European youth have been too well schooled in the pieties of multiculturalism to contemplate a protest, and those who might be so disposed know that they might end up in jail for inciting hatred—as has happened on several occasions to leaders of the English Defense League when they held counterdemonstrations protesting Muslim intimidation. And added to the fear of being either impolite or arrested is the fear of reprisals from the Muslims themselves.

A poll conducted by Le Monde reveals that 68 percent of French say Muslims are "not well integrated in society", and of these, 61 percent blame the situation on Muslim "refusal" to integrate.[27] The chief evidence for this refusal are the hundreds of Muslim "mini states" that dot Europe. In many European cities, Muslims are grouped into compact communities such as the banlieues in France, where life is centered on Islamic centers and mosques and where police do not often venture. To all appearances, Muslims in these areas prefer self-rule to assimilation. And the no-assimilation policy can be brutally enforced in what have come to be known simply as the Zones. Serge Trifkovic, author of Defeating Jihad, writes:

> Young Muslim men direct particular violence against Muslim women who try to follow French ways. Many French-born Arab girls in the ghettos resort to wearing hijab as the only protection against face-slashing and gang rapes. Not having one makes a girl a "whore" and fair game for both.[28]

Rather than Muslim assimilation into Europe, it looks as if a kind of reverse assimilation is occurring as Europeans try to accommodate themselves to the ways of Islam—the Zones, the muezzin's daily call to prayer from minarets in market towns, prayer rooms in public schools, polygamy, and forced marriage. Bat Ye'or, the preeminent scholar of *dhimmitude* (the forced subservience of non-Muslims in Islamic societies), predicts that the result will be Eurabia—a European continent dominated by Islam.

Emigration

When will Muslims become the dominant force in Europe? Predictions vary widely, but the case for its happening sooner rather than later is buttressed by a third element. To high Muslim birthrates and immigration rates, we can add the growing rate of non-Muslim emigration. In these psychologized times, we hear a lot of talk about how important it is that people feel comfortable. Well, a lot of people in Europe are feeling mighty uncomfortable about the growing influence of Islam and the growing threat to their liberty and security. A poll conducted by the respected You Gov organization in December 2007 found that more than half of all British men and four in ten British women said they would rather live abroad if given the choice. The main reasons given were antisocial behavior among a growing underclass and immigration.[29] In fact, 207,000 British citizens left the country in 2006, the highest level since before the First World War. In a show of typical British understatement, the *Telegraph* headline read, "Emigration Soars as Britons Desert the U.K."[30] A similar picture is emerging in the Netherlands, where emigration rates are at a fifty-year high—thus giving a whole new meaning to the tale of "The Flying Dutchman". According to the *New York Times*, the murder of filmmaker Theo van Gogh by a Muslim appears to have been a catalyst for increased Dutch emigration.[31]

We think of population shifts as occurring gradually over long stretches of time. But that's not always the case. Consider the rapid transformation of American cities caused by "white flight" in the sixties and seventies as municipal governments sought to achieve racial balance in the schools through forced busing. To avoid assignment of their children to non-neighborhood schools, droves of urban white families moved to the suburbs. The result was a rapid and massive population shift that radically altered the composition of many major cities. Almost overnight, Boston, Atlanta, Baltimore, Philadelphia, Detroit, Los Angeles, and Washington, DC, lost almost half their white populations.

Whether you look at white flight as purely racist, purely pragmatic, or somewhere in between, the point is that populations can move with surprising speed when the stakes are considered high enough.

Conversions

The case for Muslims' securing control of Europe sooner rather than later is also strengthened when you throw one other factor into the mix: conversions. Media interest in conversions to Islam has been piqued by the fact that so many terrorists turn out to be recent converts. You have no doubt heard of Richard Reid, the shoe bomber; Jose Padilla, the convicted terrorist; John Walker Lindh, the American who fought with the Taliban; and Adam Gadahn, the al-Qaeda media adviser sometimes known as "Azzam the American". All are converts to Islam. But how about Muriel Degaque, Jerome and David Courtailler, David Hicks, Jack Roche, Germaine Lindsay, Don Stewart-Whyte, Brian Young, and Oliver Savant?[32] Again, all are converts to Islam who have been either indicted for or convicted of terrorist activities. Germaine Lindsay was one of the London Tube bombers; Stewart-Whyte, Young, and Savant are three British citizens who were arrested for plotting to blow up transatlantic passenger jets.

Why did these young men convert to Islam? Brian Young's friends said he was troubled by the decadence of Western society.[33] David Courtrailler's lawyer said, "For David, Islam ordered his life."[34] These are the sorts of reasons ordinary converts to Islam give. A common refrain from converts is that Islam provides a complete plan for life in contrast to the ruleless and clueless life offered by secular society. As Mary Fallot, a young French convert, explains, "Islam demands a closeness to God. Islam is simpler, more rigorous, and it's easier because it is explicit. I was looking for a framework; man needs rules and behavior to follow. Christianity did not give me the same reference points."[35] If you look at the convert testimonials on Muslim websites, they echo this refrain: Islam brings "peace", "order", "discipline", and a way of life that Christianity and other religions fail to offer.

Conversions to Islam are a worldwide phenomenon. They are taking place in Canada, Australia, Brazil, Mexico, New Jersey, and California. But the trend in Europe is quite pronounced. According to various surveys, increasing numbers of Europeans are converting. The number of British converts to Islam recently passed one hundred thousand. In France, an estimated seventy thousand citizens have converted to Islam in recent years; in Spain, the number is at least fifty thousand and in Germany, twenty thousand.[36] These are respectable numbers but, as an optimist might point out, not enough to tip the population balance in favor of Islam.

On the other hand, conversion rates cannot be reliably projected into the future. In its early days the Christian Church didn't seem a good statistical bet to become the dominant faith of the Mediterranean world. For that matter, no one could have predicted how rapidly Islam would catch fire in just a few decades in the middle of the seventh century. In short, conversion rates can accelerate dramatically. The question is not what conversion rates look like now, but what they will look like in five or ten years. Are we at one of those tipping points when history "speeds up" and decades of change are compressed into months and years? Most in Europe and America would find it difficult to imagine conversions to Islam occurring on a mass scale, but once a certain point is reached, conversions can increase rapidly. At that point, the bandwagon effect kicks in. When a movement starts looking like the coming thing, more people contemplate jumping on board—especially when the competition is looking tired or on the way out.

Christianity in Decline

In 1867, Matthew Arnold famously described how the "Sea of Faith" was withdrawing from the Continent.[37] In retrospect we can see that the Christian faith in Europe had a lot more withdrawing to do. The decreasing influence of Christianity in Europe helped create the conditions that now make Islam look like the wave of the future. Europe's current malaise—drugs, welfare dependency, declining birthrates—are linked to its loss of Christian faith. The resulting moral uncertainties make Islam's ordered plan of life seem appealing—at least to some. But when those "some" start to include society's elites, the bandwagon effect is intensified. Robert Ferrigno's novel *Prayers for the Assassin* presents a fictional account of the process. He pictures an America that has by and large converted to Islam. The real breakthrough came when the elites—in our case, the sports heroes and movie stars—turned to Islam, thus setting off a cascade of conversions.[38]

The Irish actor Liam Neeson, the star of *Schindler's List* and the voice of Aslan in the *Chronicles of Narnia* films, recently revealed that he is thinking about becoming a Muslim. If so, he will add his name to a growing list of well-known people who are trading their Christian heritage for Islam. In Europe, there have already been a number of celebrity converts—sports stars, entertainers, the great-granddaughter of a British prime minister, Tony Blair's sister-in-law—but the one person whose life seems to sum up the current European situation is an elite by anyone's standards. Prince Charles is not a convert, but in recent years he has been very much a booster of Islam. The prince is the patron of the Center for Islamic Studies. He has installed an elaborate Islamic garden at his Highgrove residence. He has appeared on several occasions wearing turbans and Bedouin robes. All that could be passed off as typical of the English elites' long-standing romance with Araby. But actions speak louder than wardrobes, and the prince's actions and words over the years indicate that his predilections may be more than a passing Lawrence-of-Arabia phase.

Take, for instance, his role in the construction of the Finsbury Park mosque in North London—a mosque that subsequently became the headquarters for jihad in Great Britain. According to Melanie Phillips, in her book *Londonistan*, the mosque "owed its existence to the Prince of Wales, who persuaded King Fahd of Saudi Arabia to donate well over £1.3 million to construct [the building]".[39] The prince's public utterances on the subject of Islam are also revealing. In one speech on Islamic pedagogy, the prince contrasted Islam's "integrated spiritual view of the world" with the West's inability to achieve the same, and he opined that "we need to be taught by Islamic teachers how to learn with our hearts as well as our heads."[40] In another speech he said, "Islam can teach us a way of understanding and living in the world which Christianity itself is poorer for having lost."[41]

Prince Charles has made it known that when he becomes king, he would like to be known as "Defender of Faith", not "Defender of the Faith"—one of the traditional titles conferred on the English monarch.[42] Christianity is the faith that the crown has traditionally defended, but Charles seems to be signaling that he thinks Christianity doesn't have much of a future in England. And if he thinks that way, what is the average Christian supposed to think?

Although the majority of English regard themselves as Christians, their faith—if judged by church attendance—is not widely practiced. Peter Hitchens describes the situation this way: "The choirs and the bells gradually fall silent, the hymns are no longer sung and one by one the doors are locked and places which in some cases have seen worship for centuries become bare museums of a dead faith." [43] England today is a country of full mosques and empty churches. It is, in many senses, a post-Christian society, and Muslims are merely expanding into the spiritual vacuum that has resulted from England's turn to secularism.

From one perspective, Charles could be looked upon as a far-seeing sage who recognizes that a nation needs spiritual sustenance and who judges that the Church of England isn't doing the job. In that view, he's paving the way for a peaceful transition to a more vibrant spirituality. From another perspective, he's helping to deliver his countrymen into the hands of religious zealots who will make Oliver Cromwell and his Roundheads seem benign by comparison. Melanie Phillips is of the second opinion. She writes, "At a time when Britain's fundamental values are under attack, its future monarch is preparing to abandon them with an explicit aim of replacing them by the 'spiritually superior' forces of Islam." [44]

In the rest of the world, the Christian faith is considerably more vibrant than in Europe. In many parts of the globe, people are converting to Christianity, not away from it. But Europe is still crucial. For obvious reasons, the fate of Europe is going to weigh more heavily on global security than will the fate of Ecuador or Ethiopia.

* * *

How about the United States? At a casual glance, it would appear that we are protected from Islamization both by our demographics and by our faith. In contrast to Europe, America is a churchgoing nation with a healthy birthrate. So why worry?

Apart from the fact that we would still have to worry about a nuclear-armed Muslim Europe, there are other reasons for alarm. For example, our birthrate is not nearly as healthy as it appears. Yes, it's holding steady near the magic 2.1 replacement figure, but 41 percent of those births now occur out of wedlock. About 35 percent of white children are now born out of wedlock, as are 55 percent of Hispanic children and 70 percent of black children. And, as any cop, schoolteacher, or single parent can attest, these trends quickly translate into trouble. As the boys in these fatherless families grow up, they are prone to school failure, delinquency, and gang activity. They are particularly attracted to hypermasculine ideologies and organizations. As we are now learning, masculine supremacy is a prominent feature of Islam. Sooner or later, all those fatherless boys are going to notice that there's a lot of manly activity going on at the local mosque. So in the absence of traditional father-in-the-home families, America's respectable birthrate may only translate into more recruits for Islam. For example, a disproportionate number of fatherless boys end up in prison, and a significant number of prisoners convert to Islam. According to some estimates, between thirty and forty thousand inmates in the United States convert to Islam each year.[45] Likewise, black Muslim groups such as the Nation of Islam have been extremely effective in recruiting father-deprived young men in black neighborhoods.

The United States is not experiencing an influx of Muslim immigrants on the same scale as Europe; nevertheless, there are some troubling signs. Thanks to a State Department refugee resettlement program, the Somali population of the US is now over 200,000—more than the combined numbers of Somalis who have settled in Australia, Canada, Sweden, Norway, Denmark, and the Netherlands and second only to the 250,000 Somalis who have settled in Great Britain.[46] In addition, there is speculation that the State Department is considering a similar resettlement program for Palestinians.

But the growth of Muslim influence is not simply a numbers game. Concentration of numbers is also an important factor. For example, the population of Minneapolis–St. Paul includes 100,000 Somali residents, and Muslims make up 30 percent of the population of Dearborn, Michigan (the headquarters of Ford Motor Company).[47] Michigan residents often refer to the city as "Dearbornistan" because of its several mosques, Arabic signs, veiled women, and men in Muslim garb. A less obvious but perhaps more telling indicator of the power of convergence is that Muslims now make up at least 10 percent of the population of Washington, DC.[48]

The clustering of Muslims in and around the nation's capital suggests that, as in chess, the disposition of your pieces is as important as their numbers. During the Clinton, Bush, and Obama administrations, Muslim activist groups such as the Council on American Islamic Relations (CAIR), the Muslim Public Affairs Council (MPAC), the Islamic Society of North America (ISNA), and the Muslim American Society (MAS) worked tirelessly and with great success to gain access and influence in Washington. Muslims, some of them with ties to terrorist organizations, were appointed to important positions in government departments, including Defense and Homeland Security. Abdurahman Alamoudi, who was a frequent visitor to the Clinton White House and in charge of providing Muslim chaplains for the Department of Defense, is now serving a twenty-three-year prison sentence for terror-related activities.[49] Faisal Gill, a former deputy of Alamoudi, was appointed to the Department of Homeland Security as policy director for the intelligence division, but he resigned before an investigation into his background could be completed.[50] Since then, at least three other Muslims have been appointed to important Homeland Security positions, including Arif Alikhan, the assistant secretary for policy development, who, as deputy mayor of Los Angeles, blocked a Los Angeles Police Department project to assemble data about mosques in the LA area.[51] This is only a sampling of the Muslims with questionable backgrounds who hold security-related government positions.

Why hasn't the FBI been scrutinizing these dubious appointees more carefully? One reason might be that for years the FBI partnered with CAIR, which has since been named an unindicted co-conspirator in the Holy Land Foundation terrorism-funding trial.[52] Numerous CAIR members have also been convicted of federal crimes. If not the FBI, then maybe someone should alert the CIA. But then, again, maybe not. A recent *Washington Post* article revealed that the current chief of the CIA's counterterrorism unit converted to Islam six years ago.[53] Perhaps, then, the State Department should conduct an inquiry into the CIA. But Secretary of State Hillary Clinton's deputy chief of staff and top personal aide, Huma Abedin, is a Muslim whose mother in Saudi Arabia is reported to be a member of the Muslim Brotherhood's sister organization.[54] What about the army? During the second Bush administration the Defense Department often hosted ISNA delegations in the Pentagon and in the office of the deputy defense secretary. Like CAIR, ISNA was also named an unindicted co-conspirator in the terrorist-funding conspiracy.[55]

All of these particulars might add up to nothing. Various ethnic, racial, and religious groups have always vied to gain leverage in Washington. What sets the Muslim pressure groups apart from other special-interest groups, however, is that their special interest is world domination. CAIR, ISNA, MAS, and the like are all creations of the Muslim Brotherhood, an organization founded in Egypt in 1929 with two express goals: to spread sharia worldwide and to reestablish the caliphate (the Islamic empire). The Brotherhood's creed is: "God is our objective; the Koran is our law; the Prophet is our leader; jihad is our way; and death for the sake of Allah is the highest of our aspirations." The stated goal of the Brotherhood in North America is to engineer a "grand jihad" with the purpose of "eliminating and destroying the Western civilization from within".[56] Omar Ahmad, the cofounder of CAIR, told a Muslim audience in California in 1998, "Islam isn't in America to be equal to any other faith, but to become dominant. The Koran should be the highest authority in America, and Islam the only accepted religion on earth." [57]

In Egypt, the Muslim Brotherhood was, until recently, officially banned. Yet leaders in America have been eager to embrace it. Condoleezza Rice, while secretary of state in the second Bush administration, held the view that the Brotherhood is not only reformable, but also preferable to despots in the Middle East. When he gave his landmark speech in Cairo in 2009, President Obama insisted that ten members of the Muslim Brotherhood be invited. During the 2011 riots and demonstrations in Egypt, the Obama administration called for President Mubarak to step down, knowing full well that the Muslim Brotherhood was the group most likely to take power. Since then, various administration officials have described the Muslim Brotherhood as a "moderate" and "secular" organization that can prove a valuable ally to the United Sates. On April 4, 2012, White House officials met in Washington with a delegation of officials from Egypt's Muslim Brotherhood. White House spokesman Tommy Vietor explained, "The meeting ... is just one in a series of meetings between U.S. officials, members of Congress, and representatives of the Muslim Brotherhood." [58] Thus, the Muslim Brotherhood, which is dedicated to "eliminating and destroying the Western civilization from within", is now a power player on the world stage.

The term *Islamophobia* was invented by a Muslim Brotherhood group in Virginia. The term is now used as a convenient way of dismissing concerns like those raised above. But there is nothing phobic or irrational in worrying about the growing presence and influence of Islamic supremacists in our government or in wondering why key government officials have been so solicitous of their interests. In Europe, the rise of Islam has been a slow, incremental process—the result of decades of immigration combined with high birthrates for Muslims and low birthrates for indigenous Europeans. In America, Muslim strategists may have found a way to shortcut the long process.

Secular Seductions and Pop Christianity

Will Christians be able to counter the growing influence of Islam in America? Before answering that question, let me ask another: How well have they resisted the growth of antireligious secularism in America? Christians make up the vast majority of the population. You would think that if they were serious about their faith, it would be reflected in the larger culture. Instead America has high rates of divorce, illegitimacy, and abortion. Popular entertainment resembles the Roman circus, and sexual experimentation has become a national pastime. It seems that the number of Christians who are willing and able to resist the cultural tides must be fairly small. The question is: If American Christians can't successfully resist the steady secularization and sexualization of the culture by a handful of cultural elites, how likely is it that they will be able to resist the efforts of dedicated and well-funded cultural jihadists? Christians in America may not be as close to the falls as their brethren in Europe, but they seem to be on the same river and headed in the same direction.

According to a recent poll, self-identified Christians have fallen from 86 percent of the population in 1990 to 76 percent today.[59] This decline is not just a result of atheist and secularist attacks. Christian churches have been weakened by self-inflicted wounds—sex scandals, money scandals, and a tendency to buy into secular fads. Many Christians, for example, now subscribe to the ideology of multiculturalism, which—since it is based in cultural relativism—serves only to undercut Christian beliefs. Moreover, most Christian children are educated in public schools, where they are given the impression that Christian history mainly has to do with the Crusades, the Inquisition, the trial of Galileo, and the oppression of women and gays. Meanwhile, Christian education itself has been steeped in pop psychology ever since the early seventies. In the madrassas, children learn to pray and recite the Koran; in many Catholic religious-education programs they do role playing and sensitivity exercises. While Abdel learns about the joy of martyrdom, Adam is more likely to be learning about the joy of self-esteem and the danger of being judgmental. No doubt he is currently hearing a lot about the sin of Islamophobia.

There's no First Church of Self-Esteem in America—not yet, anyway—but it's difficult to avoid the impression that many churches suffer from a blending of faith and pop psychology. Take the Colorado church that offers thirteen different weekly support groups ranging from Debtors Anonymous to Sex and Love Addicts Anonymous to Codependents of Sex Addicts Anonymous.[60] Anonymous? Anonymity should be made of sterner stuff. The whole point of therapized religion is to talk about yourself. And while talking about their problems might be a necessary starting point for some people, Christians are eventually supposed to move away from self-absorption. How is that done? Traditionally it was accomplished through formal prayer and formal worship, spiritual discipline, penance, fasting, and good works. The emphasis was on soul toughening rather than soul baring, theism rather than "meism".

Christianity is in better shape in America than in Europe, but whether American-style, feel-good Christianity is up to the task of meeting the Islamic challenge is an open question. Let's-talk-about-me Christianity may be a good preparation for an appearance on the *Oprah Winfrey Show*, but it might not be the best preparation for a long spiritual struggle. Many Christians are still locked in an overcoming-my-personal-problems mode, while Islam's modus operandi might be better described as overcoming the world. The word *Islam* means "submission". It's not a figure of speech. It's not a symbol of something else. It doesn't have anything to do with coexistence or respecting diversity. It means that if Allah's will is to be enforced, Islam must dominate and the rest of the world must submit to it.

Misinterpreting Islam

The first order of business in confronting a danger is simple awareness that a danger exists. But as long as Christians think that all differences are a matter of misunderstanding or insensitivity, they'll fail to grasp what makes Islam different—and dangerous. Take the word *jihad*. Many Christians and Christian leaders have been led to believe that it means "inner spiritual struggle"—despite the fact that all Islamic religious authorities agree that *jihad* means "struggle against unbelievers". Nonie Darwish, who grew up in Egypt, notes:

> This "inner struggle" business is hogwash. In the Arab world there is only one meaning for jihad, and that is: a religious holy war against

infidels. It is a fight for Allah's cause. Ask anyone in the Arab street what "Jihad for the sake of Allah" means and he will say it means dying as a shahid for the sake of spreading Islam. I have never heard of any discussion of inner struggle in my thirty years living in the Middle East. Such nonsense is a PR ploy for Western consumption only.[61]

You can misinterpret or even completely ignore the belief of the Jains or the Buddhists and still rest secure that your life will go on pretty much as before. But misinterpreting Islam could turn out to be a fatal mistake. While the West has insisted on continuing to interpret *Islam* as "peace" rather than as "submission", submission to Islam has been on the rise.

In 2008, in one of many similar rulings, a court in Egypt ordered a Coptic Christian mother to turn over her two daughters, ages eight and twelve, to their Muslim-convert father so he could bring them up as Muslims.[62] In Pakistan, two sisters, ages ten and thirteen, were kidnapped, forced to marry, and forced to convert to Islam. A Muslim judge ruled that since the girls had converted, they could not be returned to the custody of their Christian parents.[63] In Iran, in 2011, many churches were ordered to cancel Christmas celebrations as a show of respect and support for the Muslim observance of the mourning period known as Ashura.[64] In countries governed by sharia, Christians have a *dhimmi*, or second-class, status. This means that they do not have the same rights as Muslims. They can practice their religion but only if they pay a special tax and accept severe restrictions: sermons are monitored, permission must be granted for meetings, evangelizing is not allowed, and courts can overrule parental rights.

One of the original intents of the institution of dhimmitude was to ensure that non-Muslims were made to feel inferior and subdued. That treatment of non-Muslims is still very much alive and has even increased in recent decades. What have also increased are the attacks against Christian churches and individual believers. The word *dhimmi* means "protected", but Christians in Muslim lands are feeling less and less protected; consequently their numbers are declining rapidly. Lebanon went from a Christian-majority nation to a Christian-minority nation in the space of two decades. Almost two-thirds of Iraq's seven hundred thousand Christians have fled in the last six years.[65] In Egypt, during the year of the Arab Spring, more than two hundred thousand Christian Copts fled their homes to avoid violence at the hands of Muslims.[66] The overall population of Christians in the Middle East has dropped from 20 percent in 1900 to 2 percent today.[67]

And there are worse fates than forced emigration. More than ten thousand Christians have been martyred in Northern Nigeria since Islamic law was imposed on the region in 1999.[68] Over two hundred thousand Christians have been murdered in East Timor since it was invaded by Muslim-dominated Indonesia in 1975.[69] Between 1983 and 1995, Muslims in Sudan killed an estimated two million Christians and displaced another four million. Crucifixions of Christians were common.[70]

Christians worldwide are facing significant persecution at the hands of Muslims, but this fact is only now beginning to register with American Christians. One effect of American individualism on Christianity is an overemphasis on the personal nature of one's relationship with Christ and a corresponding neglect of one's membership in the Church, the Body of Christ. If one's main concern is cultivating a personal relationship with Jesus, it may be difficult to notice the plight of fellow Christians in Pakistan or Egypt or to recognize the growing threat to Western freedoms.

On the other hand, cultivating a personal relationship with Jesus is a significant improvement on cultivating a personal relationship with one's self. In many cases, however, individualistic Christianity hardly rises above the general level of self-absorption in America. Too many Americans devote themselves almost exclusively to what psychologist Paul Vitz calls "the cult of self-worship". And Christians also often find themselves tempted by secular visions of self-fulfillment. If Christian bookstores are any indication of their frame of mind, many Christians seem more concerned about weight loss than about loss of freedom. A remarkable number of Christian books are devoted to explaining God's plan for you to shed your extra pounds—thus giving a whole new meaning to the term *Christianity Lite*. At the same time—once again, judging by the shelves full of books on the subject—God has plans for you to beef up your finances, improve your marriage, and succeed in business. Islam, on the other hand, seems to be well down on the list of things that American Christians worry about.

I recently attended a seminar on the threat of cultural jihad sponsored by a large Jewish community center. The presentation contained some fairly scary information. Afterward, in the crowded foyer, I overheard a somewhat distraught woman asking, of no one in particular, "Where are the Christians?" Answer: look for them on the treadmills in the gyms, in the diet aisle at Whole Foods, or at financial-planning seminars. Though a growing number of Christians and Christian leaders are waking up to the Islamic threat, too many can't see beyond the horizon of their personal cares and concerns.

3

The Cover-Up

Thanks to *The Da Vinci Code*, countless individuals now believe that there has been a worldwide conspiracy to cover up the true meaning of Christianity. For example, a *National Geographic* survey conducted a few years back revealed that 32 percent of Canadians who have read the book believe its theories are true. Although reputable historians reject the *Code* as an almost total fabrication, millions still cling to a belief in its veracity. Thus, even though Christianity markedly improved the status of women, *The Da Vinci Code*'s claim that Christianity is an oppressive patriarchy that has suppressed the truth about Jesus and Mary Magdalen is widely accepted. And the book's central claim—that Christianity is a fraud—has been cheerfully echoed in numerous books of fiction and nonfiction, as well as in countless articles, opinion pieces, and blogs.

But what if there really was an attempt by powerful people to suppress the truth about a centuries-old religion? What if that religion really does subject women to harsh oppression? What if, instead of a single albino monk, this religion could enlist legions of willing executioners to silence dissenters? And what if that cover-up was happening right now?

We would be quick to spot it, wouldn't we? Or would we? The irony is that while millions have swallowed Dan Brown's fictional account of the Catholic Church's supposed cover-up of the truth about Christianity, almost everyone is ignoring the real covering up of the true meaning of another world religion—Islam.

The cover-up is occurring at the highest levels of society: the media largely refuse to report stories damaging to Islam; presidents and prime ministers praise it as a religion of peace; and in many parts of the Western world, new laws are being proposed that would make criticism of Islam a crime. Meanwhile, school textbooks are rewritten to malign Christianity and idealize Islam; government officials in the United States are forbidden to mention the word *jihad*; and their counterparts in the United Kingdom are now required to refer to Islamic terrorism as "anti-Islamic activity".

Many of those who cover up for Islam appear to do so unwittingly and automatically. Westerners, especially Western elites, have developed a mindset that forbids them to think certain thoughts—or, if they think those thoughts, to say them. In many cases, career advancement or even simply holding on to one's job demands that one conform to the code of political correctness. And that code has put Islam off limits to criticism. A sort of diplomatic immunity has been granted to the Islamic faith, and under cover of that protection Islam has steadily advanced.

All of this came into sharper focus for many Americans after the murder of thirteen soldiers and the wounding of thirty-eight others by a Muslim officer at Fort Hood, Texas, on November 5, 2009. Many Americans went back to sleep after 9/11; and although there have been some eighteen thousand Islamic terror attacks worldwide since then, it took Fort Hood to reawaken them.[1] The Fort Hood massacre reminded us of the grave threat that Islam poses, but it did more than that. It graphically exposed the unwillingness of those responsible for public safety and national security to face the realities of Islamic fundamentalism. It also provided a clear picture of the role that multiculturalism and political correctness play in blinding us to these realities. Maj. Nidal Hasan's jihadist views were well known to senior army officers for years, but they failed to file a complaint for fear of appearing discriminatory. No one was willing to risk being branded as bigoted or Islamophobic, and no one wanted to risk the possibility of demotion. Because multicultural correctness had become the reigning orthodoxy, diversity trumped security and gave Major Hasan the opportunity to open fire upon on his unarmed fellow soldiers.

Just as disturbing as the willingness of military leaders to ignore a jihadist in their ranks was the media's willingness either to ignore or to cover up certain aspects of Islam in their reports on Hasan's shooting spree. Instead of connecting the dots between Islam's call for jihad and a devout Muslim man's invoking the name of Allah as he opened fire, the media was busy disconnecting them. If you were watching CNN or MSNBC in the days following the massacre, you would have gained the impression that this was basically a mental-health story. The major, it appeared, suffered from a newly invented syndrome—not post-traumatic stress disorder, but pre-traumatic stress disorder, as he was soon to be deployed to Afghanistan. Or was it secondhand stress, since he counseled troubled soldiers who had returned home from the front lines? The television news programs brought in a seemingly endless train of mental-health professionals to speculate about the psychological motives for the murders. The possibility that there might have been a theological motive seemed to lie outside the bounds of acceptable discourse. Days after the shooting, commentators, reporters, psychologists, and army spokesmen assured the public that they were still "searching for a motive", but for many Americans the point had been reached where such assurances carried little credibility. Out of respect for Islam, society's spokespersons had managed to cast themselves in the role of the boy who cried wolf—except that, in this case, it might be more accurate to picture a boy who cries sheep every time a wolf appears.

The selective coverage of the Fort Hood incident not only exposed the willingness of government and media to cover up for Islam; it also afforded a revealing glimpse of just how much there is to cover up. It turns out that Major Hasan was not only advanced into the heart of a military base, but in 2008 he was also invited to participate in a Presidential Transition Task Force set up by the George Washington University Homeland Security Policy Institute. Here he was given the opportunity to share ideas with members of the House of Representatives and the Department of Homeland Security.[2] Major Hasan is not the only Muslim who has been asked to consult with our national establishment. And, as Muslims in the military have increased, so have the efforts not to offend them.

Three years ago, Homeland Security banned the use of the word *jihadist* out of concern that Muslims might be offended, and it replaced the word *terrorism* with the Orwellian term *man-caused disaster*. More recently John Brennan, the deputy national security advisor, announced that those plotting attacks on the United States should not be described in "religious terms": "Nor do we describe our enemy as 'jihadists' or 'Islamists' because jihad is a holy struggle, a legitimate tenet of Islam, meaning to purify oneself or one's community."[3] Yes, except if Brennan has seen any of the various Palestinian recruitment videos featuring boys with bomb belts, he might have noticed that in those films, the preferred method for purification is with the blood of infidels slain for the sake of Allah. Another agency charged with protecting national security is the FBI, and for years the bureau has had a policy of giving preference to Muslim Arabic translators over equally qualified non-Muslims. Arabic-speaking Jews are routinely rejected. In addition, the FBI maintained close ties for many years with the Council for American Islamic Relations until CAIR's status as an unindicted co-conspirator in a terrorist-funding case finally led the agency to have second thoughts. CAIR has long been involved in training airport and other security personnel in the fine art of sensitivity to Muslim concerns.

Get the picture? Sadly, it seems that many of those responsible for our nation's security do not. For example, in 2008 Maj. Stephen Coughlin, the Pentagon's top authority on Islamic law, was fired for not softening his views on the connection between Islamic law and jihad. Coughlin was fired at the behest of Hesham Islam, a special assistant to the deputy secretary of defense, who, along with other Muslims in the Pentagon, branded Coughlin as a "Christian zealot".[4] To put it in terms that *Da Vinci* fans would appreciate, you might say that the major was getting too close to uncovering the truth about a powerful religion—a religion that had firmly implanted itself in the corridors of power. Naturally, he had to be silenced.

Major Coughlin's conclusions about the Islamic doctrine of warfare against unbelievers were confirmed only a year later by another army major. In effect, Major Hasan offered the world a short course on Islam. At the same time, the media offered the world a short course on deception. *The Da Vinci Code* asserts that powerful interests have long been covering up the true nature of Christianity. There's hardly any evidence for that claim, but in our society it's the kind of provocative formula around which one can build a bestseller and do so without any fear of being decapitated by angry Christians. But it's beginning to look as though the real story of our time is a desperate attempt by the media and other influential institutions to cover up the aggressive nature of Islam.

Why would they do that? Because many in our society, particularly those who have the power to control information, have a religious belief of their own that they desire to maintain. They believe steadfastly in the beneficial effects of multiculturalism. Christians believe that Jesus saves, but multiculturalists are convinced that diversity saves. And one of the central doctrines of multiculturalism is that all religions are roughly equal. Any evidence that Islam is essentially warlike would undermine what for many elites has become their central belief system—a system around which many have organized their lives and their careers.

There is another reason, and an ironic one, why some media people keep the wraps on Islamic aggression—fear of inciting Muslim violence. When the maker of the end-of-the-world disaster movie *2012* was asked why he showed Christian holy places being destroyed but not Muslim ones, he said that he did not fear upset Christians declaring fatwas calling for his death but that he could not say the same about upset Muslims.

Given this combination of multiculturalism and fear, it was almost inevitable that most of the news media would report that the Fort Hood massacre had nothing to do with Islam. Or, if a commentator did admit that Islam was a factor, he was quick to add that it was only because Hasan had misinterpreted his religion. Thus the *Nation* opined: "No one knew on Thursday afternoon whether stress, fear, anger over mistreatment, mental illness or *a warped understanding of his religion* might have motivated Major Hasan" (emphasis added).[5]

If you are thoroughly convinced that Islam is a religion of peace and brotherly love, then Hasan's views would indeed be warped. But Major Hasan appeared to be thoroughly well grounded in the tenets of his religion. He was able to quote copiously from Islamic texts in support of his beliefs. A year before his attack at Fort Hood, he gave an articulate presentation on Islam to his medical colleagues. The presentation was peppered with quotes from the Koran and from Islamic authorities.

Hasan is no exception. The more we find out about jihadists, the more it seems that they understand Islam very well and the more it seems that the media are the ones guilty of misinterpretation. Take Umar Abdulmutallab, the "underwear bomber" who attempted to blow up Northwest flight 253 over Detroit on Christmas Day 2009. He also was labeled a "misunderstander" of Islam by the press. Yet Abdulmutallab was president of the Islamic Society of University College, London, and in high school he was known as "the scholar" for his extensive knowledge of Islam. In the preceding three years, three other presidents of university Islamic societies in the UK had been convicted on terrorist charges. As Spencer points out, "It is extremely rare—if not impossible—to find a jihadist who does not cite the Koran to justify his actions."[6]

Yet our country's official spokespersons never tire in their efforts to maintain a strict wall of separation between Islam and terror. When Faisal Shazhad was identified as the Times Square bomber, the initial reaction was to portray him as just another emotionally burdened "lone wolf" who happened to have a Muslim name—although this time it appeared that the lone wolf also had money problems. Accordingly, numerous columnists grabbed on to reports that Shazhad faced foreclosure on his home. And that was all the explanation that many in the media required. Shazhad's attempt to blow up New Yorkers was just another case of mortgage meltdown. Judging from the news coverage, turning one's car into a bomb is one of those things that financially distressed people do all the time.

So, for the longest time, the media kept alive the hope that the Times Square incident had nothing to do with Islam. His court appearance, however, suggested that Shazhad had other things on his mind besides meeting the monthly mortgage payment. He not only pleaded guilty; he pleaded guilty "one hundred times", and he read out a combative statement in which he portrayed himself as a "Muslim warrior". Moreover, he was not nearly as isolated as he was at first made out to be. Rather, he had close ties with terrorist leaders in Yemen and Pakistan. Not coincidentally, Shazhad also expressed confidence that his actions were in compliance with the Koran and the sunna.[7]

The media narrative dictates that Islam must be given the benefit of the doubt and acquitted of any connection to violence. Thus, Muslim terrorists such as Faisal Shazhad, Nidal Hasan, and others like them are described as off-balance loners whose isolated actions result from personal problems and not from the dictates of their religion. Christians, on the other hand, receive a different kind of treatment. If a terrorist has any link, no matter how slight, to Christianity, the media are quick to emphasize the Christian connection.

Almost immediately after Anders Behring Breivik massacred ninety people in Oslo, Norway, in July 2011, the mainstream media launched an all-out effort to discover a Christian motivation behind his crime. In his rambling manifesto, Breivik described himself as a "cultural Christian", but didn't consider belief in Christ or God to be a necessary condition for being one. Breivik didn't go to church, didn't aspire to be a religious person, and didn't cite any Christian teaching that would justify his actions. He did, however, cite several agnostics and atheists who had influenced his thinking, and he expressed an interest in forming an alliance with Muslim terrorists. Nevertheless, numerous Western newspapers repeatedly described Breivik as a "Christian fundamentalist". Typical was the *New York Times*, which ran the headline: "As Horror Emerges, Norway Charges Christian Extremist".[8] The *Washington Post* carried an op-ed piece titled "When Christianity Becomes Lethal".[9] In other words, Breivik's tenuous link to Christianity was enough for the media to indict the Christian faith, while the claims made by Muslim terrorists, that they are acting in the name of Allah, are considered irrelevant to their crimes.

The slanted story is one way to cover up for Islam; the missing story is another. On the anniversary of D-Day, June 6, 2010, a group of eight thousand people held a rally near the site of the World Trade Center to protest a plan to build a thirteen-story mosque and Islamic center next to Ground Zero. There are, to say the least, a number of major media outlets in New York City. Moreover, big colorful rallies are the sort of thing the media like to cover. In addition, this one took place at a highly symbolic site in the nation's cultural capital on one of the most important remembrance days of the year. Yet none of the mainstream national media covered the story.[10]

Three months later, on September 11, the anniversary of the terrorist attack on the World Trade Center, a similar rally was held to protest the construction of the mosque. This time the demonstrators numbered over twenty-five thousand, and this time the media did decide to cover it—but only because of a nearby counterdemonstration in support of the mosque. The counterdemonstrators numbered roughly nine hundred, but despite the huge disparity in the size of the two rallies, the media managed to convey the impression that just as many people were for the mosque as were against it. The true sizes of the crowds were concealed by extensive use of close-up shots, as well as by the deceptive caption "dueling rallies", which accompanied the story on the major news channels. It was the kind of coverage one usually associates with government-controlled media in a one-party state.[11]

When a story is slanted, you always have the option of rendering your own judgment or of checking out the facts, but when a story is not covered, you simply don't know what you aren't told. Some people follow the unfolding jihad story daily through the Internet, but it's a good bet that the majority of Americans know only a fraction of the news about Muslim violence. A week after the Fort Hood murders, another devout Muslim—this time a graduate student at Binghamton University—stabbed and killed a Jewish professor while shouting "Allahu Akbar".[12] Despite the similarities between this assailant and the one who shot up Fort Hood, the news coverage was minimal. Likewise, when the founder of a Buffalo, New York, television station dedicated to improving the image of Muslims beheaded his wife, the story initially made hardly a ripple outside Buffalo.[13]

There may be "eight million stories in the naked city", as the old television series informed us, but the news producers are the ones who decide which ones you will hear. For example, how many Americans know about the Texas and Arizona honor killings,[14] or about the five Muslims who were arrested on charges of trying to poison the food supply at Fort Jackson, South Carolina?[15] How many know that Jews are routinely intimidated by Muslims on American campuses? How far along is the Islamic jihad in this country? Thanks to the media's non-coverage, it's hard to say. "What you don't know won't hurt you" is a catchy phrase, and sometimes it's true. But sometimes what you don't know can hurt you very badly.

What about that other world religion? That would be the one described by Dan Brown in *The Da Vinci Code*—the one that trains up young monks in the art of assassination, controls the Paris police, has spies and agents everywhere, and will stop at nothing to keep the world from discovering the secret of the grail. In the case of the Catholic Church, the media always seem to be on full alert. When reporting the Fort Hood incident, the *Globe and Mail* said that the shootings were "the work of a man, not a belief system, and must not lead to open season on Western Muslims and their beliefs."[16] Apparently, however, the same rule doesn't apply to coverage of crimes committed by Catholics. When a priest goes astray, he is not usually portrayed as a "misunderstander" of his religion but as a typical representative of it. When news broke in late March 2010 about decades-old sex abuse cases in Germany and in Milwaukee, the media immediately tried to link Pope Benedict to the crimes. Without waiting for the facts to come in, the *New York Times*, the *National Post*, the *Washington Post*, and other newspapers invited readers to accuse the pope of protecting child molesters and of presiding over "a culture of silence" when he was a cardinal. Anyone who has been closely following the abuse story knows that this is pretty much the reverse of the truth. From the point in 2001 when the sex abuse cases were transferred to his office and he became fully aware of their extent, Cardinal Ratzinger moved swiftly and deci-sively to clean up what he referred to as "the filth" in the Church.

But the most disturbing aspect of the media attacks on the pope was the attempt to link the crimes to Catholicism itself. Several col-umnists, including Maureen Dowd of the *New York Times*, suggested that the trouble lay with the Church's policy against married priests, the Church's prohibition of women's ordination, or the Church's repres-sive attitude toward sexuality. While the media made every effort to avoid implicating the religion of Islam in Major Hasan's crimes, they took every opportunity to implicate the whole Catholic faith because of the crimes of a few. Opinion makers used the incidents to suggest that there is something intrinsically wrong with Catholicism.[17]

The media blitz against the Catholic Church is part of a larger attack on Christianity itself—an attack so obvious that even atheist authors such as S. E. Cupp have begun to deplore it.[18] Why the animus against Christians? Read between the lines of a typical assault column, and you'll find that what usually offends the columnist is not the moral failings of Christian leaders, but the fact that Christianity still proposes moral absolutes. It is not sexual misbehavior that galls, but rather that the churches dare to put limits on sexual behavior. Christian churches are the main obstacle to the dominance of secular gods such as moral relativism and sexual liberation. Pope Benedict, for example, has long been critical of what he calls the West's "dictatorship of relativism", and he has frequently warned about the moral breakdown that results from it. The pope has some profound and important things to say about the precarious state of the West, but due to the repeated attacks on him, many will be tempted to ignore his message. That, of course, is the idea. While Christians and non-Christians should be rightly disturbed by the sex scandals in the Catholic Church, they also ought to be disturbed by the motives behind those who try to blame them on the faith itself.

One other reason to suspect the media's motives is that there is a noteworthy exemption from media condemnation of child abuse. It appears that the abuse of children is much more acceptable to the opinion makers when it is protected by the shield of multiculturalism. The media has been much less willing to criticize adult-child sex when it occurs in Islamic cultures or to note that, in the case of Islam, such behavior is sanctioned. For example, although one can find plenty of criticism of the Ayatollah Khomeini's political views, rarely does one see a condemnation of his views on sex. The one-time spiritual leader of Iran not only endorsed sex with children in his writings, but also took to himself a thirteen-year-old bride.

Here we come to a turning point in world history, of which the frenzied assaults on the Catholic Church are only a part. The drive to undermine the Church's moral authority and the threat posed by Islam are linked in an ironic way. For many centuries, the Catholic faith was the main bulwark against the Islamization of Europe. Now that Christianity is in decline in Europe, Islam is on the move again. And with the growing presence of Islam has come an increase in the sexual abuse of children—or, to be precise, what the West considers sexual abuse. The sexual exploitation of children is considered a far less serious offense in Islamic societies and is often protected by the force of sharia law. Muhammad, who consummated his marriage with Aisha when she was nine years old, is considered by all Muslim authorities to have provided a "beautiful pattern of conduct". That's why whenever a Muslim country tries to ban marriages to children (as recently happened in Malaysia and in Yemen), the imams rise up to insist on their right to marry minors.

And the exploitation of girls is only half the story. There also appears to be some justification in the Koran for the culture of pederasty, which Phyllis Chesler points out is "epidemic in the Muslim world".[19] A 2010 edition of PBS's *Frontline* reported on the phenomenon of the dancing boys of Afghanistan—youngsters who are recruited, usually at age nine or ten, to provide entertainment and sex for men.[20] While Islam frowns on homosexual relations between adults, pederasty is a different matter. Perhaps this has to do with passages in the Koran that promise men that in addition to the dark-eyed maidens in paradise, "there shall wait on them young boys of their own" (52:22). Since the boys are mentioned in conjunction with the maidens, and since they are described in the same way—"graced with eternal youth", "fair as virgin pearls"—it seems likely that they are there for the same purpose. However one interprets these verses, there is ample evidence from literature, history, and sociology that pederasty is both tolerated and accepted in many parts of the Muslim world.[21]

The dancing Muslim boys haven't yet been sighted in Europe or America, but the West's waltz with multiculturalism has already whirled it into unfamiliar territory. A United Nations NGO study estimates that there are now ten thousand cases of female genital mutilation in

Switzerland, with hundreds of thousands of cases elsewhere in Europe. According to a report by British police, an estimated seventeen thousand girls and women in the UK are victims of honor crimes or forced marriages each year.[22] In the British Midlands, girls in their early teens are routinely flown to Pakistan to marry men they have never met.

When it comes to the sexual abuse of minors, Western elites are exercising a double standard. When Catholic clerics are accused of molesting children, they and the whole Church are put on trial. When Muslims are accused of sexual abuse, there is not the same vigorous response. In fact, some of those who point out the abuse—for example, Lars Hedegaard and Elisabeth Sabaditsch-Wolff—are themselves put on trial. While abuse is often portrayed by the media as being somehow intrinsic to Catholicism, the same media, along with governmental authorities, take pains to disassociate Islam from practices such as honor killings and genital mutilation. For example, government organizations that condemn the practice of female genital mutilation go to great lengths to explain that it represents a misinterpretation of Islam.[23]

Judging by the way sex abuse cases are handled, it's difficult to avoid the impression that Western elites want to damage the Church as much as possible and offend Islam as little as possible, which, when you think about it, betrays an almost suicidal impulse. It really does seem that the fate of Western societies is bound up with the fate of Christianity. Europe and America are in trouble because they have rejected their Christian heritage and embraced moral and cultural relativism instead. And in the end, cultural relativism is a suicidal policy. As the climate of opinion changes in a relativist society, so will the consensus about what's right and what's wrong. If Catholic Christianity is swept aside in the West, the climate of opinion will increasingly be dictated by Islam—in which case the protection of children from adults will be treated as a less serious matter.

Secular militants are acting as though Christians are a threat to our culture. And they don't confine themselves to writing venomous columns in newspapers. If you're a representative of traditional Christian beliefs, media attacks aren't the only thing you need to worry about. In Dearborn, Michigan, four Christians were arrested for distributing Gospel leaflets near an Arab street festival. It didn't seem to matter that the Christians were also Arabs.[24] They were the wrong kind of Arabs. In Canada and Europe, Christian pastors have been fined or jailed for expressing their beliefs from the pulpit. In Workington, England, a street preacher was jailed for saying that homosexual conduct was a sin—a comment he made not in his sermon but in a conversation with a passing shopper.[25] Not even the pope is safe in England. Geoffrey Robertson, a high-ranking United Nations jurist, called on the British government to detain Pope Benedict when he visited England in September 2010. Robertson, who was commissioned by celebrity atheists Richard Dawkins and Christopher Hitchens, wanted the UK to send the pope to the International Criminal Court to be tried for "crimes against humanity".[26]

The multicultural elites want to silence not only Christians but also any who question the politically correct view of Islam. Oriana Fallaci in Italy, Brigitte Bardot in France, Mark Steyn in Canada, Geert Wilders in Holland, Elisabeth Sabaditsch-Wolff in Austria, and numerous others have been brought up on charges of defaming Islam. In *The Da Vinci Code*, the daring duo who are trying to uncover the "true" nature of Christianity are in constant danger of arrest. In the real world, the ones who are chased by the law are those who are trying to say something about the true nature of Islam. Many in government and media are intent on imposing a religion of diversity on the rest of us, but it's becoming apparent that the religion that will ultimately be imposed as a result of their efforts will have nothing to do with the multicultural creed. The main beneficiary of the attempts to silence Christians and the critics of Islam will almost certainly be Islam. A lot of people find it difficult to fathom the motives of suicide bombers. It may be time to ponder the motives of the suicide politicians and pundits who have declared open season on the religion that built their civilization, while treating as a protected species the religion that aims to supersede it.

In the opening chapters of *The Da Vinci Code*, Robert Langdon and Sophie Neveu find a series of baffling clues near the body of Jacques Sauniere, the curator at the Louvre Museum. One of these is a mysterious message: "So dark the con of Man". The clue is an anagram for *Madonna of the Rocks*, a Leonardo da Vinci painting that in turn provides other clues. But "So dark the con of Man" has a double meaning. It is also meant to point to the sinister con job supposedly perpetrated by Christian church leaders on mankind over the centuries. Well, yes, it's beginning to look as if we are all the victims of a massive con job—although not quite the one Dan Brown had in mind. So dark the con of man? Just so. But who is conning whom?

PART II

ISLAM'S ENABLERS

4

Secularists: Lights Out for the Enlightenment

In celebration of the 2007 winter solstice, the Connecticut Valley Atheist Association erected a ten-foot-tall sign on the village green in the small town of Vernon, Connecticut. The sign showed the World Trade Center prior to 9/11 and the message "Imagine No Religion", taken from John Lennon's song "Imagine".[1] The destruction of the Twin Towers was carried out in the name of a particular religion, but the sign and the song don't seem to evince any interest in fine distinctions or even broad ones. It's a good example of the all-religions-are-the-same mentality in action. The only good religion, in short, is no religion.

It's a good bet that the Connecticut Valley Atheists have read up on the gospel according to Richard Dawkins, Daniel Dennett, and other best-selling atheist authors, and so it's also a good bet that they believe that without religion the world would be not only physically safer, but also safer for our freedoms. As these writers have been insisting, a secular society not only makes the world more peaceful, but also better protects our freedoms of speech and expression. Only there's not much evidence that that's the way the world really works.

Take the case of Ayaan Hirsi Ali. In 2006 she put her signature on a manifesto calling for "resistance to religious totalitarianism and for the promotion of freedom, equal opportunity, and secular values for all". The document also speaks of "universal values", "universal rights", and "Enlightenment" with a capital *E*. But how sturdy are Enlightenment values once they are cut off from their Christian roots? Can jihad be resisted solely on the basis of secular values? Hirsi Ali's own experience provides some perspective. In her autobiography, *Infidel*, she describes her harsh childhood in Somalia, where genital mutilations and forced marriages are a way of life for girls, and then relates how she eventually escaped her tribe and family and made her way to Holland and freedom. Not content with having won her own liberty,

Hirsi Ali then began a public campaign to bring attention to the mistreatment of Muslim women (mostly by their own families) in Holland. She ran for and won election to the Dutch parliament. Then in 2004 she collaborated with Theo Van Gogh on the fateful film *Submission*, which featured Muslim women in Holland who had been humiliated, beaten, and forced to marry in the name of Islam.[2]

Shortly after the film's release, Van Gogh was murdered by an Islamic radical in broad daylight. The threatening note stabbed to his chest was addressed to Hirsi Ali; it warned that she should expect the same fate. Ali's illustrious career in Holland began to unravel. She went into hiding under government protection, but by this point, her welcome was wearing thin: because of her criticism of Islam, she had become an embarrassment to many in the Dutch government. In April 2006 a Dutch court ordered her to leave her safe house, and shortly after that the government threatened to revoke her citizenship (on the pretext that she hadn't been entirely truthful when she applied for refugee status). Holland, which had originally been so welcoming, was suddenly less so, and Hirsi Ali took refuge once again—this time in the United States.

During her stay in Holland, Hirsi Ali fell in love with the thinkers of the Enlightenment—with "Spinoza, Locke, Kant, Mill, Voltaire—and the modern ones, Russell and Popper".[3] At the same time, she lost her religion: "The little shutter at the back of my mind . . . snapped open after the 9/11 attacks, and it refused to close again."[4] Then she opened *The Atheist Manifesto*. "Before I'd read four pages I already knew my answer. I had left God behind years ago. I was an atheist."[5] As Hirsi Ali puts it, "We froze the moral outlook of billions of people into the mind-set of the Arab desert in the seventh century. We were not just servants of Allah, we were slaves."[6]

Given her very bad experience with religion, it's not surprising that Hirsi Ali would reject all religions, although she says that Jews and Christians have a more humane concept of God than do many Muslims. But for her, as for the Connecticut atheists, the ideal is no religion. Her real faith is in the Enlightenment. The problem of substituting Enlightenment humanism for religion, however, jumps out from the pages of *Infidel*. On the one hand, Holland is the "peak of civilization" and "no nation in the world is more deeply attached to freedom of expression than the Dutch."[7] On the other hand, Hirsi Ali's colleagues warn her to keep her opinions to herself; and in the end, the

enlightened Dutch force her out of Holland precisely for freely expressing her thoughts about Muslim treatment of women. Ironically, Hirsi
Ali's next port of refuge was the American Enterprise Institute, a conservative think tank that numbers quite a few traditional Christians
among its scholars.

The Italian journalist Oriana Fallaci had a similar experience with
"enlightened" Europe. A feminist, a secularist, a leftist, and an atheist,
Fallaci was celebrated for her daring interviews and essays until she
focused her critical talents on Islam. After the publication of her books
The Rage and the Pride and *The Force of Reason*, Fallaci faced charges in
Switzerland and Italy for the crime of "defaming Islam". Because of
European Union extradition laws, it became unsafe for her to live any-
where in Europe, and she, like Hirsi Ali, moved to the United States.

Unlike Hirsi Ali, however, Fallaci began to doubt that secular values would be able to protect Western freedoms. As Mark Steyn put it:

> This year [2006], a dozen intellectuals including Ayaan Hirsi Ali and
> Salman Rushdie, published a manifesto against Islamism and in defense
> of "secular values for all".... But La Fallaci, a lifelong atheist, had come
> to the conclusion that secular humanism was an insufficient rallying cry,
> that it had in some sense led to the gaping nullity of contemporary Euro-
> pean identity, which Islam had simply steamrollered. By the end, she
> was, if not a Christian, then (as she formulated it) a "Christian atheist." [8]

Before her death of cancer in 2006, Fallaci had a private audience
with Pope Benedict XVI, one of the few contemporary leaders for
whom she had respect. In an interview a year before that meeting, she
said she had found support for her view of Europe in the writings of
Joseph Ratzinger. "I am an atheist, and if an atheist and a pope think
the same things, there must be something true. It's that simple!" [9] One
of the things they both thought is that there is something "great and
pure" at the heart of European culture, something worth defending. [10]
Primarily that something is respect for human dignity—out of which
flows respect for human rights.

In a series of books and essays, Joseph Ratzinger, now Pope Benedict XVI, argued that the case for human dignity rests not on the Enlightenment but on something prior to the Enlightenment—the Genesis
account of creation, which says that we are made in the image of God.
Not that he discounted the contribution to political philosophy made
by the Enlightenment; on the contrary, he praised it. "The Enlightenment

has a Christian origin," wrote Cardinal Ratzinger, "and it is not by chance that it was born specifically and exclusively within the sphere of the Christian faith."[11] Enlightenment thinkers were not the first to ponder human freedom and the just limits of human authority. Studying the Scriptures and the works of ancient philosophers, great Christian minds had considered these matters for centuries. Thus, continued Ratzinger, "it was and remains the merit of the Enlightenment to have drawn attention afresh to these original Christian values and to have given reason back its own voice."[12] Ratzinger suggested, however, that Western societies will lose their freedoms if they try to set up the Enlightenment as a self-sufficient value system without reference to Christianity. And that's the problem of modern Europe in a nutshell: contemporary Europeans think they can have the fruits of the Enlightenment—a free press, free speech, democracy, reason—without the roots. Without Christian roots, argued Ratzinger, society can't sustain the claim for human specialness upon which all those freedoms rest.

Nevertheless, in 2004, the European Union drafted a new constitution that excluded mention of Christianity's contribution to European civilization. That constitution affirms "the universal values of the inviolable and inalienable rights of the human person, democracy, equality, freedom and the rule of law".[13] The trouble is, as George Weigel pointed out in The Cube and the Cathedral, secular Europeans can't explain why those values should be affirmed. Modern Europeans are shaped primarily by philosophies of scepticism and relativism, but scepticism and relativism don't provide any reason for believing in the "inalienable rights of the human person". Christians, by contrast, can give reasons for believing in human dignity and human freedoms, if simply because, as Weigel put it, "God requires this of Christians."[14] As Marcello Pera wrote in his introduction to Ratzinger's Christianity and the Crisis of Culture, "We act in liberty and equality as if we were all sons of God; we respect each other as if we were made in the image of God; we love one another as if we were responding thereby to an order given by God".[15] While under the leadership of Cardinal Ratzinger, the Congregation for the Doctrine of the Faith, in its document Instruction on Christian Freedom and Liberation (1986), summed up human freedom this way: "God wishes to be adored by people who are free."[16]

Go back to Hirsi Ali and—given her background—her perfectly understandable love affair with Holland. Of Holland she wrote, "Society worked without reference to God, and it seemed to function perfectly. This man-made system of government was so much more stable, peaceful, prosperous, and happy than the supposedly God-devised systems I had been taught to respect." [17] Yet when push came to shove, the Dutch society that "worked without reference to God" decided it was more expedient to kick out Hirsi Ali than to defend her rights to free speech. Dutch society circa 2006 had committed itself to a version of the Enlightenment that was more attuned to relativism and multiculturalism than to any transcendent vision of human rights and freedoms.

Actually, it's helpful to think in terms of two Enlightenments: the Enlightenment that was nourished by Christianity and the Enlightenment that cut itself off from God. The former led to the American Revolution, the Declaration of Independence, the abolition of slavery, and the civil rights movement. The latter led to the French Revolution, the Reign of Terror, the suppression of church by state, and the godless philosophies of Marx and Nietzsche and their offspring—National Socialism and communism. More recently the abandonment of God has led to the regime of cultural relativism that regards rights as arbitrary constructs.

It's this second Enlightenment tradition that Cardinal Ratzinger referred to when he wrote, "The radical detachment of the Enlightenment philosophy from its roots ultimately leads it to dispense with man." [18] Actually, this transition happened not "ultimately" but almost immediately. The first instance occurred when Enlightenment worship of abstract "reason" and "liberty" degenerated quickly into the mass murders committed during the antireligious Reign of Terror in France. "Liberty, what crimes are committed in your name", said Madam Rolande as she faced the statue of Liberty in the Place de la Revolution moments before her death at the guillotine. She was one of the early victims of a succession of secular systems based on rootless notions of "liberty", "equality", and "reason".

As many historians have pointed out, the atheist regimes of modern times are guilty of far more crimes than any committed in the name of religion. Communist governments alone were guilty of more than one hundred million murders, most of them committed against their own people. Thanks to the new crop of atheist boosters, we hear a lot about the five-hundred-year-old crimes of the Inquisition, but as Dinesh D'Souza points out, "Less than two decades after the collapse of 'godless Communism', there is an eerie silence about the mass graves of the Soviet Gulag." [19]

As Stalin remarked, "One death is a tragedy; a million deaths is a statistic." It's a little difficult to grasp the enormity of one hundred million murders, which is why atheists are still able to make hay out of the much smaller number put to death by the Inquisition. Although the Inquisition was inspired by religious zeal, it was also restrained by the inquisitor's awareness that he too could be judged by God's laws. Over a 350-year period, an estimated four thousand persons were put to death by the Spanish Inquisition. That's four thousand too many, but for some perspective, consider that within a few months of coming to power in 1936, the Socialists and Communists of Spain murdered over four thousand priests, monks, and nuns, many of whom were first tortured and humiliated.[20]

The manifesto "Together Facing the New Totalitarianism"—signed by Hirsi Ali, Salman Rushdie, Ibn Warraq, and nine other writers—starts off this way: "After having overcome fascism, Nazism, and Stalinism, the world now faces a new totalitarian threat: Islamism".[21] Strangely, the next sentence issues a "call for resistance to religious totalitarianism and for the promotion of freedom, equal opportunity and secular values for all".[22] The sentence is strange because fascism, Nazism, and Stalinism were thoroughly secular ideologies, not examples of "religious totalitarianism". Moreover, much of the initial resistance to Nazism and communism came from Christian church leaders. For example, at the behest of Pope Pius XI in 1931, eight German bishops wrote a pastoral letter criticizing Nazism because "the ideology proclaiming superiority of race and the anti-Semitism deriving from that ideology were contrary to Christian teaching".[23] Or consider that in his first encyclical, *Summi Pontificatus*, Pope Pius XII rejected Nazi anti-Semitism so forcefully that allied aircraft dropped eighty-eight thousand copies of the encyclical over Germany in an attempt to encourage anti-Nazi sentiment.[24] As for communism, the Church rejected it from the start—something that many secular intellectuals still are not able to do (witness the manifesto's use of the term *Stalinism* rather than *communism*). Pope Pius XI, in his 1937 encyclical *Divini Redemptoris*, condemned communism, and, as is well-known, Pope John Paul II probably did more than any other individual to end Communist Party rule in Eastern Europe.

In short, it might not be a good idea to place all your bets on "secular values for all" as the main resistance point to totalitarian Islamism. Modern Western culture owes a lot to the Enlightenment, but at crucial historical junctures, it was Christian activists working on Christian principles who did most of the heavy lifting. Enlightened secularism didn't put an end to the Atlantic slave trade. That was the work of Christians in England—men such as John Newton and William Wilberforce. It wasn't the Enlightenment that put an end to slavery in the United States. It was six hundred thousand Union soldiers marching to the tune of "The Battle Hymn of the Republic" and inspired by the writings of Christian abolitionists such as Harriet Beecher Stowe. Nor did enlightened secularism give us the civil rights movement in the sixties. That was the work of the Rev. Martin Luther King, Jr., and other Christian leaders who directed their appeal to the Christian conscience. And finally, it wasn't Enlightenment thinking that broke the resolve of Communist Party rulers in Eastern Europe. That was the work of the Catholic Solidarity movement, Pope John Paul II, and various priests and pastors in Poland, Czechoslovakia, East Germany, and other countries who kept alive the spirit of resistance, sometimes at the cost of their lives.

It's unlikely that secularism—even a humanistic, enlightened secularism—can be the foundation for resisting an aggressive Islam, because it was enlightened secularism that produced the vacuum that in Europe is now being filled by Islamists. In his book *The Cube and the Cathedral*, George Weigel contrasts two cultures—the one that produced the colossal and starkly modernist Arche de la Défense in Paris and the one that produced Notre Dame Cathedral. Which culture, he asks, is more likely to protect human rights and human freedoms? He answers, "A thoroughly secularized culture from which transcendent reference points ... have disappeared is bad for the cause of human freedom and democracy because democracy, in the final analysis, rests on the conviction that the human person possesses an inalienable dignity and value and that freedom is not mere willfulness." [25]

For proof of what he says, look at what happened to Ayaan Hirsi Ali when she spoke out about abused Muslim women in Holland. Look at what happened to the free-speech rights of Oriana Fallaci. And that's just the tip of the iceberg. Suits against writers are routine now in Europe. Former actress Brigitte Bardot faced up to a year in jail when a French court convicted her in 2004 for criticizing immigration policies that, she said, were bringing about an "Islamification of France". Instead of jail, Bardot got off with a five-thousand-euro fine. The publisher of her book was also fined five thousand euros. [26]

In the summer of 2007, Cambridge University Press stopped printing *Alms for Jihad: Charity and Terrorism in the Islamic World*, a book that draws a connection between wealthy Saudis and the funding of terrorists. Why? Because wealthy Saudi banker Khalid bin Mahfouz filed a libel claim against the book. Cambridge University Press declined to fight the case in court, paid substantial damages to the plaintiff, and recalled all unsold copies of the book. Mahfouz has brought successful suits against three other books in England, where libel law distinctly favors the plaintiff. All the books in question were written by Americans. In one case, terrorist expert Rachel Ehrenfeld, author of *Funding Evil: How Terrorism Is Financed—and How to Stop It*, was required to apologize to Mahfouz and pay a fine of $225,000. Ehrenfeld, who refused, won't be traveling to England anytime soon, but then, neither will her book. And as a result, English readers won't get the chance to find out whether she makes a convincing case about terrorism funding.[27]

The suit against Ehrenfeld did have one good effect. It led to the passage of the SPEECH Act—a law that protects American authors and publishers from foreign libel suits. Still, the succesful lawsuits have had a chilling effect on people in publishing. Andrew McCarthy is the former assistent US attorney who led the 1995 prosecution against the man who attempted to blow up the World Trade Center and other New York landmarks in 1993. When his Encounter Books decided to publish his *Willful Blindness: A Memoir of the Jihad*, editor Roger Kimball received the following note from one of Encounter's distributors for Canada and Britain:

> Can you please let us know if there are any references to Saudis and terrorist[s] in the book. We are just concerned that this book, could potentially create libel lawsuits as it could offend Saudis living in England and this has happened with many other US publications and we do not want to be jeopardized in selling this book.[28]

Just prior to the outbreak of World War I, British Foreign Secretary Sir Edward Gray said to a friend, "The lamps are going out all over Europe; we shall not see them lit again in our lifetime." Mark Steyn thinks we're in a similar situation today, but with a difference: "To reprise Sir Edward Gray, 'The lamps are going out all over Europe'—one distributor, one publisher, one novelist, one cartoonist, one TV host at a time." [29]

The lamps are flickering in Canada too. Steyn himself was sued along with *Maclean's* magazine, which had published an excerpt from

Steyn's book *America Alone*. The Canadian Human Rights Commission, the British Columbia Human Rights Commission, and the Alberta Human Rights Commission began proceedings against Steyn (a Canadian who lives in New Hampshire) because of complaints from the Canadian Islamic Congress about Steyn's "flagrant Islamophobia". The charge didn't go much beyond the fact that Steyn cited statistics suggesting that Europe will someday be a predominantly Muslim continent. Those charges seemed pretty thin, but who knows what might happen in a Canadian court these days. In 2001 a Saskatchewan newspaper and a private citizen were found guilty of inciting hatred and fined for publishing an ad listing four Bible verses about homosexuality. The ad didn't carry the verses themselves, only the number of the verses, as in "1 Corinthians 6:9–10". To find the "offending passages", you would have to open your Bible and look up the references yourself, but that was enough provocation for the court.[30] In 2002 an Ontario court ordered a Catholic school to admit a homosexual teen and his older male lover to the school prom. The court also refused the school's request to cancel the prom.[31] As the Canadian poet and humorist Robert Service wrote, "There are strange things done in the midnight sun."

The strange things done in human rights commissions, however, couldn't withstand the glare of publicity brought by the Steyn trial. Up until that point, the Canadian human rights commissions had an alarming 100-percent conviction rate. But once their Star Chamber methods came under public scrutiny, the commissions prudently decided to drop the charges against Steyn and *Maclean's*—although it took nearly a year for the British Columbia commission to realize that Steyn would be no easy prey like the assortment of small-town pastors, backwoods newspapers, and fringe bloggers they had been accustomed to putting through the "human rights" wringer.

But the situation in Canada is mild compared with another midnight-sun country, Sweden, where in 2004 a pastor was sentenced to a month in prison for "hate speech" for a sermon he preached citing biblical references to homosexuality. In the same year, lawsuits were threatened against a Belgian cardinal and a Spanish cardinal for similar criticisms of homosexuality. And the year before that, Irish clergy were warned that they could face prosecution if they distributed a Vatican publication on same-sex relationships.[32] In Norwich, England, in 2009, a grandmother who complained about a gay-pride march near her home was visited by the police and subsequently received a letter from the city council informing her that her complaint might constitute a hate crime.

Still, if you had to choose between offending gays and offending Muslims, the former might be the safer bet. After all, homosexuals are leaving former gay meccas like Amsterdam in droves. That's because Amsterdam is becoming more like the real Mecca—which means that it won't long remain a mecca for gays. The greater risk lies in offending against Islam because the European courts are, in effect, upholding Islam's blasphemy laws. Recently a number of people were tried for criticizing Islam in what Mark Steyn aptly termed "heresy trials". "Officially," writes Steyn, "Mrs. Sabaditsch-Wolff and Geert Wilders and Lars Hedegaard [were] in the dock as heretics against post-Christian Europe's new religion of 'multiculturalism'." [33] In each case, the courts made it clear that truth is no defense. As the spokesperson for the Openbaar Ministerie put it, "It is irrelevant whether Wilders' witnesses might prove Wilders' observations to be correct. What's relevant is that his observations are illegal." [34] In other words, telling the truth about Islam is against the law in Holland.

Lars Hedegaard, president of the Danish Free Press Society, was put on trial because of remarks he had made in a private conversation about widespread sex abuse in Muslim families. Despite an initial acquittal, he was re-tried, found guilty of racist statements, and fined approximately one thousand dollars. [35] In Austria, Elisabeth Sabaditsch-Wolff, a mother and a member of Pax Europa, a human rights organization, was put on trial for the charge of "incitement to hatred" because of negative comments about Islam she made in a seminar presentation. She was acquitted on that charge but was then convicted for "denigration of the teachings of a legally recognized religion" and fined 480 euros. The specific denigration was to refer to Muhammad as a pedophile (although she had never used that particular word). This, said the judge, was factually incorrect because Muhammad was attracted to women of all ages.

Meanwhile, back in Hirsi Ali's enlightened Holland, the trial of Geert Wilders dragged on for years. As Hirsi Ali once was, Wilders is a member of the Dutch Parliament and one of the most popular politicians in the Netherlands. Like Hirsi Ali, he produced a short documentary film that Muslims found offensive. In January 2009, the Amsterdam Court of Appeal ordered Wilders' prosecution for "incitement to hatred and discrimination". He was prosecuted for, among other things, proposing an end to "non-Western immigration" to the Netherlands. At one point, the prosecuting attorneys decided to drop their case, but the judges insisted that the trial continue. Eventually, in June 2011, the court decided that Wilders' opinions fell within the limits of legitimate speech.

By American standards, these challenges to free speech seem extreme; but that's the point. In America, Christianity is still fairly robust. In May 2011, at the Cornerstone Church in Nashville, Tennessee, Wilders spoke at length about the connection between free speech and the Judeo-Christian tradition. "I am especially happy to be in your midst," he told the congregation, "because here I can say what I want to say without having to fear that I will be dragged to court upon leaving this church. My dear American friends, you cannot imagine how we envy your First Amendment."[36]

The fact that freedom of speech is more robust in America tends to confirm Weigel's thesis that human rights and freedoms will be better protected in a Christian environment than in a purely secular one. By contrast, Canada, Sweden, England, Denmark, Austria, and the Netherlands are essentially post-Christian states. Judging by the various legal attacks on Christians, they might even be considered anti-Christian states. As a result, freedom of speech and freedom of religion aren't nearly as secure in Canada and Europe as they are here. In short, there seems to be a connection between loss of faith and loss of freedoms.

We hear a lot these days about the dangers to our freedoms posed by Christians who are supposedly legalistic and oppressive. But the Church won't throw you in jail or fine you if you criticize or disagree with it. For an interesting contrast, look at the treatment of French Archbishop Marcel Lefebvre at the hands of the Church and at the hands of the state. Lefebvre, who appears to have been oppositional by nature, condemned the Second Vatican Council, defied three popes, refused to recognize papal authority over him, and eventually broke with Rome, bringing thousands of followers along with him. After twelve years of negotiations, admonitions, and attempted compromises, the Church finally excommunicated him in 1988 for ordaining bishops without authority. And the state? In 1990 Archbishop Lefebvre was convicted in a French court and sentenced to pay five thousand francs for some provocative remarks he had made a few months earlier about the dangers of Muslim immigration.[37] The lesson? If you're looking for due process and serious deliberation, disagreeing with the Church is a better bet than disagreeing with the state.

Whether they result in convictions or acquittals, the numerous libel and hate-speech actions against critics of Islam put a damper on free speech. Authors, translators, publishers, and speakers are thinking twice about saying anything critical of Islam or even anything that could be construed as critical, such as demographic trends. Before discussing Islam, authors and publishers must be brave enough to risk a fatwa; in addition, they must be able to come up with tens or even hundreds of thousands of dollars to defend themselves in court. And so a lot will choose to remain silent.

This self-censorship, in turn, increases the leverage that activist Islamic groups can employ. As Muslim groups try to extend their influence in society, any resistance to their agenda will be branded as racist or Islamophobic, and the threat of legal proceedings will always be hanging in the air. Muslims make up only about 5 percent of the European population, and a smaller percent in Canada and the United States; but with the help of the courts and the silence of authors and journalists, they are able to have a much greater impact on public policy than their numbers would suggest. For an analogy, consider how successful homosexual activists have been in shaping public policy and school curriculums in North America and Europe despite the fact that they make up only 2 to 3 percent of the population in any given country. Overwhelming numbers are not required to create a societal change. A small but determined minority can have an outsized impact—especially if it has the support of the courts and the press.

Or, if it has the support of the universities. If political correctness has managed to slow the free flow of information on Islam in the publishing world, in the academic world it has reduced it to a trickle. You cannot learn about this from your alumni magazine, but fortunately there are now dozens of books and studies documenting the anti–free speech agenda on American campuses. David Horowitz's *Indoctrination U*, Alan Charles Kors and Harvey A. Silverglate's *The Shadow University*, and Dinesh D'Souza's *Illiberal Education* are examples of books that examine how universities have invented speech codes that prohibit "hate speech" to ensure that only certain views receive a hearing on campus. Whether in the United States or abroad, universities are among the least-free institutions in society. In the last forty years, they have become increasingly ideological and doctrinaire in their opposition to Western civilization. It shouldn't be surprising, then, that some of the most vocal apologists for jihadists come from the ranks of college faculties.

University of Colorado professor Ward Churchill made the news when he claimed that the 9/11 victims got what they deserved. An extreme case, yes, but not—according to evidence uncovered by the David Horowitz Freedom Center—untypical. They might not believe in a personal devil, but a hefty chunk of the nation's professoriate subscribe to the "Great Satan" school of historical interpretation. In Damascus and Islamabad, the Muslim in the street believes 9/11 was a Jewish conspiracy. In the faculty clubs at Columbia and Duke, they have a more sophisticated theory: the attack was planned not by the Jews, but by the US government—as in the "9/11 was an inside job" bumper sticker sometimes seen in upscale college towns.

Then again, maybe some academics do blame the Jews. American universities are decidedly protective of Muslim sensitivities and decidedly unsympathetic toward Jewish feelings. Films, speakers, and presentations that denounce Jews as the source of the world's problems have become an established feature of campus life. On the other hand, films, speakers, and advertisements that suggest a connection between Islam and terrorism are regularly rejected by campus officials.

For example, *Gaza Strip*, an anti-Israel documentary film about the Second Intifada in 2001, has been shown at several universities, including Princeton. Yet numerous student groups, including Jewish student associations, have been denied permission to show *Obsession*, a documentary about Islamic jihadism, on their campuses. Likewise many campuses host "End Israeli Apartheid Week" but vigorously resist David Horowitz's attempt to initiate an "Islamic Fascism Awareness Week".[38] Moreover, although Horowitz is regularly denied a speaker's platform, a Holocaust denier and anti-Semite like Mahmoud Ahmadinejad had no trouble finding an audience at Columbia University. "Anti-Semitism and anti-Israel hatred are not only tolerated in our universities," says Horowitz, "they are in vogue."[39] Despite the high-sounding talk of academics, there is, in reality, more freedom of expression in a bar or barbershop than there is on the average college campus—particularly when it comes to discussing Islam.

Some of this favoritism toward Islam may have to do with Saudi money. Saudi Arabia donated $20 million to Georgetown to establish the Prince Alwaleed Bin Talal Center, $20 million to create a Middle Eastern studies program at the University of Arkansas, $22.5 million to Harvard, $11 million to Cornell, $5 million to Rutgers, and $5 million to Columbia.[40] And this is only the short list. Moreover, the Saudis are committed to the Wahhabi brand of Islam, which means the centers they sponsor are beholden to exponents of a fairly hard-line version of the Islamic faith.

Does this mean the universities are being bought off with Saudi dollars? Not necessarily. There is at this point a sort of natural gravitation in the academic world toward anything that is perceived as anti-Western or anti-Christian. Money or not, a lot of academics would still sympathize with radical Muslims whom they think of as freedom fighters striving to break free of Western imperialists.

How did the universities come to this pass? Why are they so ready to align themselves with violent and oppressive movements? What happened in the universities is essentially what happened in Europe. Both suffered a loss of faith, and in the process of losing their religion, both lost their understanding of the source and purpose of freedom. Many of the prestigious American universities began as seminaries or as denominational colleges and over the course of time became secularized. But for a long time they still kept up some of the vestiges of faith. For instance, there is a large Latin inscription over the entrance to Harvard Law School that translates, "Not under Man, but under God and the Law". In the last forty years, however, the process of secularization accelerated, and a substantial number of colleges became in effect not merely agnostic but anti-Christian. Many colleges now have officially branded various Christian teachings as "intolerant", and conduct orientations to disabuse students of core Christian beliefs. The real and growing danger on American campuses is not Islamophobia but Christophobia.

America itself is not Christophobic or post-Christian, but wherever you find enclaves of Christophobia—such as in universities—you're pretty sure to find far less freedom of thought and expression than in America at large, as well as far more receptivity to Islam. Still, one might ask, why should it matter if academia wants to live in an insular fantasy world? It matters because universities have become powerful propaganda and indoctrination centers—powerful and yet strangely naïve. They are populated by the kind of people Lenin referred to as "useful idiots". They can be easily co-opted by those for whom ideology is more than an academic pose. Nonie Darwish, an Egyptian writer who left Islam, thinks the process has already begun. She writes:

> Before I began actively appearing and speaking on college campuses in support of Israel, I was of course aware of the activism on U.S. campuses by the Muslim and Arab organizations, but when I actually began experiencing it firsthand I was stunned. Radical Islam is not just powerful in the Middle East but is thriving inside the free world, especially in the institutions of higher learning in America.[41]

In Europe, according to Melanie Phillips, the takeover is well under way. Universities there, she maintains, have become the main centers for Islamic recruitment and radicalization.[42] So, to the list of the lamps that are going out all over the world we can add the light of free inquiry, which universities are supposed to keep lit.

Ayaan Hirsi Ali deserves gratitude for calling attention to the plight of Muslim women, but she's wrong to think the Enlightenment is going to bring them justice. For example, Western radical feminists— daughters of the atheistic Enlightenment—have shown little concern for their Muslim sisters. They are, for the most part, AWOL when it comes to the oppression of Muslim women. A 2007 review of women's studies programs on eight campuses revealed that none of the many course offerings focused on oppression of women under Islamic law.[43] In the same year, Christiana Hoff Sommers, a scholar at the American Enterprise Institute, noted that the websites of major women's groups, such as the National Organization for Women, the Ms. Foundation for Women, and women's centers at leading universities, seldom mentioned women in Islam, although many other issues were addressed.[44] Radical feminists are not altogether silent about the abuse of Muslim women, but what they have to say is usually framed in the context of the moral-equivalence paradigm. For example, Katha Pollitt of the *Nation* sees a "common thread of misogyny" in both the Taliban and Christian evangelicals, and compares death by stoning in Nigeria to evangelical attempts to ban abortion.[45] In a similar vein, Eve Ensler, author of the *Vagina Monologues*, goes about the country giving a lecture titled "Afghanistan Is Everywhere", which proposes that "we all have different forms of enforced burqas" and they're all equally bad.[46] A color-coded map in *The Penguin Atlas of Women in the World* shows the United States along with Somalia, Uganda, Yemen, Niger, and Libya as places where women are kept in their place by "patriarchal assumptions" operating in "potent combination with fundamentalist religious interpretations".[47] In short, feminists who are trapped in the multicultural ideology can't seem to distinguish between the sufferings of Somali women and the difficulties of suburban housewives in America. Worse, many feminists are unable to pass any judgment on non-Western cultures. A number of feminist authors have suggested that what appears to the Western mind as oppression is not perceived as such by Muslim women and is therefore not really oppression. According to this view, Western notions about the violation of individual rights do not apply in cultures where, as one professor puts it, "closeness to God" and "community" are more meaningful values.[48]

And what about the Hollywood elites, who are so outspoken about so many injustices? Do they stand up for the right to question or criticize Islam? Well, they failed to mention filmmaker Theo Van Gogh when they read out the list of that year's departed on Oscar night. Is it possible that the movers and shakers in the film world were afraid? Or were they simply engaging in what Orwell called "crimestop"—the automatic exclusion of unorthodox thoughts? Whether the locale is Hollywood or Holland, Orwell seems more relevant than ever. In the Netherlands, a Rotterdam artist created a mural to commemorate and condemn the murder of Theo Van Gogh. The painting depicted an angel and carried the biblical message "Thou shalt not kill." But an imam in a nearby mosque complained that the mural was "racist", so the Rotterdam police showed up, demolished the painting, arrested the TV crew that was filming it, and then erased the tape.[49] The incident is reminiscent of the bad old days in the Soviet Union, when some party figure or other would be airbrushed out of a group photo because he had fallen out of favor and been eliminated. The contemporary version of airbrushing takes the form of disappearing videos—not just videos erased by police in Holland, but also the numerous videos that are obligingly removed from YouTube, lest Muslims complain.

Imagine no religion? We don't have to imagine. We've already seen what "no religion" looks like. It looks like the Soviet Gulag and the mass murders carried out by Mao and Pol Pot. It looks like the Reign of Terror in France. It looks like the steady erosion of freedoms that is now taking place in secularized Western societies.

John Lennon also asked us to imagine "nothing to kill or die for". In today's Europe, that also requires little in the way of imagination.

Having lost their religion, many are discovering that post-Christian values may not, after all, be worth fighting and dying for—all the more so for those who are getting on in years and are hoping the really bad things won't happen in their lifetimes. The new motto for many middle-aged Europeans could be "Après moi le dhimmitude." The West is threatened both by a resurgent Islam and by its own home-grown relativistic ideologies. The answer to these threats is not to imagine no religion, but to remember the religion that has proven itself the best guardian of liberty.

Which culture is more likely to protect human rights and freedoms against totalitarian movements? A thoroughly secular culture that has cut itself off from all transcendent reference points? Or a culture imbued with the Judeo-Christian belief that human beings possess an inalienable, God-given dignity? It's one of those non-academic questions to which the wrong answer might prove fatal.

Atheists: The Descent of Man

The plan to have the pope arrested when he visited England in September 2010 didn't pan out, but suppose the plan—hatched by Richard Dawkins and the late Christopher Hitchens—had been successful. Suppose Dawkins and Hitchens had their dearest wishes fulfilled—not only to jail the pope but also to rid the West of Catholic Christianity. What would happen then? Dawkins is and Hitchens was an outspoken critic of Islam, but if Catholicism were to be cleared out of Europe, what would replace it as a buffer against Islam? In large part, Catholicism is the repository of Europe's highest values—values necessary to resist not only Islamization, but also the relativism that has allowed Islam to spread throughout Europe. What exactly do Dawkins and Hitchens have to offer in its place?

The answer—strange as it may seem—is Darwinism. Once you've dismissed God, you have to have some belief system to fill up all that empty space, and many atheists have hit on materialist evolution as the best substitute. Thus, Darwinism is now almost as popular as it was during the eugenics movement of the 1920s and 1930s. And it seems likely that if Western societies become less Christian, more people will fall back on Darwinian explanations of life. This has interesting implications for the future of Western societies. One consequence of taking Darwinian evolution to heart is the conclusion that Islam deserves to rule. Whether you subscribe to a crude "survival of the fittest" form of Darwinism or to Richard Dawkins' more sophisticated idea of cultural evolution through replicating "memes", it seems that Islam has developed a highly successful system for passing its values to the next generation.

Darwinists do not commonly draw this conclusion but rather oppose the spread of Islamic law on the grounds that it violates human rights and freedoms. But what does Darwinian evolution contribute to the cause of upholding human rights? The short answer is, it contributes nothing. This lack is evident in Ibn Warraq's book *Why I Am Not a Muslim*, which was inspired by Bertrand Russell's *Why I Am Not a Christian*. Warraq does a fine job of exploring all the ways in which Islam violates human rights, but then, to debunk the idea of God as Creator, he wanders off into a long explanation of Darwinian evolution, complete with lengthy quotes from Darwin, Huxley, and Dawkins. The gist of it all, as Warraq patiently explains, is that there is nothing special about man, who "was descended from some apelike ancestor, and certainly was not the product of special creation". He continues, "man is, at present, classified under the order Primates, along with tree shrews, lemurs, lorises, monkeys, and apes." [1] This sounds very scientific, but it's not too far removed from the Islamic claim that some of us infidels are the descendants of pigs and monkeys. How do such animals claim to have special rights?

The contradiction inherent in the atheist/Darwinian critique of Islam is even more pronounced in the work of Christopher Hitchens. On the one hand, Hitchens was a bold defender of the West; on the other hand, his views on human nature don't seem to lend much support to Western values. Although you have to admire his courage in standing up to Islamic attacks on human rights and liberties, you have to wonder what he saw in Darwinian evolution that can possibly be used to buttress the case for human rights. In his book *God Is Not Great: How Religion Poisons Everything*, Hitchens advances the idea that the story of evolution is far more satisfying than what he calls "God stories". Among the consoling comforts provided by evolution, we learn that the pig "is one of our fairly close cousins" because it "shares a great deal of our DNA". [2] Not since *Charlotte's Web* have pigs been portrayed so sympathetically. They "display many signs of intelligence", continues Hitchens, and when granted enough space "keep themselves very clean, arrange little bowers, bring up families, and engage in social interaction with other pigs". [3] Hitchens devotes a whole chapter to pigs and declares his solidarity with them by describing himself, along with various other historical figures, as nothing more than a mammal. Thus, Saint Francis and Muhammad are mammals; the Bible was put together by "crude, uncultured human mammals"; and Martin Luther King, Jr., though a great preacher, was "a mammal like the rest of us". [4] This might be a good argument for abstaining from ham sandwiches, but it doesn't help the case for human specialness or human rights.

Hitchens spends considerable time dismissing the belief in the father-hood of God as a piece of irrational nonsense and then ends up assert-ing that pigs are our cousins—all of which substantiates G. K. Chesterton's observation that when people stop believing in God, they start believ-ing in anything. Take for another example Richard Dawkins' views on the origin of life. In a filmed interview, Ben Stein asks Dawkins how he explains the existence of life on earth if there is no intelligent designer such as God. Amazingly, Dawkins concedes that there might indeed be some kind of designer, but that it couldn't possibly be God. Rather, he suggests, "highly evolved" aliens from another planet could have brought life to earth. Stein doesn't ask the obvious next question. He doesn't have to. It will occur to even the slowest film viewer to wonder how life got started on the alien planet. By other still more highly evolved aliens from a galaxy far, far away? Is it possible that the world's premier atheist is proposing an infinite regression of ETs as the explanation of life's origin? [5]

While presenting themselves as the party of rationality, the atheists proffer evolutionary theories that seem more faith-based than most reli-gious creeds. Aside from the "just so" story of life's origins, the most egregious example of "just believe" is the Darwinian assertion that human nature is simply part of nature and in no way distinct from it. That is a stunningly narrow view of human life. To accept it, you have to ignore language, literature, art, music, culture, free will—the things that make humans human. You also have to ignore the massive score gap between men and other animals in the achievement exams administered by time. The distance that separates man from the animals is not just a leap; it is a chasm. Animals may be plodding along under the rule of some natural evolutionary scheme, but humans seem to be progressing by a different set of rules. "We talk of wild animals," wrote Chesterton, "but man is the only wild animal. It is man that has broken out." [6] In some ways humans fit into the natural scheme of things, but in other ways they decidedly do not. This, and not the shape of a finch's beak, is exhibit A in the evolution debate, but Darwinians studiously avoid it. To have missed the main point does not speak well of their powers of observation.

Thus, it might be wise to question whether Hitchens, Dawkins, and the others have any plausible answer to the problems that plague the West. What they are saying, in effect, is that if only we can rid our-selves of religious superstitions, we can all rally around the idea that human life is purposeless and meaningless. Is this the well of wisdom from which the West will summon up the will to resist Islamization? It's difficult to see how you can effectively counter a vision of man as a slave of Allah with another vision of man as a slave of biology.

One of the ironic things about atheist apologetics is that it cuts away the rational basis for all the blessings the atheist wants to confer on mankind. Atheist writers like Hitchens and Dawkins want to free people from ignorance and superstition, but what's wrong with ignorance and superstition if they help you fit into your environment? Aren't they simply evolutionary adaptations? For that matter, what's wrong with genital mutilation, honor killings, child abuse, and genocide? Atheists deplore these things but can't provide any reason why one mammal should pass judgment on another mammal for obeying the promptings of its impulses. Hitchens, in particular, is full of outrage on behalf of his fellow mammals who have been the victims of pogroms, inquisitions, and witch hunts throughout the ages. There are a lot of implicit "shoulds", "oughts", and "thou shalt nots" scattered through his work. But it's not easy to figure out where they come from. Hitchens says we ought to behave morally but then falls back for support on Darwin, who was not a moralist but a biologist. Hitchens seems to believe in something like the dignity of human life, but he has thrown out the main case for it—the one that tells us we all are made in the image of God.

As Pope John Paul II observed, "When the sense of God is lost, there is also a tendency to lose the sense of man, of his dignity and his life." [7] Hitchens' book is titled *God Is Not Great*, but it just as well could be titled *Man Is Not Great*. After reading three hundred pages of his complaint that most of mankind is ridiculous, pathetic, and absurd, his audience may find it difficult to feel much warmth for the poor, deluded mammal. It doesn't help when Hitchens keeps insisting on our links to the animal kingdom. Take this passage:

> Elsewhere, a group of dedicated and patient scientists had located, in a remote part of the Canadian Arctic, several skeletons of a large fish that, 375 million years ago, exhibited the precursor features of digits, proto-wrists, elbows, and shoulders. The Tiktaalik ... joins the Archaeopteryx ... as one of the long-sought so-called missing links that are helping us to enlighten ourselves about our true nature. [8]

Enlighten ourselves about our true nature? By looking at a dead fish? In the Judeo-Christian vision, God is great and man has the potential for greatness because of his close relationship with God. In the gospel according to Hitchens, God is not great, and neither is man—unless you can find greatness in tracing your ancestry to a prehistoric fish or find meaning in "the proteins and acids which constitute our nature".[9]

Kudos to Hitchens for taking Islam to task for its many violations of human dignity. But how, one might ask, do you build the case for human dignity on a foundation of "proteins and acids"? How do you build a case for making simple distinctions between right and wrong? Darwinists argue that humans are just animals—our own kind, to be sure, but considered scientifically, there is nothing special or sacred about them. As for morality, that is also a product of evolution. Thus, from a Darwinian viewpoint, there can be no fixed, objective morality. There's a chilling ten-minute segment in Ben Stein's documentary film *Expelled* that shows how Darwinian ideas were used to justify the Nazi Final Solution. In one scene, the camera follows Ben Stein to a site once used to kill "defectives". When Stein asks the curator what was the biggest influence on the doctors who did the killing, she replies, "Darwinism".[10] No surprise there, given the Nazi superior-race theory and its dependence on the notion of evolutionary struggle. It's also no surprise that respect for human rights had no place in the Nazi program to hasten the process of natural selection.

Toward the end of his life, notable British historian Christopher Dawson began to worry that the West was living off the accumulated capital of Christian culture, and he wondered what would happen when that capital was used up. Christopher Hitchens' outraged sense of morality seems to draw on that dwindling account; even though he rejected Christianity, he grew up in a culture that still transmitted it. And his attempt to substitute what might be called "mammalian morality" for Judeo-Christian morality is not in the least convincing. The real problem comes when mammalian morality has the field to itself. Ever since Hitchens' native England became a post-Christian nation, the crime rate there has risen dramatically. The chances that any given citizen will be a crime victim are now significantly higher in England than in the United States. It's striking when you consider that not long ago, *England* was almost synonymous with order, security, and unarmed bobbies. Maybe increased criminality is one of the things that happens when a people comes to believe they're only a set of chemical reactions living in a world of random chance and decides to act accordingly.

Hitchens' attachment to human dignity might better be described as sentimental rather than rational. A much clearer view of where Darwinian thinking leads is provided by Lee Harris in his book *The Suicide of Reason: Radical Islam's Threat to the West*. Harris dispenses with high-sounding talk about "dignity" and "universal human rights" and goes right to the Darwinian heart of the matter. He maintains that in a life-and-death struggle for survival, "the law of the jungle that governed all animal existence on the planet" takes precedence over Enlightenment values.[11] In fact, says Harris, Enlightenment values are a handicap in such a struggle. For example, the West's "exaggerated confidence in the power of reason" leads it to underestimate the power of "fanaticism" and "tribalism".[12]

Harris takes pains to explain that he doesn't use the term *fanatic* as a term of moral reprobation, or *rational actor* as a term of approval. From a strictly Darwinian viewpoint, it doesn't make any sense to talk about "good" and "bad"; it makes sense to talk about only "winners" and "losers". In the struggle for survival in which Harris thinks we are already engaged, the independent rational actor will be the loser: "Rationality, at this point, requires group solidarity. It involves the surrender of moral autonomy and the fanatical embrace of the tribe."[13]

In an echo of Dawkins' appeal to cultural memes, Harris asserts that Islam has created an "artificial tribe", which, because of its fanaticism, has a tremendous evolutionary advantage in the struggle for survival. If the West hopes to resist Islam, says Harris, it must develop a similar fanatical tribal mindset:

> You must unconditionally support your own tribe or pack, and you must be prepared to act with utter ruthlessness toward those who belong to other tribes or packs. You must see members of the enemy tribe not as individuals or as fellow humans; you must see them as your existential enemy. That is all you need to know about them in order to be willing to kill them, torture them, or mutilate their corpses. When the laws of the jungle rule, the very idea of humanity is forgotten.[14]

I don't think we need to give up on the idea of humanity or to reduce ourselves to the level of "our pack versus your pack" in order to defeat supremacist Islam, but I do think we need to be clear, *contra* Hitchens, that we can't justify the rightness of our values by reference to biological theories. We should oppose sharia law because it violates human rights—not just our rights but the rights of Muslims also. That view of universal human rights is not rooted in evolutionary theory; it's rooted in the Judeo-Christian belief in the sanctity and equality of all men. If that vision fades in the West, expect to see more converts to the "law of the jungle". Harris says that the struggle for survival needs to be brutal and ruthless. If the Darwinian view of human nature is the correct one, Harris has drawn a logical conclusion.

6

Multiculturalists: Why Johnny Can't Read the Writing on the Wall

In America, multiculturalism is a widely held creed, whose promotion has become the chief mission of our schools. In most European countries, multiculturalism is an official state policy, and deviation from it might land you in jail. But in Europe this situation might be changing. Recently, the leaders of Europe's three most powerful nations pronounced multiculturalism a failure. Britain's Prime Minister David Cameron called it a "failed policy", German Chancellor Angela Merkel said that multiculturalism had "utterly failed", and French President Nicholas Sarkozy declared that the concept is "clearly . . . a failure".[1]

How is it that a concept that until yesterday was hailed as the best hope for unifying diverse peoples is now under fire from the very people who encouraged it? The answer, in brief, is that multiculturalism doesn't unite people; it divides them. As Cameron put it, "Under the doctrine of state multiculturalism, we have encouraged different cultures to live separate lives, apart from each other and the mainstream."[2] Sarkozy's statement was more pointed: "If you come to France, you accept to melt into a single community, which is the national community, and if you do not want to accept that, you cannot be welcome in France".[3]

What prompted the three leaders to reverse course? In a word, Islam. The combination of multicultural openness and Muslim assertiveness had proven to be a disastrous mix. Many Muslims were not only failing to abide by European customs; they were failing to abide by the law. In Sweden the vast majority of rapes and other violent crimes are being committed by members of the Muslim immigrant community. In France Muslims have established 751 "no-go zones", Islamic enclaves—some as big as small cities—in which native French and police dare not set foot. In England Muslim terrorist groups are flourishing. And everywhere, previously harmonious societies with shared values have been splintered into hostile camps.

Why doesn't multiculturalism work? The answer is that multiculturalism is essentially a form of relativism in which morality is relative to culture. The corresponding belief is that the members of one culture have no right to make judgments about the rightness or wrongness of another culture's traditions or practices. Thus, even commonsense observations about group behavior can leave one open to charges of racism, homophobia, or Islamophobia. In Germany Thilo Sarrazin lost his position on the board of the Deutche Bundesbank for writing a book critical of Muslim immigrants who refuse to integrate into German society. In Denmark, Lars Hedegaard, the president of the Free Press Society, was put on trial for observing that Muslim families in his country exhibited a high incidence of child abuse. The fact that he made the comment during the course of a private conversation didn't seem to matter. Throughout the West, critics of Islamic laws and customs at odds with those of the host society are routinely subject to coercion and intimidation by their own government. Pope Benedict's phrase "dictatorship of relativism" is an apt description of these attempts to control thought and speech in the name of tolerance.

Because of its inherent divisiveness, the multiculturalist model would eventually fail in any society. But it is particularly fatal to a society that has in its midst an aggressive cultural group that refuses to subscribe to relativism. By neglecting to stand up for their own values, traditions, and religious heritage—indeed, by denigrating them— European countries left themselves almost defenseless against a resurgent Islam. Islam's success in Europe has been built in large part on European self-doubt.

In America it is not yet a crime to offend against multicultural pieties, but, as in Europe, our attachment to multiculturalism has severely hampered our ability to defend against stealth jihad. The most obvious example is the Fort Hood incident. Major Hasan's army and medical-school superiors didn't report his threatening behavior because they didn't want to criticize a Muslim. Instead they found reasons to praise him. As one evaluation put it, the major's work had "extraordinary potential to inform national policy and military strategy".[4] Unfortunately, after Major Hasan had completed his "work", the army chose to remain uninformed. The Defense Department's report on the lessons of Fort Hood came out several months after the shooting, but it had nothing to say about Islam, Muslims, or jihad; it did not even mention Major Hasan by name. As Dorothy Rabinowitz wrote in the *Wall Street Journal*, the failure to name the threat posed to our armed forces by militant Islamists in the ranks is "a signal to the entire Defense bureaucracy that the subject is taboo".[5]

Despite the many criticisms of the Defense Department's Fort Hood report, the government still seems committed to policies that let diversity trump security. The latest example is the congressional repeal of the "Don't Ask, Don't Tell" policy. Homosexuals will now serve openly in the military; and it is highly probable that once affirmative-action policies kick in, the culture of the military will be permanently changed. Several high-ranking officers have made it known that soldiers who can't adopt a gay-positive attitude will be forced out of the service. Once that happens, the term *army camp* may well take on an entirely new meaning. No one knows what the effect of the new policy will be on recruitments and reenlistments, but it seems safe to say that a lot of young men and women will think twice before signing up. If troop levels should sharply decline as a result of diversity policies, would the multiculturalists come to their senses? It seems unlikely. Very few are willing to question the multiculturalist faith. After the Fort Hood shooting, Gen. George Casey, the Army chief of staff declared, "As horrific as this tragedy was, if our diversity becomes a casualty, I think that's worse".[6] How about the loss of our ability to defend ourselves? Would that be a lesser tragedy than the loss of our diversity? That seems to be the logical conclusion of the multiculturalist thought process.

The Catholic Church, along with many other Christian churches, teaches that homosexual behavior is sinful. That has quickly become a minority point of view and should therefore qualify as a diverse opinion. But, apparently, some diversities are more equal than others. A bill pending in the Legislative Assembly of Alberta, Canada, would make it illegal for private schools, Catholic schools, and homeschools to teach that homosexual acts are sinful. A representative of the Education Ministry explained: "We do not tolerate disrespect for differences ... a fundamental nature of our society is to respect diversity".[7] It does not seem to have occurred to the ministry that Catholicism is also a diversity; or if it did occur to them, it seems that they do not consider Catholicism to be a very important form of diversity.

In the multiculturalist scheme of things, the morals of traditional Christians don't count as much as those of other groups. The same goes for their holidays. Recently the European Union sent schools three million calendars that listed Muslim, Chinese, and Hindu holidays but left out Christmas and Easter.[8] When criticized, EU bureaucrats said it was a mistake, but it's the kind of mistake that seems consistent with a certain mindset. The Christmas crèche on the town green is mostly a thing of the past. Public schools long ago banned Christmas plays, Christmas carols, and even Christmas vacation, which has been renamed winter vacation. As for Christmas cards with mangers, shepherds, and wise men, you'll have to look harder for them, or possibly special order them. Most retailers prefer to stay on the right side of the multiculturalists, and that means no Christian images at Christmas time.

These multiculturalist attacks on Christmas make perfect sense, because the anti-Christian thrust is not incidental to multiculturalism but central to it. If multiculturalism has a core belief, it's a belief in unfallen human nature—the antithesis of the Christian belief in Original Sin. In the days when they needed to demonstrate in order to get what they wanted, multicultural activists used to chant, "Hey, hey, ho, ho, Western culture's gotta go." Why must we say goodbye to the West? Because one of the chief sins of the West was to introduce Christianity to an innocent world.

According to multicultural mythology, the non-Western world was a happy place before European Christians introduced their notions of right and wrong, moral and immoral, good and evil. Multiculturalism is mainly an invention of modern educators, many of whom cling to Rousseau's belief in the existence of the Noble Savage—that naturally virtuous primitive man who seems to hang around the imaginations of the perpetually naïve. From the Rousseauian viewpoint, man fell not from a state of grace but from the state of nature. Consequently, multiculturalists dismiss the Judeo-Christian story of the Fall and replace it with their own myth of original innocence destroyed. According to this story, non-Westerners lived in an unspoiled state of nature, and Columbus and other colonists were the serpents in the garden who introduced greed, war, slavery, and guilt-ridden Christianity.

Multiculturalists seem to be enamored of what might be called blue-lagoon anthropology, an idealized vision of society not unlike Margaret Mead's doubtful description of Samoa. What they have in mind is not any real culture, but a nonexistent ideal. In this mythical culture, people live in harmony with each other, get along fine without technology, swim in blue lagoons, and have guilt-free sex under the palm trees. Thus, a good portion of the multiculturalist curriculum is devoted, not to studying the achievements of the West or learning about current world cultures, but to eulogizing past cultures such as those of the Mayan and American Indian.

Another good chunk of the typical school curriculum is devoted to celebrating alternative lifestyles. Sexual liberation à la Rousseau is a main part of the multiculturalist agenda. All those thoughts about unspoiled human nature were bound to lead to thoughts about unspoiled sex—natural, guilt-free, and uneventful. Uneventful because, as Rousseau helpfully pointed out, if any children come along, the state—or, as contemporary Rousseauians like to say, the "village"—can take care of them. According to multiculturalist theory, sex was meant to be natural and happy, and it would have been if it weren't for the Christians who gummed it all up with things like weddings and lifelong vows.

One of the striking things about multiculturalist education is the extent to which it celebrates sexual diversity along with cultural diversity and, if anything, celebrates it more enthusiastically. For example, *It's Elementary*, a documentary video that's widely screened to teachers, demonstrates how schools can be made gay-friendly and gay-affirmative (by, for example, revealing to primary-grade students that songs from *The Lion King* were written and sung by gay men). The success of such efforts may be gauged by the fact that in 2007 the Gay, Lesbian and Straight Education Network claimed that over 3,500 schools had gay-straight alliances registered with them.[9] It's probably safe to assume that this is somewhat more than the number of school-supported traditional family clubs.

All this attention to sexual diversities and pre-Columbian tribes left the multiculturalists unprepared for the major cultural-diversity story of modern times. While multiculturalist educators in the United States were busy arranging "coming out" days for gay students, over in Afghanistan, Yemen, and Saudi Arabia, the imams and mullahs were perfecting their own educational ideology—one that raises up jihadists to wage war against the West. It's difficult to conceive of a more disastrous combination of events than the simultaneous emergence on the world stage of a fiercely passionate ideology dedicated to conquering the West, and of another, dangerously naïve ideology, eager to dismantle it from within. Yet the majority of multiculturalist educators do not seem to recognize the *danse macabre* in which they are caught up. But that's understandable. Multiculturalism was an anti-intellectual project from the beginning. An offshoot of the self-esteem movement, it wasn't designed to deepen knowledge of other cultures, but to make students and teachers feel good about themselves by affirming other cultures and other lifestyles. The trouble was, there were so many cultures and so many lifestyles in need of a hug that by century's end, the diversity educators still hadn't gotten around to Islam.

The multiculturalists had been too busy studying the Mayan to know much about the Muslim. So when New York and Washington were hit on September 11, multiculturalists had to take at face value the instantaneously established consensus among elites that Islam is a religion of peace. Nobody, least of all the multiculturalists, had bothered to study what Islam actually taught. Moreover, because of their anti-Western bias, they were prepared to believe that the attackers had turned to violence only because of valid grievances against Western imperialism. Thus, even the explosive force of 9/11 did nothing to shatter the multiculturalist presumption against the West. If we were attacked, it must have been our own fault. "Why do they hate us?" (with its implication that they must have had good reason) became the watchword of the day.

True to form, on the first anniversary of the attack, the National Education Association prepared a special website with links to lesson plans that counseled teachers, "Do not suggest any group is responsible"; "Discuss historical instances of American intolerance"; and "Explore ... current examples of ethnic conflict, discrimination, and stereotyping at home and abroad." [10] While most of the nation was wondering when and where the next blow would fall, the educational establishment seized on 9/11 as the perfect opportunity to preach about the dangers of stereotyping. In short, Manhattan has just been bombed; therefore, it must be time for another unit on the internment of Japanese-Americans during World War II.

Multiculturalists used 9/11 as an occasion to haul out and dust off every questionable or shameful incident in the American past. Such an approach is dubious even in times of peace, but when the nation is under attack, it seems suicidal. If you insist on telling students that their culture is contemptible, eventually they will take you at your word and conclude that their culture deserves to perish. Robert Spencer recounts what a university student told her American Indian professor: "I don't see anything about my culture to be proud of. It's all nothing. My race is just nothing. . . . Look at your culture. Look at American Indian tradition. Now I think that's really great. You have something to be proud of. My culture is nothing."[11] Commenting on this incident, Spencer writes, "American high schools, colleges, and universities have now created millions of Americans who think and speak like Rachel. They have been subjected to decades of anti-American, anti-Western and anti-Christian conditioning by our educational establishment. And many like Rachel are today in positions that affect public policy."[12]

Here's an example of the kind of Western-culture bashing Rachel was probably exposed to. It's from a Silver Burdett grade-6 reader:

> Like many Native American children who lived on reservations, Pablita and Patrick went to mission schools. . . . They lived at the mission schools and rarely saw their families. They were not allowed to speak their own languages or to take part in activities related to their people's past, because the schools wanted them to give up their traditional ways. Both Pablita and Patrick, however, kept their love for their people's ways in their hearts.[13]

So the mission of the mission school was to wipe out the beautiful cultural inheritance of Native Americans. Undoubtedly there's an element of truth here. Some cultural erasure did occur. That's what happens when cultures rub up against each other. But were there no positive benefits for Pablita and Patrick? Is it not possible that Christian faith is beneficial to those who accept it? Is it not possible that some natives *wanted* their children to learn skills that would give them a better life? What about all the Christian missions all over the world that build hospitals, dig wells, and encourage equal education and opportunities for girls and boys alike?

It's one thing to make a point about the failings of Western/Christian culture and then move on. But for multiculturalist educators, denigrating Western civilization is the whole point. Elementary readers abound with stories like that of Pablita and Patrick—stories about deeply spiritual and harmonious cultures that get wiped out by the Westerners. But wait a minute! What's the mission of the multiculturalists? On the one hand, they argue that the worst thing you can do is take away someone's culture, and on the other hand, all of their courses and textbooks are aimed at depriving Western students of their own multimillenia cultural inheritance. As Mark Steyn observes, multicultural education is a "cult of tolerance in which you demonstrate your sensitivity to other cultures by being almost totally insensitive to your own." [14]

It's understandable that Johnny can't read the writing on the wall. After studying American Indian spirituality for four years in a row in grade school, and racism and sexism awareness for four years in high school, it's a little difficult to see the big global picture. And when you don't know anything about your own culture except to feel guilty about it, you won't have the conviction to defend it. And, just as important, you won't have the conviction to extend it—not even to the next generation. Go back for a minute to the student who thought more of Native American culture than of her own. She's not a good prospect for resisting Islamic aggression. But it goes beyond that. She's not a good prospect for motherhood either—not in the sense of lacking motherly qualities but in the sense of lacking the desire to bear and raise children who will keep her own culture going. As columnist Don Feder observes, "Confident societies have babies. People with a sense of mission have children. Nations with a sense of destiny and faith in the future fill maternity wards, and nurseries, and cradles." [15] It's a good description of Islamic societies perhaps, but not, unfortunately, of contemporary Western ones.

America's schools seem bent on undermining our confidence in Western civilization. At the same time, they have no qualms about obliging Islam. For example, a Harvard University training program for primary and secondary teachers encourages student activities such as memorizing Islamic principles, appointing imams, and acting out prayer at a mosque. A sample lesson plan encourages students to monitor newscasts that stereotype Muslims. [16] In a similar fashion, textbooks have been revised to include mostly positive portrayals of Islam. Consider the following items in some widely used textbooks. Prentice Hall's *World History* defines *jihad* as "Struggle in God's service ... usually a personal duty for Muslims who focus on overcoming immorality within themselves." [17] Another Prentice Hall text describes jihad as "a person's inner struggle to achieve spiritual peace." [18] McDougal Littell's world-history text tells us, "The persecuted people often welcomed the [Muslim] invaders and chose to accept Islam. They were attracted by the appeal of the message of Islam, which offered equality and hope in this world." [19]

Moreover, in contrast to the descriptions of other religions, the claims of Islam are taken at face value. Thus, in McDougal Littell's *Modern World History* we read, "Muhammad's teachings, which are the revealed word of God ... are found in the holy book called the Qur'an." [20] Referring to Jesus, the book states, "According to the New Testament, Jesus of Nazareth was born around 6 to 4 B.C." and "According to Jesus' followers, he rose from the dead." [21] The subtle suggestion that the Bible is a collection of stories while the Koran is a revelation from God is reinforced in McDougal Littell's *World Cultures and Geography*: "Judaism, Christianity, and Islam all share common traits. Judaism is a story of exile. Christians believe that Jesus was the promised Messiah. The Qur'an is the collection of God's revelations to Muhammad." [22]

In addition to misinterpretations, there are significant omissions in the textbooks. While the Atlantic slave trade is discussed at great length, the Arab slave trade is largely ignored, although it was of much longer duration, involved the enslavement of many millions more, and continued into the first half of the twentieth century. According to Gilbert T. Sewall of the American Textbook Council, "Textbooks mention Islamic slavery only obliquely, as with the janissary soldiers, or not at all". [23]

Because it is impossible totally to ignore the violent side of Islam, another multiculturalist tactic is to play the game of moral equivalence. While there is some violence in Islam, a book might state, there is violence in all religions. Thus, the fifth edition of *Religion in America*, a widely used college text, informs its readers:

- "A recent study of ... Judaism, Christianity, and Islam ... notes that all three exhibit a profoundly ambiguous attitude about violence". [24]

- "In the current situation, there are no clear cut 'good guys' and 'bad guys' ". [25]

- "It is important to remember that, worldwide, the last decade has seen violence perpetrated by people who claimed affiliation with religions other than Islam". [26]

- "Most of our religious traditions and faith communities have elements of both [peace and militarism] in their history, and

> most have been involved in overt violence, either in the past or currently".[27]

"Either in the past or currently"? Yes, but we all happen to live in the "currently", and for the last couple of decades, about 95 percent of terrorist attacks have been perpetrated in the name of Islam. One can argue that textbooks can't be expected to keep up with the latest news events, but the author can't very well claim that she didn't have sufficient data. The fifth edition of *Religion in America* was published in 2006—after 9/11, after Beslan, after Madrid, after the London Tube bombings, after the Bali bombings, and after the almost daily bombings of mosques, markets, and civilians in Iraq. But old theories die hard. Educators may talk about the importance of change and adaptability, but a good many of them have failed to notice that the world has changed, and changed in ways that were never envisioned in multiculturalist theory.

In one of his columns, Mark Steyn makes the observation that a suicide bomb is a weak weapon, except in a suicide culture. In a culturally confident society like Israel, a long campaign of terrorism serves only to stiffen resolve. In other parts of the West, it's a different story. In Spain, a single hour of train bombings in Madrid put the country into surrender mode. In the United States, the September 11 bombings set the whole nation to wondering, in good multiculturalist fashion, what we had done wrong. One of the first things that leaders in England, Canada, and the United States did after 9/11 was to hasten to local mosques to assure Muslim leaders that our peoples were not Islamaphobic.

Long before the jihadists began their campaign of suicide bombings in the West, the multiculturalists had installed the cultural equivalent of suicide bombs in nearly every classroom in the United States, Canada, and Europe. While radical madrassas around the world schooled Muslim children to despise non-Muslims, the diversity educators took pains to teach their students that no Western society was worth defending.

In retrospect, it looks as though our students would have been better served if they had spent less time studying the Battle of Wounded Knee and more time studying the Battle of Lepanto, less time understanding the beauty of diversity, and more time understanding the misery of dhimmitude. Of course, they don't know anything at all about dhimmitude, which means they will be ill prepared to prevent that fate from befalling them.

A couple of decades ago, the Ayatollah Khomeini offered some insights into Islam that were apparently overlooked by the multiculturalists:

> Islam makes it incumbent on all adult males . . . to prepare themselves for the conquest of countries so that the writ of Islam [sharia] is obeyed in every country in the world. . . . Those who know nothing of Islam pretend that Islam counsels against war. Those are witless. Islam says: Kill all the unbelievers just as they would kill you all! . . . Islam says: Whatever good there is exists thanks to the sword and in the shadow of the sword! People cannot be made obedient except with the sword! The sword is the key to Paradise, which can be opened only for the Holy Warriors![28]

This leads to the question: Who are you going to believe—the multiculturalist apologists for Islam, or the ayatollah and any number of other Islamic religious authorities who have made similar pronouncements? It seems that devout adherents of Islam don't want to live in a multicultural society. They want to live in an Islamic society, and they want you to live in one too.

The reason the multiculturalists are blind to all of this is that multiculturalism itself is a kind of religion—and a very parochial one at that. Rather than taking the perspective of other cultures, multiculturalists actually look at the world through Western eyes. They assume that the taken-for-granted qualities that developed in the West can be taken for granted anywhere. In other words, they assume that the Western concern with justice and ethics, with equality and freedom, with tolerance and inclusiveness is just a natural human evolution rather than a difficult cultural achievement. A while back, I mentioned that multiculturalists have a core belief in unfallen human nature. That means they tend to ignore the role played by culture, and particularly Christian culture, in helping people to overcome their natural tendencies to dehumanize, exploit, and enslave one another.

The multiculturalist faith in human nature also leads to a denial of sin—or, to put it more exactly, to a denial of non-Western sins. It shouldn't be too difficult to say that the massacre of pilgrims en route to shrines in Iraq is evil, that the idolization of suicide bombers by Palestinians is evil, or that the slaughter of innocent children in a Russian elementary school is evil, yet *evil* is not a word with which the commenting class is comfortable.

In Beslan, Russia, in 2004, thirty-two heavily armed Muslim terrorists took hostage twelve hundred adults and children in an elementary school. They executed twenty hostages within the first few hours and warned police that they would kill twenty hostages for every hostage taker wounded. As a result of the ensuing three-day siege, nearly 350 hostages were killed, over half of them children. When commentators first tried to grapple with the Beslan atrocity, it was evident that they were not used to thinking in terms of good and evil. They fell back on the usual clichés to describe the killers as "radicals", "separatists", and even "activists". Dutch Foreign Minister Ben Bot described Beslan as a "deep human tragedy".[29] But a tragedy, like a car accident, is something that no one really intends. To use the word in the context of the Beslan massacre shifts the focus away from the moral depravity of the terrorists.

General Casey referred to the Fort Hood massacre as a tragedy. The media now routinely describe the 9/11 attacks as a tragedy. The Church, however, is not so quick to relieve men of their moral responsibility by framing all events as Greek tragedies in which men are controlled by their Fates. The multiculturalist depiction of Christian history as a series of Inquisitions and Crusades is a caricature, but its main objection to Christianity is accurate enough. Christianity *is* judgmental in the sense that it brings men face-to-face with their sins. Wherever it spread, it did bring a sharper sense of right and wrong, good and evil. The mission of the Church, however, is not to condemn men for their sins, but to bring them to repentance and a new relationship with God. And the world is better off when men realize the depth of sin and their responsibility for it. Karl Marx had Christianity in mind when he called religion the opiate of the people. But Christianity didn't put people to sleep; it woke them up. It was Christians who stood against the Roman practice of infanticide. It was Christians who tried to wake up the world to the evils of slavery, Nazism, communism, and more recently, abortion and euthanasia. Christians themselves are often involved in evil; they too are sinners. But there are no Christian principles that can justify sinful actions.

Multiculturalism, by contrast, doesn't provide any ground on which to resist or even recognize evil. The theory is too mired in relativism to be of any use in distinguishing good from evil. If you're looking for an opiate of the people, multiculturalism fits the bill. By substituting slogans—"racism", "intolerance", "Islamophobia"—for thought, it induces a kind of intellectual and moral stupor. Melanie Phillips describes the process in her book *Londonistan*:

> The British education system simply ceased transmitting either the values or the story of the nation to successive generations, delivering instead the message that truth was an illusion and that the nation and its values were whatever anyone wanted them to be.[30]

Phillips goes on to explain the result of this process:

> This moral inversion has been internalized so completely that the more Islamic terrorism there is, the more hysterically British Muslims insist that they are under attack by "Islamophobes" and a hostile West.[31]

As for the police, they

> have been paralyzed by the fear of giving offense to any minority group and being tarred with the lethal charge of prejudice.[32]

As for assimilation:

> So when Muslims refused to accept minority status and insisted instead that their values must trump those of the majority, Britain had no answer.[33]

Well, they did have an answer of sorts—more multiculturalism. For example, the London Metropolitan Police Authority recruitment targets for 2009–10 required that 27 percent of all new police recruits must be "black and minority ethnic" and 41 percent must be female.[34] One result of the fewer-men/more-women policy is the risk-averse approach that the London Police now seem to follow. During the summer 2011 riots in London, police watched passively as rioters smashed windows, looted, and burned. The police were under orders to "stand and observe".[35] On the other hand, the police can be very zealous when it comes to enforcing multiculturalist strictures against homophobia and Islamophobia. As Mark Steyn observes, "In Britain, everything is policed except crime".

"At the heart of this unpicking of national identity", writes Phillips, "lies a repudiation of Christianity, the founding faith of the nation and the fundamental source of its values".[36] But Christians themselves are hardly immune to the lure of multiculturalism. The prime example is the current Archbishop of Canterbury, Dr. Rowan Williams, who has called for the recognition of some aspects of Muslim law and said that the adoption of sharia law in Britain is "unavoidable".[37] As Phillips notes, "In Britain ... the Church of England has been in the forefront of the *retreat* from the Judeo-Christian heritage. At every stage it has sought to appease the forces of secularism, accommodating itself to family breakdown, seeking to be nonjudgmental and embracing multiculturalism." [38]

Why do so many Christians embrace multiculturalism despite its essentially relativistic and anti-Christian nature? The answer is that multiculturalism bears a surface similarity to Christianity. In fact, it can almost be considered a Christian heresy. As Robert Spencer maintains:

> Multiculturalism is one of the most successful heresies in history: it is as dominant in America and Western Europe today as Calvinism ever was in Geneva, or Anglicanism in Elizabethan London. Multiculturalism is the entrenched ruling dogma of the United States of America. The victory of the multiculturalist idea is so complete that those in thrall to its dogma do not even seem to notice the grotesqueries in which it involves them.[39]

Multiculturalism seems close enough to Christianity to serve for some as a substitute for Christianity, except that those who subscribe wholeheartedly to the multiculturalist faith don't look upon it as a substitute, but as an obvious way of fulfilling their Christian duties. Multiculturalism seems Catholic in its embrace of all ethnicities. It seems to accept the stranger. It seems to seek social justice for all. It seems to be tolerant and nonjudgmental. In short, it seems to mesh with Christian values. Consequently, the multiculturalist agenda—with all its destructive potential—has been welcomed by many Christians. Multiculturalist education is now as prevalent in Christian schools as it is in their public counterparts.

A recent book for Catholic children illustrates some of the problems inherent in the multiculturalist approach. Pauline Books has published *My Muslim Friend*—a book that it hopes will give Catholic children, their parents, and their teachers "a new understanding and appreciation of Islam".[40] *My Muslim Friend* does deal with some of the differences between Islam and Christianity, but the reader soon finds that commonalities trump differences by a wide margin. The two friends in the story are like peas in a pod. Mary goes to church; Aisha goes to mosque. Mary has her rosary beads; Aisha has her prayer beads. Mary believes in one God; so does Aisha. Mary's church reveres the Virgin Mary; Aisha's faith has great reverence for Mary as well. Catholics believe in Jesus as the Son of God; Muslims honor Jesus as one of God's greatest prophets. Similarities are even drawn between the pilgrimage to Mecca and a visit to Lourdes. In both cases, we are told, pilgrims often take holy water back home with them.

A child reading this book will come away with the impression that the things we have in common are more important than the things that separate us. No doubt this is what the author intends. She has constructed her story in such a way that the only fitting conclusion for the reader to draw is, "Why can't we all just get along?"—or some variant thereof. Given the high-tension times we live in, it's tempting to gloss over the differences between Catholics and Muslims; but if, in fact, there are substantial differences, too much emphasis on the similarities can be both misleading and confusing.

Take the matter of revelation. *My Muslim Friend* starts off on the right foot by stating that Muhammad "believed" that the voice he heard came from the angel Gabriel and that his followers "came to believe" that Allah was calling Muhammad to be a prophet. But this qualified assertion soon slides into the unqualified mode. Thus, "God's messages to Muhammad became the Qur'an", and "Aisha prays five times, as Allah instructed Muhammad to do." [41] Of course, the author of *My Muslim Friend* doesn't come out and say that Muhammad's revelation was a valid one, but neither does she do anything to counter the possibility that many children might arrive at that conclusion. This is one of the problems inherent in the multiculturalist approach. Multiculturalist education primes children to believe that there are many truths and many valid traditions. The ethic of nonjudgmentalism prohibits even a Catholic text from questioning the validity of another religion's revelation. This approach is fine for creating an atmosphere of good feelings, but it doesn't do much to sharpen a youngster's ability to make distinctions. And the distinction in this case is a crucial one—the Koranic teachings about Jesus flatly contradict Christian beliefs. If you accept one, you have to reject the other.

And how about the cultural differences? One wonders if there will be a UK version of *My Muslim Friend* with the story set in some Yorkshire town with a large Muslim population such as Bradford or Leeds. Aisha, being thirteen, would be just about of age for a flight to Islamabad and marriage to a thirty-year-old first cousin—a custom that is the norm in Muslim Bradford, but for which there is, as far as I know, no Christian counterpart.

The notion that Muslims and Christians share much in common is misleading on many counts, but the main one is that it makes Christians think they understand Islam when they don't. It's similar to the Russians-are-people-just-like-us-so-their-ideology-can't-be-that-bad mentality that passed for deep thinking among college students during the Cold War days. Yes, the Russian people were like us in many ways, but as even the Russians now admit, communist ideology was deadly.

Too much emphasis on commonality is misleading in another sense. It makes it difficult to believe that Christian churches are really serious about their own beliefs. After all, if Mary is nice, and Aisha is nice, and the people at Aisha's mosque are just as nice as the people at Mary's church, and if their religions have so much in common, then what's the difference? Why be Christian? Such an approach suggests to students that Christ doesn't really matter. Naturally, the author doesn't say this, but children can draw their own inferences. If there are many roads to heaven, maybe it doesn't really matter which one you take. The "Note for Catholic Teachers" that concludes *My Muslim Friend* only adds to the confusion. It suggests a number of activities, including a day of fasting at Ramadan, so that "Christian students will have an opportunity to share in the Islamic experience." [42]

Multiculturalist religious education is a self-defeating enterprise. If students gain the impression that there is no substantial difference between Christianity and Islam, they might well conclude that it's better to align themselves with the faith that's confident and on the rise. Here and there, one hears reports of North American Christians converting to Islam. Expect that to increase. In Latin America Islam is one of the fastest-growing faiths; and in Europe Islam is winning converts at a rapidly increasing rate. As the geopolitical winds keep blowing in the direction of Islam, Christians will come under increasing pressure to make the switch. Books such as *My Muslim Friend* will make it that much easier for them to make the necessary adjustments and accommodations.

Multiculturalist education seems designed to make everyone, with the exception of Western Christians, feel comfortable about their culture. The lesson seems to have sunk in. A few years ago, a Los Angeles Police Department plan to identify Muslim enclaves that might incubate terrorists was shelved when several Muslim groups complained. "There was a clear message from the Muslim community that they were not comfortable with it. So we listened", said Mary Grady, a spokeswoman for the LAPD.[43] If we follow that line of thought to its conclusion, it means that our society will make concessions whenever Muslims claim to feel uncomfortable. This approach will make things more comfortable for non-Muslims too for a time, because there will be less friction. But one day, the non-Muslims will wake up and feel not so comfortable anymore.

Christian Enablers

Islam has many enablers in the secular world. Just as disturbing is the fact that many Christians act as unwitting enablers of the Islamist agenda. Critics of Christianity such as Sam Harris, Kevin Phillips, and Chris Hedges have warned that Christians are a major threat to American freedoms. In a way they may be right—though certainly not in the way they intend. There is no danger of Christians imposing a Christian theocracy on America, but there is a danger that Christians, in their naïveté and in their desire to be thought tolerant, may inadvertently pave the way for an eventual Islamic theocracy in the West.

The paving process is already under way. Many priests, ministers, and Christian groups unthinkingly rally behind every initiative to advance Islamic law—whether it be the building of a mosque at Ground Zero, a protest against Congressional hearings on Muslim radicalization, or the launch of an Islamic stock exchange. But the main way in which Christians are smoothing the path to sharia is through sheer complacency. Rather than taking the effort to examine the nature of Islam, too many Christians have fallen back on the simplistic proposition that Christians and Muslims share much in common. Let's look at some examples of this fixation on finding common ground.

The way the average church member is most likely to encounter the common-ground argument is through participation in an education program held in conjunction with a local mosque. These programs are intended not only to educate congregants about Islam, but also, in many cases, to provide them with an opportunity to show their solidarity with Muslims. Islamic apologists have done a good job of framing their causes as civil rights issues, and this has great appeal to the many Christians who see the pursuit of social justice as their main mission. These Christians may feel that supporting and defending the rights of Muslims is the same as linking arms with civil rights marchers in the 1960s. What they may not realize is that Islam is not simply a religion but a system of law and social organization at odds with our own.

The typical church information program hosts a Muslim spokesman who explains Islam to the congregation. Naturally, the spokesman presents Islam as a religion of peace and love. And naturally, in their desire to be loving and accepting, the Christians tend not to question or challenge the speaker. According to Faith McDonnell of the Institute of Religion and Democracy,

> Many churches are obsessed with making themselves likeable to Islamists ... such churches opt for sessions of feel-good dialogue with the local mosque, gushing about how much Christianity and Islam have in common, and never challenging Muslims to serious debate on those so-called commonalities.[1]

One such program was conducted on July 24, 2010, at the Lamb of God Church in Fort Myers, Florida. The guest speaker was the imam Shaker Elsayed of the northern-Virginia mosque Dar Al Hijrah—the same mosque where two of the 9/11 hijackers prayed and where the imam Anwar Al-Awlaki mentored Major Nidal Hasan, the perpetrator of the Fort Hood massacre. Another frequenter of Dar Al Hijrah was Ahmed Omar Abu Ali, who is in prison for providing material support to al-Qaeda. Imam Elsayed was an unofficial spokesman for Ali's family during his trial. Elsayed was also a secretary general of the Muslim American Society (MAS), an organization that has been linked to the Muslim Brotherhood.

At Lamb of God Church, Imam Elsayed's presentation was politely received by the four-hundred-person audience; when a handful of ACT! for America members asked tough questions during the question-and-answer session, however, the audience became visibly disturbed. Apparently the sympathies of the audience were with the representatives of Islam and against anyone who would question them.

So too were the sympathies of their pastor, Rev. Walter Fohs, who told a reporter that Christians who fear Islam don't understand their own religion. There are more violent chapters in the Bible than in the Koran, Fohs said, implying that Islam is not the only religion with violent tendencies.[2] This moral-equivalence argument sits well with many Christians who, along with Americans in general, have been taught multiculturalist myths about the essential equality of different cultures and religions. So they have no reason not to nod in agreement when they are informed by an Islamic cleric (or by their own pastor) that the new mosque in their neighborhood is no more a threat to their way of life than is the church or synagogue down the street. For too many Christians, the essence of enlightened Christianity is tolerance and nonjudgmentalism. Probing for differences between Islam and Christianity strikes them as inappropriate.

It seems safe to assume that the congregants at the Lamb of God Church are sincere Christians who want to do the "Christian thing". But what exactly is the "Christian thing" to do in regard to an increasingly aggressive Islam? In recent decades, the notion has grown that the Christian approach is always one of acceptance, inclusiveness, and nonjudgmentalism. In the long run, that approach could prove to be fatal, because it constitutes one of the main obstacles to recognizing and resisting the threats we face. It's important, then, to call into question the idea that we must be accepting of all differences. The simplest way to do this is to point out that, by contemporary standards, Christ could be both intolerant and judgmental—and this was especially true of his dealings with religious authorities. "What would Jesus do?" is a question that Christians often ask themselves. The question seems a bit presumptuous because Christ's responses were rarely what people expected. In many cases we simply don't know the answer. But as to the question, "How would Christ respond to Islam and its clerical representatives?" there is considerable evidence that he would not be nearly as accepting as many contemporary Christians are. The evidence lies in his treatment of the Pharisees.

On numerous occasions, Christ lashed out at the Pharisees. He upbraided them for hypocrisy and iniquity; for laying burdensome rules on men's shoulders; for neglecting justice and mercy and focusing instead on minor ritual observances; and for "teaching as doctrines the precepts of men" (Mt 15:9). We tend to forget the way Jesus treated the religious authorities of his day. He warned them, he insulted them, and on several occasions he provoked them. Even when the Pharisees asked what seemed to be reasonable questions, Jesus often cut them short or rebuked them. He called them "liars", "hypocrites", "blind guides", "whitewashed tombs ... full of uncleanness", "serpents", "vipers", "children of hell", and worthy of "being sentenced to hell".

So how would Jesus respond to Muslim clerics who are more pharisaical than the Pharisees ever were? Consider *Reliance of the Traveller*, thought to be one of the definitive manuals of Islamic law and as close to an official summation of traditional Muslim practice as one can find.[3] It is certified as reliable by Al-Azhar University, the principle center of Islamic scholarship, and despite its bulk, it has gone through numerous printings in recent years. The guide is over one thousand pages long and contains minute and detailed descriptions of the proper way to pray, to dress, to wash, to eat, to fast, to buy and to sell, and to conduct relations with one's wives. Islamic law, in short, is very much concerned with cleansing the outside of the cup; when it comes to "justice and mercy"—the "weightier matters of the law" (Mt 23:23)—however, Islam falls far short of the Christian standard. Moreover, as regards interfaith information programs, it's useful to know that Muslims are allowed to practice *taqiyya*, or deception, in promoting their faith. If Christ was hard on the Pharisees and Sadducees, would he be favorably disposed to Muslim apologists? If he thought the Pharisees were deceivers and hypocrites, what would he think of imams who say one thing in English and something quite different in Arabic? Once again, there is no certainty about what Jesus would do, but it does seem that the burden of proof is on those Christians who think that the "Christian thing" is to seek for common ground with Islam while overlooking its oppressive laws.

Two thousand years into the Christian era, Islamic law still stipulates that a woman caught in adultery should be whipped or stoned to death. Sharia also punishes thieves with amputations, permits forced marriages of youngsters, allows honor killings of wayward wives and daughters, treats women and children as the property of men, and punishes apostates with the death penalty. Islamic law imposes the very second-class citizenship that the civil rights advocates marched against. In societies ruled by Islamic law, non-Muslims are not only considered inferior; they are considered unclean. Do Christians want to enable the spread of these laws in America? Would that be the "Christian thing" to do?

So it may be that Harris, Phillips, and Hedges will turn out to be right after all when they say that Christians pose a major threat to society—only it won't be for the reasons they adduce. The threat comes not from "Christian" militias and theocrats, but from all those well-meaning Christians who act as unwitting enablers for Islam—and also from their pastors. Shepherds are supposed to protect their sheep from wolves, but at the Lamb of God Church and places like it, the pastors are handing the lambs over to the wolves. "Beware of false prophets, who come to you in sheep's clothing but inwardly are ravenous wolves" (Mt 7:15). It's an apt warning for our times. Unfortunately, too many Christians and their pastors live in a bucolic dream world where thoughts of wolves and false prophets are never entertained.

The tendency to look at Islam favorably can be found even among Christians who are ordinarily astute and reliable about theological and social issues. For example, both Dinesh D'Souza and Peter Kreeft have written outstanding books of Christian apologetics, but both seem to think that Islam and Christianity have enough in common to make them natural allies. Both authors seem to think that we can join together with Muslims in what Kreeft calls an "ecumenical jihad" against our common enemies—sin and secularism. D'Souza's claim that traditional Americans and traditional Muslims are natural allies will be examined in a later chapter. For now, let's look at the argument in Kreeft's recent book *Between Allah and Jesus: What Christians Can Learn from Muslims*. The book, which is written as a dialogue between several characters, features a Muslim graduate student named Isa (the Arabic name for Jesus) as the principal character. In his introduction, Kreeft maintains that the "Islam of the Qur'an ... is a religion of peace ... and of divine justice", which has been getting bad press and which has furthermore been perverted by "terrorist Islam". In truth, says Kreeft, Islam has much in common with Christianity—so much so that they are both "high and honorable faiths."[4] "Beneath our differences," says a Jesuit priest who is one of the characters in the dialogue, "we all believe in God and morality and justice and peace and goodness, don't we?"[5]

Because of this commonality, says Kreeft, we have a lot to learn from Islam. By looking at the example of Muslims, Christians can recall or better understand their own faith. In his introduction he writes, "I also say Islam has great and deep resources of morality and sanctity that should inspire us and shame us and prod us to admiration and imitation".[6] For example, says Kreeft, one of the most important things Christians "should learn from Muslims, or be reminded of by Muslims" is "the sacredness, of the family and children".[7] Here and in other parts of his book, Kreeft seems to be inadvertently transposing Christian notions onto Islam. While there are some Muslims who look at marriage and family in a sacred light, this is not the picture of family life that emerges in the accounts of ex-Muslims such as Nonie

Darwish, Ayaan Hirsi Ali, and Wafa Sultan. Here's Nonie Darwish on first seeing a church wedding in an old Hollywood movie:

> I was very touched by the holiness of the marriage vows, especially when the husband promised to love, honor, and cherish his one and only wife "till death do us part".... I now realize that my innocent mind was touched not only by the romance of the marriage vows but also by the way a Christian woman was honored and elevated by her husband and society.... In sharp contrast, Muslim weddings are more about sex and money. They do not convey the holy covenant of marriage.[8]

Darwish illustrates the point with a standard Egyptian marriage contract, complete with questions about the bride's virginity, the amount of the dowry, and three spaces for the husband to record the names and addresses of wife number one, wife number two, and wife number three. To a Westerner overdosed on multiculturalism, that last item might seem to be just another bright thread in the rich tapestry of diversity. But how do such arrangements work out in an actual marriage? Wafa Sultan recounts how her grandfather in Syria forced her grandmother to solicit a young woman to be his new bride. And, to compound the humiliation, when the wedding took place, she was forced to "welcome the bridal procession by dancing before it with a bowl of incense on her head".[9] After the wedding, writes Sultan, her "grandmother was reduced to the status of a servant in her own home. She served my grandfather, his wife, and the ten boys that wife would bear for him."[10]

Though individual Muslims may treat women as equals, legal systems based on Islamic law do not require such treatment, but permit men to look upon their wives and daughters essentially as commodities—possessions for the father or husband to dispose of as he sees fit. The result, according to ex-Muslims who talk about their experiences, is a tangle of family pathologies. Significantly, many of the pathologies can be traced back to the example set by Muhammad, who had eleven wives and several slave-girl concubines. As is well known, Muhammad married a nine-year old; what is less well known is that one of his conquests was his own daughter-in-law. Seeing Muhammad's evident interest, his adopted son graciously, or perhaps prudently, divorced his wife to clear the way for the marriage. On another occasion, Muhammad "married" (took to bed) an attractive captive on the same day that his troops killed her husband, father, and brother in battle. Yet the characters in Kreeft's book keep referring to Muhammad as a man of "honor" and "compassion" and "a great moral reformer" who gave the Arab world "morality and peace and universal justice and mercy".[11]

In his view of Muslim marriage, Kreeft seems to be conflating Islamic concepts with Christian beliefs. The same seems to be true of his treatment of jihad. In his introduction, Kreeft berates the secular media for portraying Muslims as hate-filled, violence-prone and fanatical. Isa tells his friends that the secular media has created the false impression that jihad is a duty to wage war against unbelievers, when in reality jihad is simply "the inner struggle against evil".[12] The trouble is, the evidence for this interpretation is minimal. In one of the hadith—the collected sayings of Muhammad—Muhammad is reported to have said, "The most excellent jihad is for the conquest of self." This statement supports Kreeft's interpretation, and perhaps he hopes that this view could become the dominant one if enough Mulsims adopted it. Unfortunately, many scholars say this hadith is of doubtful provenance: and, in any event, the Koran makes it quite clear in several places which is the more excellent jihad. For example: "Do you pretend that he who gives a drink to the pilgrims and pays a visit to the Sacred Mosque is as worthy as the man who believes in God and the Last Day, and fights for God's cause? These are not held equal by God" (9:19–20). According to Islam expert Fr. Samir Khalil Samir, S.J., the notion that jihad is to be understood as primarily a spiritual struggle is a recent innovation "that corresponds neither to Islamic tradition nor to modern language". "From the Qur'an onward," he observes, "the ordinary meaning of *jihad* is unequivocal. The term *jihad* indicates the Muslim war in the name of God to defend Islam".[13]

Kreeft seems to project onto Islam the Christian notion of an interior spiritual struggle against sin. Or maybe he is attempting to pull out of a Muslim concept a glimmer of a Christian one. Sadly, however, many former Muslims report that there is very little sense of inner struggle in Islam. Recall Nonie Darwish's observation that she had never heard any discussion of it in her thirty years of living in the Middle East.[14] It would appear that Western-style soul-searching is a rare commodity in Muslim lands. As Raphael Patai points out in his study *The Arab Mind*, "One of the important differences between the Arab and the Western personality is that in Arab culture, shame is more pronounced than guilt."[15] In other words, there is less sense of personal sin and personal responsibility in the Arab world. One behaves oneself to avoid censure, not to undergo spiritual transformation. Some

Sufis have a more spiritualized interpretation of Islam, but theirs is not the most common form of Islam. Thus, Isa's preoccupation with the "war against evil within" seems more Christian than Muslim. Kreeft is right in his contention that many Christians have lost the sense of sin and spiritual struggle, but there is little reason to believe that they are going to find it again by looking to Islam.

Isa's attitudes may be unrepresentative of the majority Muslims, but, unfortunately, Kreeft's favorable disposition toward Islam *is* representative of many influential Christians. He is not alone in his attempt to "reach across the aisle" and find common ground with Muslims. A few years ago, over three hundred prominent Christian leaders signed a letter (which appeared as a full-page ad in the *New York Times*) seeking "reconciliation" and "common ground" with Islam. After asking "forgiveness of the All-Merciful One" for the Crusades and other Christian sins, the letter speaks of "deep affinities" and "common ground" between the two faiths, though the only common ground that's ever specified in the lengthy statement is "love of God and neighbor".[16] And even here it is questionable whether there is common ground since "love of neighbor" in Islamic teaching extends only to other Muslims.

Three years ago, Pope Benedict XVI also stressed the common ground between Islam, Christianity, and Judaism. Speaking to Muslim leaders in May 2009 at the Dome of the Rock in Jerusalem, the pope observed: "Here the paths of the world's three great monotheistic religions meet, reminding us what they share in common. Each believes in One God, Creator and ruler of all. Each recognizes Abraham as a forefather, a man of faith upon whom God bestowed a special blessing. Each has gained a large following throughout the centuries and inspired a rich spiritual, intellectual and cultural patrimony."[17]

Broadly speaking, the pope is correct, but that's the problem—it's difficult to get beyond generalities when speaking of our common ground with Islam. Moreover, a large chunk of this commonality disappears when one considers that the Catholic Church does not, after all, accept the claim that Muhammad received a revelation from God. In short, the common-ground thesis lies atop a deep fault line.

In his defense, it should be kept in mind that the pope has to choose his words carefully, especially in speaking to a Muslim audience. There are millions of Christians living in the Muslim world, and an ill-considered word could put them in danger, as happened after his 2006 lecture at the University of Regensburg. Muslims throughout the world staged mass protests against his speech; churches in the Middle East were attacked; and a Catholic nun doing charity work in Somalia was killed. Yet, without regard to context—for the pope's concern for Christians living in precarious circumstances—words such as *common*, *share*, *great*, and *rich* may lead some Catholics to be uncritical in their assessment of Islam and jump to unwarranted conclusions.

The issue here is not so much the effect on Muslims, but the effect on Christians. Most Catholics don't pay close attention to papal talks in faraway places. But they do pay enough attention to get a general impression; and the general impression conveyed by media coverage of the pope's Middle East visit was that the pope is okay with Islam, from which the average Catholic might conclude, "So I guess I can be okay with it too."

Of course, Catholics can always dig a little deeper. They could, for example, consult the *Catechism of the Catholic Church*. Catholics are usually well advised to consult the *Catechism* when they need a better understanding of the Church's position; but on the subject of Islam, the *Catechism* has very little to say. In fact, there is only one sentence: "The plan of salvation also includes those who acknowledge the Creator, in the first place amongst whom are the Muslims; these profess to hold the faith of Abraham, and together with us they adore the one, merciful God, mankind's judge on the last day." [18] When a Catholic reads "together with us they adore the one, merciful God", he might conclude that the Allah of the Koran and the God of the Bible are one and the same. He might also conclude that he ought to accept the fashionable assumption that the true Islam has been hijacked by a handful of radicals.

A Catholic might dig deeper still and consult *Nostra Aetate*, the Second Vatican Council document that outlines the relation of the Catholic Church to non-Christian religions and continues to serves as the primary Catholic guide to interreligious dialogue. But the section on the "Moslems" whom "the Church regards with esteem" is only two short paragraphs. Like the *Catechism*, it states that "they adore the one God" and adds that Muslims "revere [Jesus] as a prophet", "honor Mary", and "value the moral life". Like the *Catechism*, the document contains very little information on Islam, and the little information there is emphasizes the common ground between Christians and Muslims. The document does mention that Muslims "do not acknowledge

Jesus as God". It states that more than "a few quarrels and hostilities have arisen between Christians and Moslems" but says nothing about the causes of these quarrels and urges all to "forget the past".[19]

An unfortunate result of the shared-spiritual-brotherhood approach, which is prevalent in the leadership circles of both Catholic and Protestant churches, is that Christians are much less aware than they should be about the current threat from Islam. Western Christians have been lulled into complacency by the oft-repeated emphasis on the similarities between their faith and the faith of Muslims. But if, in reality, there is little common ground between Islam and Christianity, Christians will find that they have been put at a serious disadvantage. The time that Christians are wasting in pursuing false hopes is time that Islamic activists are using to press their agenda. Instead of finding common ground with Islam, Christians will find that they have lost ground—in both the cultural and geographical sense.

And there is more at stake. Sooner or later, Christian laymen are going to notice the discrepancies between the assurances of common ground and the realities of Muslim behavior. What's the interfaith common ground on jihad? On the equality of men and women? On slavery? On amputation for theft? On the fate of apostates? On the status of non-Muslims? For that matter, where's the common ground on the Islamic belief that, in the last days, the Muslim Jesus will return and destroy Christianity? Most Christians read the news, and they can see that the news about Islam is often disturbing. Why should Christians have respect for Islam when so many of Islam's devotees are prone to violence and so often contemptuous of Christianity? For church leaders to express respect for Islam won't do anything to increase respect for Islam, but it might serve to lessen the respect that Christians have for their own leaders. Church leaders who continue to fall back on multicultural clichés such as *respect* and *affinities* in the face of an ever-more-aggressive Islam will risk undermining their credibility with their own flock.

In glossing over the unpleasant facts about Islam, the Catholic Church in particular may well be setting itself up for another scandal—one that could rival the sex abuse scandals. Much of the damage from those scandals was caused by the revelation that some priests and bishops had covered up for the abusers. The Church's current policy of seeking common ground with Islam is a well-intentioned interreligious gesture. It's not meant as any sort of cover-up; but, in effect, it minimizes the rather large gap that divides Islam and Christianity. As that gap becomes more evident to ordinary Catholics, the credibility of the Church may once again come into question. As the threat from a resurgent Islam becomes more apparent, Catholics may well begin to feel that they have been misled on an issue vital to their security. The complaint against the Church will shift from "Why didn't Church officials do more to protect children?" to "Why didn't they tell us the rest of the story about Islam?"

In addition to confusing Christians about current dangerous realities, the common-ground approach has another unintended effect. If you were looking for a way to strengthen the hand of atheists and strident secularists, it would be difficult to top the tactic of trumpeting Christianity's common ground with Islam. That's because it was precisely by claiming that Christianity and Islam are essentially the same that atheists were able to make so much hay in the aftermath of 9/11.

The atheist argument is not that Islam is a bad apple among world religions, but that it is just like all religions—irrational, cruel, and unjust. Atheists such as Hitchens and Dawkins made a particular point of portraying Islam and Christianity as evil twin brothers. The Bible, they insisted, is bloodier than the Koran, and Christians and Muslims are equally intolerant. There is a good deal of evidence that the tactic has been effective in undermining confidence in Christianity. The number of self-identified Christians has dropped precipitously in recent years. At the same time, the number of those identifying themselves as atheists, agnostics, or of no religion has risen year by year. When Christian clergy identify themselves with Muslim clerics, it serves only to strengthen the atheist argument that there is little difference between the two faiths.

Now that we are getting a clearer picture of Islam in action, it might be wise to reconsider the degree of affinity between Islam and Christianity. Islam scholar Raymond Ibrahim recently posted on his website a video of excerpts from sermons delivered by Muslim preachers in the Middle East. Here is a supplication by popular Egyptian preacher Sheik Muhammad al-Zoghbi regarding fit punishment for infidels:

> May Allah cut your tongue out! May he freeze the blood in your veins! May he inflict you with cancer and allow you no reprieve. . . . Allah, strike them with all sorts of disease, afflictions and pain! . . . Allah destroy them! Allah destroy them! Allah destroy them![20]

Another excerpt showed Muslims circumambulating the Ka'ba, the holiest site in Mecca, while the following supplications issued from a loudspeaker:

> O Allah, vanquish the unjust Christians and the criminal Jews, the unjust traitors; strike them with your wrath; make their lives hostage to misery; drape them with endless despair, unrelenting pain and unremitting ailment; fill their lives with sorrow and pain and end their lives in humiliation and oppression; inflict your tortures and punishments upon the unjust Christians and criminal Jews. This is our supplication; Allah, grant us our request![21]

Needless to say, these are not the type of prayers offered up in Christian churches. While it's true that Christians and Muslims share a common humanity, it's time to question the idea that they share similar theologies. The truth is, Islam is built on a rejection of basic Christian beliefs—the Trinity, the divinity of Christ, the Resurrection, even Christ's crucifixion. The following section presents a comparison of core Muslim beliefs with core Christian beliefs.

PART III

THE COMPARISON

8

Questioning the Koran

At a point in history when Christians ought to be thinking very hard about the Muslim religion, many can hardly bring themselves to think about it at all. After the attacks on New York and the Pentagon; the bombings in London, Madrid, and Mumbai; the riots in Paris; the threats against the pope; and the escalation of Muslim anti-Semitism throughout the world, one would expect to find more curiosity among Christians about the book that is used to justify the terror. The prevalent attitude, however, is still one of live and let live, in the manner of, "They have their holy book and we have ours, and all holy books ought to be respected." Not all Christians are so complacent, of course, but enough are to raise concern.

Unfortunately the resurgence of militant Islam happened to coincide with the rise of the multiculturalist philosophy and its admonitions about respecting diversity. The cult of cultural relativism asserted that all religions and traditions are equally valid, and many Westerners, Christians included, went along with it. As a result, even many churchmen developed a rather uncritical attitude toward Islam. When the Ayatollah Khomeini pronounced a death sentence on Salman Rushdie for his unflattering portrayal of Muhammad in *The Satanic Verses*, the Vatican newspaper, *L'Osservatore Romano*, criticized Rushdie for offending millions of Muslims. Many prominent Christian leaders and Jewish rabbis also scolded him for his irreverence.[1]

Prominent Muslims, on the other hand, have few scruples about finding fault with other faiths. Many of them consider the Koran far superior to the Jewish and Christian Scriptures and believe that the refusal to accept Islam is the result of either insanity or a spiritual blindness inflicted by Allah.

The Muslim attitude is more honest than the Christian one. And it's considerably more realistic than the multiculturalist belief that differences don't matter. For example, the Koran and the New Testament flatly contradict each other on essential matters. It's logically impossible to assign equal validity to the two, unless you think they are both equally wrong.

A real respect for Muslims would require Christians to be more truthful about their own beliefs and more faithful to them. So it's time for Christians to stop pretending they have great respect for a book that most of them have never read and that denies many of the main tenets of their own faith. It's time to stop worrying about hurting Muslims' feelings concerning their holy book and start worrying about all the people—many of them Muslims—who are being blown up in the name of that book.

In A.D. 610, when he was about forty years old, Muhammad claimed that the angel Gabriel visited him with revelations from God. The revelations continued until Muhammad's death at age sixty-two. The primary message of these revelations, which came to be known as the Koran, is that there is only one God and Muhammad is his final prophet, commissioned to call everyone to obey and worship God. Initially, the revelations were conveyed by Muhammad to his companions, who committed them to memory or wrote them on scraps of parchment. Within about two decades after Muhammad's death, the Koran was collected into a single volume. In its present form, the Koran is about four-fifths the length of the New Testament and is divided into 114 suras (chapters), which are, in turn, divided into verses. The word *Koran* means "recitation" in Arabic. In Islam, the Koran is considered to be a word-for-word dictation from God, given to Muhammad to recite to his followers.

Sometime fairly soon after the Koran was compiled, Muslim clerics and caliphs reached a consensus that it was uncreated, eternal, immutable, and not to be subjected to critical examination. Muslim scholars can and do debate and discuss the meaning of Koranic passages, but it would be a mistake to suppose that they carry on their work in the same spirit of inquiry as that of their Christian counterparts, who are free to question every jot and tittle of the Bible. The Christian scholar who concludes that the Bible is a myth may well be rewarded with a book contract and an endowed chair, whereas the Muslim scholar who asserts that the Koran is a myth risks being rewarded with an electric chair, or whatever the local instrument of execution happens to be. The possibly lethal consequences of too closely questioning the Koran suggest that it might not hold up well to the kind of questions Bible scholars ask.

Of course, you don't have to be a Scripture scholar to ask the most basic question: Is the Koran of divine origin? A Christian, unless he believes that God is sending contradictory marching orders to Christians and Muslims, would have to answer no. But one doesn't have to rely solely on faith to make a judgment. Read a few suras at random, and you will quickly see that the Koran itself is extremely defensive about its own authenticity. Hardly a page goes by without some reminder that it is a genuine revelation, not a fake one. Here is a sampling:

"This Koran could not have been devised by any but God" (10:37).

"Will they not ponder on the Koran? If it had not come from God they could have surely found in it many contradictions" (4:82).

"If they say 'He [Muhammad] has invented it [the Koran] himself,' say to them: 'Produce ten invented chapters like it'" (11:13).

"This is no invented tale, but a confirmation of previous scriptures ..." (12:112).

"Some say 'it is but a medley of dreams.' Others: 'He has invented it himself'" (21: 5).

"This Book is beyond all doubt revealed by the Lord of the Universe.... Do they say: 'He has invented it himself'?" (32:1–2).

"When our clear revelations are recited to them they say ... 'this is nothing but an invented falsehood'" (34:43).

"Do they say: 'He has invented it himself'?" (46:8).

And so on. The Koran is full of admonitions about its own authenticity. While allowances can be made for statements of this nature appearing occasionally, there are literally hundreds of such passages in the Koran.

How does this defensiveness compare with the Bible? The Koran's very first sura after the Exordium begins with the words "This Book is not to be doubted." By contrast, the first words of Genesis are "In the beginning God created the heavens and the earth." The author of Genesis has his mind on God and his creation; the author of the Koran has his mind on his book. True enough, in some Old Testament books, there are plenty of passages in which the author asserts the divine authority for what he has to say ("Thus saith the Lord"), but in the Koran, the issue of authenticity is almost the chief preoccupation.

It can be objected that unlike the Bible, which contains a variety of literary genres, the Koran is mainly a collection of prophetic utterances—a form that more naturally calls for the invocation of divine warrant. The point here is that the Koran differs from other scriptures in that the assertion of divine authority is not simply a rhetorical device or a necessary preliminary for delivering a divine lesson; rather, much of the time, it *is* the lesson. In other words, the authenticity of the Koran is one of the central themes of the Koran. This cannot be said of the Bible or of any individual books of the Bible. Such a preoccupation with one's own authority suggests a basic insecurity either on the part of Allah (which would be a self-contradictory notion) or, more likely, on the part of Muhammad. In this regard, there is a significant difference between "Thus saith the Lord" and "This is no invented tale." The latter phrase betrays a degree of defensiveness that seems unsuited to the Lord of the Universe.[2]

The Koran is, in fact, one of the most self-conscious books ever written. It's fair to say that far more space is devoted to justifying the revelation than to telling what the revelation is. The content of the revelation is, in fact, quite skimpy, leading Christopher Hitchens to observe, "There is nothing—absolutely nothing—in its teachings that can even begin to justify such arrogance and presumption."[3]

Not surprisingly, Hitchens doesn't have much use for any revelations: the Old Testament, the New Testament, and the Koran are pretty much alike in his books—all obvious fabrications. But if they are all fabrications, they are significantly different sorts of fabrications. You don't have to subscribe to the truth of the New Testament, for example, to see that the New Testament is nothing like the Koran in either content or style. It can't easily be jammed along with the Koran into some filing box labeled "dubious revelations".

Nowhere are the differences between the Koran and the New Testament more evident than in the matter of self-consciousness. In a word, the author of the Koran is self-conscious; the authors of the Gospels are not. Matthew, Mark, Luke, and John do not engage in constant fretting about whether their account seems to be made up. They have something to report, and they simply report it. The tone of the New Testament authors is not the tone of those who feel insecure about their message. On the contrary, it's a tone of self-assurance. And when Christ speaks, it is with an air of supreme confidence. One of the things that people found most remarkable about Christ was that he spoke with such authority.

Muhammad, by contrast, is obsessively concerned with his authority, even to the point of repeatedly defending his own sanity: "Has it never occurred to them that their compatriot [Muhammad] is no madman, but one who gives plain warning?" (7:184); "Your compatriot is not mad" (81:21); "By the grace of God, you are neither soothsayer nor madman" (52:29). The cumulative effect of all these assertions that Muhammad is not mad, not a soothsayer, not an inventor of tales, is to cast doubt on him. He seems to be conscious not only that others would doubt him, but that they would doubt him with good reason. In *The Sword of the Prophet*, Serge Trifkovic observes of the Koran that "it looks, feels, and sounds like a construct entirely human in origin and intent, clear in its earthly sources of inspiration and the fulfillment of the daily needs, personal and political, of its author." [4] Muhammad's continual reiteration of his messengerial authority suggests that he was well aware that his "recitations" fell far short of the "perfected Gospel" they were supposed to be.

Clearly, the Koran's oft-repeated claim to be an authentic revelation doesn't establish that claim. What other case, then, is made on its behalf? For Muslims, one of the main proofs of the Koran's divine authorship is its inimitable style. They say that the Koran is a literary masterpiece, which could never have been produced by an illiterate merchant such as Muhammad. The Koran itself makes this claim in the form of a challenge: "If you doubt what We have revealed to Our servant, produce one chapter comparable to it" (2:23). The challenge is repeated in several verses. In a nutshell, the Koran must be the word of God because only God could have said it so well.

Some of the Koran is impressive. Here and there are flashes of poetry, and there are many lyrical, sometimes powerful, passages describing God's creation. But for the most part—at least for the Western reader—it falls short of other great literature. Much of it is tedious, repetitive, and didactic. While it's true that a lot is lost in translation, how much could have been lost from: "Prophet, we have made lawful to you the wives to whom you have granted dowries and the slave-girls whom God has given you as booty: the daughters of your paternal and maternal uncles and of your paternal and maternal aunts who fled with you;

and any believing woman who gives herself to the Prophet and whom the Prophet wishes to take in marriage" (33:50). No matter how skillfully translated, such passages lack literary punch.

Many readers also find parts of the Bible to be tedious, repetitive, and didactic. But this is not a problem for Christians, who do not claim that the Bible is a word-for-word dictation from God. Christians believe that the men who wrote the books of the Bible were divinely inspired, but it does not follow that they always wrote in an inspired style. For Christians, the literary merit of Scripture is not a crucial issue, but Muslims who believe that every word in the Koran is from the very mouth of God are stuck with the task of defending the Koran as a work of incomparable expression and perfect prose.

Given that many Arabic scholars say the Koran has its share of grammatical errors and given its many mediocre passages, proving the Koran's literary perfection is not an easy assignment. Although there are some striking passages in the Koran, it is not the literary breakthrough that one would expect if God himself took up pen and paper. It's a bit too derivative for that. For example, the poetic passages resemble the poetry of Umayya ibn Abi al-Salt, a contemporary of Muhammad, while the prophetic language echoes that of the Old Testament.[5] Muslim apologists like to argue that because the Koran is a relatively recent revelation, it is therefore more progressive, but stylistically it is, for the most part, a period piece harking back to an age that long preceded it.

Though, for Christians, the authenticity of Scripture doesn't hinge on its literary excellence, there is a sort of literary argument that can be made for the Gospels—not that they are composed in perfect prose but that they are unique. If you're looking for a literary breakthrough— something completely new in its day—you have to look at the books written by the four evangelists: Matthew, Mark, Luke, and John. Although they were written six hundred years before the Koran, they sound closer to our age than the Koran does. Compare any dialogue involving Jesus in the New Testament with any of the utterances of the Jesus of the Koran. The Jesus of the New Testament has believable conversations with believable people; the Jesus of the Koran says things like, "Blessed was I on the day I was born and blessed I shall be on the day of my death and on the day I shall be raised to life" (19:35). Moreover, in line with the general air of unreality in the Koran, these words are delivered from his cradle. When the Jesus of the Koran speaks—which isn't often—it's in this formulaic style. In fact, almost all of the Koran is composed in a formulaic style.

If there is a literary "miracle" in holy writ, it is to be found in the New Testament. As the renowned literary critic Erich Auerbach pointed out in his classic work *Mimesis*, the Gospels, if taken merely as fiction, constitute an extraordinary mystery since they anticipate the development of the realistic modern novel by about eighteen hundred years.[6] This is not to say that the Gospels are better literature than, say, *The Iliad* or *The Odyssey*. In fact, *The Odyssey* is a far more artfully constructed narrative than any of the Gospels. The startling thing about the Gospels is that they break with the classical rules of style by mixing everyday realistic scenes with the most profound and tragic themes. As Auerbach observes, "A scene like Peter's denial fits into no antique genre. It is too serious for comedy, too contemporary and everyday for tragedy, politically too insignificant for history—and the form which was given it is of such immediacy that its like does not exist in the literature of antiquity."[7] C. S. Lewis made a similar point, observing that if the Gospels are not history, "then they are realistic prose fiction of a kind which actually never existed before the eighteenth century."[8] When you step into the Gospels or the Acts of the Apostles, you step inside a changed world. Something revolutionary had happened, and to describe it, the New Testament writers were forced to break through the boundaries of classical writing.

The only-God-could-have-said-it-so-well school of Koran defense presents a dual problem. For one thing, the supposedly unique Koran is unable to transcend ancient literary forms and formulas. For another thing, even within the boundaries of those forms, it fails to match the level of achievement set by other ancient authors. To put it bluntly, the Koran is not as well written as Scriptures composed by human authors such as David, Isaiah, or Solomon. Many passages in the Old Testament soar above the Koran—the Psalms, the scene of the dry bones that come to life described in Ezekiel (Ezek 37), the Lord answering Job out of the whirlwind (Job 38), the "set me as a seal upon your heart" passage in the Song of Solomon (Song 8:6), the temptation scene in the Garden of Eden, and the vivid prophecies of Isaiah.

The same holds true for the New Testament. Christians readily admit its human authorship. After all, the first book in it is titled "The Gospel According to Matthew", not "The Gospel According to God". Yet Matthew does a pretty good job of it. So do Mark, Luke, and

John. There is nothing in the Koran to compare with the moving scenes in the Gospels—and nothing to compare with the profundity of its message. Take the opening passage in John's Gospel: "In the beginning was the Word, and the Word was with God, and the Word was God. He was in the beginning with God; all things were made through him, and without him was not anything made that was made. In him was life, and the life was the light of men. And the light shines in the darkness, and the darkness has not overcome it" (Jn 1:1–5).

Reading something like this, or like the Psalms, or like the prophecies of Isaiah, one is left with the logical problem of explaining how various human beings were able to express themselves as eloquently as—or perhaps even more eloquently than—God himself in his supposed dictation of the Koran. And it's not just a question of style but also of originality and depth. To paraphrase Samuel Johnson, what is original in the Koran is not deep, and what is deep is not original. Saint John's observation that "God is love, and he who abides in love abides in God, and God abides in him" (1 Jn 4:16) is beyond the level on which the Koran operates. So are Saint Paul's profound philosophical/ theological discourses on nature and grace, and on the relationship between sin, law, freedom, atonement, and redemption. Of course, the most profound and provocative passages in the New Testament belong to Christ. For example, "I am the resurrection and the life; he who believes in me, though he die, yet shall he live, and whoever lives and believes in me shall never die" (Jn 11:25–26).

The passage is well known the world over, but it's likely that not too many Muslims are familiar with it. Why not? The New Testament is not recommended reading in most Muslim countries, and in some it's actually forbidden reading. But there's another reason. The Jesus presented in the Koran is an almost totally uninteresting person. Although he is described as a great prophet, he speaks on only about six occasions, and then very briefly and primarily to deny that he ever claimed to be God. All the depth and originality of the Gospels is completely absent in what he has to say. He appears mainly in the role of one of Allah's official spokesmen. But *appears* is really too strong a word. This Jesus doesn't attend weddings or go fishing with his disciples or gather children about him. He has practically no human interactions, and what he has to say is formulaic and repetitive. He is more like a disembodied voice than a person. Forget for the moment all the other motivations Muslims have for avoiding the Gospels; the Jesus of the Koran is such a cipher that he offers no incentive to want to find out more about him.

The Jesus of the Koran seems to be there for one purpose: to discredit the claims of Christianity in favor of Islam's. But this stripping away of all the interesting claims about Christ leads to a ticklish but fundamental question: What exactly does the Koran have to reveal? The essential thing about a revelation, one supposes, is that it reveals something, something that people didn't know or couldn't figure out for themselves—something, for instance, like the revelations about Christ in the Gospels. Whether or not they represent a true revelation, the Gospels certainly live up to our expectations of what a revelation ought to be. They proclaim that a carpenter of humble origins is the long-awaited Messiah; that God's son became one of us, died for our sins, rose from the dead, and made it possible for us to become sons and daughters of God and heirs of his kingdom. All of this, to put it mildly, caught people by surprise. Not only was the gospel message unanticipated; parts of it were unfathomable. It was outside the existing frames of reference. Whatever one may think of the claims of Christianity, they can't be brushed aside as same old, same old. There is a reason the message was called the "good news".

The Koran, by contrast, has practically nothing to add to existing revelations. For the most part, it seems to be borrowed—from the Old Testament, from the Talmud, from apocryphal Christian sources, and from the writings of the Zoroastrians and Hindus. From the earliest days of Muhammad's prophetic career, the complaint was voiced that the Koran was a hand-me-down revelation; and Muhammad was candid enough to record the criticism: "Whenever Our revelations are recited to them, they say: 'We have heard them (before). If we wished we could say the like. They are but fables of the ancients'" (8:31). In the Koran you can find the familiar stories about Adam and Eve, Noah and the ark, Joseph and his brothers, Moses and Aaron, Jonah and the whale. They are told in somewhat different versions, true, but they add nothing essentially new. Even the description of the afterlife as a garden of earthly delights is not new. Similar descriptions can be found in Greek, Hindu, and Zoroastrian writings. There is a great deal of emphasis in the Koran on the oneness of God and the necessity of submitting to his will, but, again, these were not new ideas (although they may have been new to some of the desert Arabs to whom Muhammad preached).

What is new in the Koran? If you boil it down, it comes to this: Muhammad is God's latest, greatest, and final prophet. Over and over the reader is admonished to "Believe God and His Prophet" and to "Obey God and His Prophet." That is pretty much the sum of the revelation. All the rest is basically reminder, not revelation. So we are left with the fact that the core of the Koranic revelation is nothing more than the claim that Muhammad is God's messenger, who ought to be believed and obeyed.

After that there are a number of secondary "revelations" that concern rules for prayer and fasting, the duty of charity, Muhammad's dealings with other tribes, and his relations with his wives. But none of these can be considered new in the sense of being significantly different from existing practices. In Muhammad's time, there was nothing new about prayer, fasting, almsgiving, pilgrimages, or polygamy. If the Koran is God's final and fullest revelation, why does it have so little to say? Why is it so lacking in depth? The Koran may be, in parts, a fine example of literature, but it is also a fine example of what, in literature, is called an anticlimax. After all the spectacular and shattering revelations of the Old and New Testaments, it comes as a letdown.[9]

The problem is not limited to the lack of originality in the Koran. It extends beyond that to a lack of coherence. There is no beginning, middle, or end to the Koran because, according to one of its translators, "scholars are agreed that a strictly chronological arrangement is impossible".[10] Instead the Koran is arranged according to the length of its chapters, with the longest coming first and the shortest, last. Accordingly, the Koran skips back and forth between accounts of Jesus, Moses, Joseph, Abraham, and Noah as though all these figures lived in some kind of time proximity instead of being separated by hundreds or even thousands of years. In one sura alone (Jonah), the narration encompasses the Creation, Muhammad, Jesus, Noah, Moses, Aaron, and finally Jonah. Besides the strange juxtapositions of the stories and persons, hardly any of the stories are fully developed. They are more like story fragments. And the logical transitions between episodes are often missing. As one scholar of the Koran pointed out long ago, the extended narratives of the Koran are lacking in "indispensable links, both in expression and in the sequence of events . . . and nowhere do we find a steady advance in the narration." [11] One is reminded of Mark Twain's joke that Fenimore Cooper broke all the rules of literary art, including rule one, "A tale shall accomplish something and arrive somewhere", and rule two, "The episodes of a tale shall be necessary parts of the tale and shall help to develop it." [12]

In response to these criticisms, Muslim apologists say one should think of the Koran as more like a body of sermons than an organized history. But even on this level, the Koran lacks coherence. When we listen to a sermon, we expect that the end of it will have something to do with the beginning of it. This is quite often not the case with the Koran. If you think there ought to be some logical connection between paragraph one and paragraph two or between paragraph two and paragraph three, you might have some difficulty in following the Koran.

If you are the Lord of the Universe or his prophet, you are apparently under no obligation to connect your thoughts. Nevertheless, apologists for Islam have developed some elegant explanations for the Koran's discontinuity. Here's the one offered by Malcolm Clark, an authority on comparative religions: "The Qur'an is like a montage of different images or a kaleidoscope, in which different elements recur but in different arrangements." [13] That's one way of putting it. Another way is this: "A wearisome confused jumble, crude, incondite; endless iterations, long-windedness, entanglement; most crude, incondite;— insupportable stupidity, in short!" [14] That description is from historian Thomas Carlyle, and he was fairly sympathetic to Islam.

However you try to explain it, you would think that God could make a better effort. If you believe that the Koran is dictated by God, you are faced with the difficulty of explaining why the Author of Creation seems to lack the literary touch—that is, the knack for storytelling, sequence, composition, and drama that we expect in accomplished human authors. Yes, there are beautiful passages in the Koran, but as an exercise in composition it would not pass muster in most freshmen writing courses. Muslims rankle at perceived insults to Allah, but isn't it an insult to Allah to attribute to him such a "confused jumble" of a book?

If any imam or mullah is wondering why the whole world hasn't already beaten a path to Islam, he ought to know that the Koran strikes literate Westerners not as a Great Leap Forward, but as a Great Leap Back. Both in content and coherence the Koran falls short of what Judeo-Christian civilization has come to expect of scriptural revelations. The fact that many Muslim clerics don't seem to know this can be attributed in part to the effectiveness of multicultural conditioning, which restrains Western scholars from making potentially painful comparisons.

The incoherent, anticlimactic nature of the Koran undermines not only the arguments of Koran apologists but also those of people like Christopher Hitchens, who claim that all scriptural revelations are cut from the same cloth. It's particularly ironic that Hitchens, who claimed to know so much about literature and textual criticism, missed the enormous differences between the Judeo-Christian revelation and the Koran.

If the Christian revelation is a fabrication, as Hitchens and others have claimed, it is a supremely crafted fabrication. For example, it accomplishes what the Koran only purports to accomplish—namely, the fulfillment of prophecies. Koran 10:37 asserts, "This Koran could not have been devised by any but God. It confirms what was revealed before it and fully explains the Scriptures", but the Koran doesn't do any such thing. There is very little sense in which it can be said that the Koran confirms or fulfills any earlier prophecies or events mentioned in the Old or New Testament, other than the promise made by God to send prophets (though not to the Arabs). By contrast, the life of Christ fulfills in detail numerous prophecies. Christ is described as the new Adam who lifts the curse of the first Adam (1 Cor 15); Abraham's willingness to sacrifice his son is a foreshadowing of God's willingness to sacrifice his only-begotten Son (Heb 11:17); as the Israelites are saved by the blood of the lamb sprinkled on the doorposts, so mankind is saved by the blood of Christ (Rev 7:14); as Jonah spends three days in the belly of the whale, Christ spends three days suffering, dying and descending into hell (Mt 12:40); Christ is the "man of sorrows", prophesied by Isaiah, who "was wounded for our transgressions" and upon whom the Lord has laid "the iniquity of us all" (Is 53:3, 5, 6); Christ is the Good Shepherd foretold in the Twenty-Third Psalm. And so on. The life of Christ actually conforms to earlier Scripture.

What's more, Christ effectively eliminates the need for further prophecy. Muslims say that Christ is a great prophet—one in a line of prophets that leads up to the greatest prophet of all, Muhammad. But Christ doesn't claim to be a prophet. He's not pointing to someone else; he's pointing to himself. He says he is the culmination of all prophecies, the Alpha and the Omega. He says in effect, "I am the one you have been waiting for."

Well, to be truthful, there is some prophecy. Christ does prophesy the manner of his death, his resurrection, the coming of the Holy Spirit, the destruction of Jerusalem, and his second coming at the end of time. Where does that leave Muhammad? There is no mention of him in the Gospels. He's not even hinted at—unless Christ's warnings about "false prophets" might apply. Even the various hidden gospels of the Gnostics don't reference Muhammad. Muslim apologists insist that in the original, untampered-with, and long-lost version of some gospel, Jesus does prophesy the coming of Muhammad. But no document of this description exists, and there is no evidence that it ever did. Prior to the Koran, there is simply no reference to Muhammad, let alone to his claim to be the last of the prophets. To paraphrase all those hotel desk clerks in all those Hollywood mystery movies, "I'm sorry, sir, but there's no one by the name of Mr. Muhammad registered in our book."

Of course, the astonishing number of linkages between Old Testament prophecies and New Testament events could all be an elaborately constructed hoax made up by Christ's disciples after the fact. In this scenario, a local wonder-worker had a small group of followers who exaggerated his deeds and words after his death and artfully tied them to various scriptural prophecies. Such a hoax is possible, but it would have been a highly difficult undertaking requiring exceptional feats of coordination and deception, as well as an ability to create dialogue and concepts of startling originality. It would take a very elaborate conspiracy theory to explain how the disciples of Jesus managed to pull it off, given the number of people involved, and the fact that the events described in the Gospels happened in the full light of history. Nevertheless, Hitchens claimed that the New Testament was fabricated. He referred to the process as "reverse-engineering", and he seemed to believe that this elaborate deception was a simple sleight of hand instead of the stuff of spy novels and coded message mysteries.[15]

Others who have tried their hand at revising the Christian story could have informed Hitchens of the difficulties involved. Despite its numerous historical and cultural inaccuracies, *The Da Vinci Code*, with all its improbable scenarios and its labyrinthine twists and turns, unintentionally offers a more realistic assessment of what "reverse-engineering" the life of Christ would really entail. It would not, in short, be the easy task that Hitchens seemed to imagine.[16]

Interestingly, there does exist one well-known attempt to reverse-engineer the life of Christ, and it has to be rated both a tremendous

success and an unconvincing failure. In order for Muhammad to establish himself as God's final and most important prophet, it was first
necessary for him to deal with the person of Christ, because if Christ
is who Christianity says he is, then there is absolutely no need for
another prophet or another revelation. John the Baptist said of Jesus,
"He must increase, but I must decrease" (Jn 3:30). Muhammad preferred it the other way around. For him to increase, it was necessary
that Jesus decrease. So Muhammad invented his own version of
Christ—a Christ whose stature is greatly reduced and who seems eager
to deny any claim of divinity: "Glory be to You [Allah]. . . . I could
never have claimed what I have no right to [equality with God]. If I
had ever said so, You would surely have known it. You know what is
in my mind, but I know not what is in Yours. You alone know what
is hidden. I told them only what You bade me" (5:117). Beyond that,
the obliging Jesus of the Koran has very little to say.

Muhammad's portrait of Christ was not entirely cut from whole
cloth; he had some familiarity with the Christian story, but his knowledge of Christianity seems to have come mainly from heretical Christian sects that denied the Trinity, such as the Nestorians and the
Gnostics.[17] Moreover, his cryptic portrayal of Jesus simply mirrors the
nebulous depiction of Christ in Gnostic scriptures and stories. In any
event, Muhammad was extremely successful in selling this hazy version of Jesus to his followers—mainly because most Muslims through
the ages have had little or no acquaintance with the canonical Gospels
and the Jesus who is the Christ. Yet Muhammad's reengineering of
Jesus doesn't work at all on an artistic or literary level, and certainly
not on the level of historical narrative. Compared with the Christ of
the Gospels, the Jesus in the Koran is a stick figure completely lacking
in credibility.

The contrast between the two Christs brings us back to Christopher Hitchens and his penchant for equating the Gospels with the
Koran. One would have to be wedded to a rigidly fundamentalist
form of atheism to fail to see the world of difference between the
two. For one thing, the Jesus of the Gospels is a recognizable person,
not a strategically placed chess piece. For another, the Gospel revelation has a much better claim than the Koran to being a final revelation. It ends in a climax—the kind of dramatic ending one would
expect of God's final message to humanity. The Koran, on the other
hand, comes across as an afterthought on God's part.[18]

Finally, and this is perhaps the most important distinction, the Christian revelation is the revelation not of a book but of a person. God reveals himself in the person of Christ. To a Christian, Christ is the revelation, the Word Incarnate, the "good news". If God is the Author of the Universe, the Creator not only of the natural world with all its beauties, but also of artists like Beethoven, Chopin, Rachmaninoff, Michelangelo, Donatello, Saint-Gaudens, Renoir, Van Gogh, Euripides, Shakespeare, and Tolstoy, then he must be a bit of an artist and dramatist himself—perhaps even primarily an artist. And it seems more fitting from the point of view of art and drama that his revelation would culminate in the dramatic entrance of a dramatic person, not a book. Had he not been so intent on dismissing all revelations, Christopher Hitchens, being a man of letters himself, might have appreciated the point.

9

Jesus of Nazareth versus Jesus of Neverland

The claim that Christians and Muslims share much in common is based in part on the fact that the Koran regards Jesus as a prophet. Many Christians take comfort in knowing that Jesus holds a place of honor in Islam. They reason from this that the gap between Christianity and Islam cannot be that great.

But, as indicated in the previous chapter, the Koranic Jesus is quite different from the Jesus of the Gospels. Jesus is not presented as an unusually important prophet in the Koran, but rather as one of many. He is certainly not in the same league with Muhammad, who is mentioned on almost every page. In fact, Jesus plays a relatively minor role in the Koran. Moses, who is also considered a prophet of Islam, figures far more prominently in the Koran than does Jesus. Some indication of the status of Jesus in the mind of Muhammad is that during the prophet's dream journey to paradise, he encounters Jesus in the second heaven, while other prophets are encountered at higher levels—Moses in the sixth heaven and Abraham in the seventh. It seems reasonable to ask whether the Jesus in the Koran and the Jesus in the Gospels are the same person. The Isa of the Koran bears only a slight resemblance to the Jesus of the New Testament. His message is different, and so is his mission. A final question that must be raised is this: Is the Koranic Jesus a real person at all? Did Muhammad simply get the facts wrong about Jesus, or did he deliberately create an alternative Jesus to contradict the New Testament account? In short, is the Koranic Jesus nothing more than a fictional creation?

The simple fact that there is a Jesus in the Koran naturally invites a comparison with the Jesus of the Gospels. What do Christians believe about him, and what reasons do they give for their belief? And what do Muslims believe about Isa—the Muslim Jesus?

According to the New Testament, Jesus is the Son of God and the Savior of the world, who, through his death and resurrection, atoned for the sins of men and opened for them a new life of grace. He came down from heaven and became one of us so that men might become brethren of Christ and children of God. But how do you make the case for believing this?

Well, you could start with the miracles. Seems like a weak place to start? Not really. Religion, we like to say, is a matter of faith. True— and clearly Christ asked his disciples for faith; but he did not ask for blind faith. Instead, he offered them good reasons to believe in him. He gave sight to blind people, cured lepers, healed paralytics, multiplied loaves and fishes, brought the dead back to life, and offered various other jaw-dropping displays of power. And why not? What he had to say about himself was fairly incredible. He claimed equality with God. A reasonable man would want some proof, and Christ offered it.

Some high-minded types think Christianity would be better off without the miracles. For example, President Thomas Jefferson, scissors in hand, created his own version of the New Testament by removing all the miracles and references to Christ's divinity. Jefferson somehow thought this would be an improvement; but, as Catholic author John Zmirak points out, "What resulted was a book in which a rabbi dispenses wildly impractical advice such as 'sell all you have, and give it to the poor'— but offers no reason at all why anyone should listen to him." [1]

The miracles are not there just to impress the local peasants who can't grasp the higher ethical teachings; they are there for every rational person who wants to see some evidence for the seemingly fantastic claims made by Christ. As Jefferson's cut-and-paste experiment proves, you can't take the miracles out without unraveling the whole fabric of the Gospels. Miracles are an integral part of Christ's mission. Christianity, as C. S. Lewis observed, "is precisely the story of a great Miracle".[2]

Consider some of the following statements in the context of no miracles:

"Destroy this temple, and in three days I will raise it up" (Jn 2:19).

"Before Abraham was, I am" (Jn 8:58).

"I am the way, and the truth, and the life" (Jn 14:6).

"I am the bread of life" (Jn 6:35).

The normal human response to such statements is not a resounding hymn of praise, but a resounding "hmmm". Christ was well aware of the normal human response, and that is why he performed miracles—to provide confirmation of his authority. Take the case of the paralytic who was lowered down to Jesus through an opening in the roof:

> And when Jesus saw their faith, he said to the paralytic, "Child, your sins are forgiven." Now some of the scribes were sitting there, questioning in their hearts, "Why does this man speak like this? It is blasphemy! Who can forgive sins but God alone?" And immediately Jesus, perceiving in his spirit that they questioned like this within themselves, said to them, "Why do you question like this in your hearts? Which is easier, to say to the paralytic, 'Your sins are forgiven,' or to say, 'Rise, take up your pallet and walk'? But that you may know that the Son of man has authority on earth to forgive sins"—he said to the paralytic—"I say to you, rise, take up your pallet and go home." And he rose, and immediately took up the pallet and went out before them all; so that they were all amazed and glorified God, saying, "We never saw anything like this!" (Mk 2:5–12)

In short, the miracles and the preaching are intimately connected. And just as Jesus did a lot of preaching, he performed a lot of miracles—dozens and dozens of them. In fact, his fame—which was widespread not just in Galilee and Judea but in other regions such as Idumea, Decapolis, and Phoenicia—owed as much to his power over nature as to his preaching. When the news got around about his itinerary, sick people would line up in streets and marketplaces in advance of his coming (Mk 6:54–56). The crowds became so unmanageable in some places that "Jesus could no longer openly enter a town, but was out in the country" (Mk 1:45).

When Christopher Hitchens was asked what he would say if, after death, he found that there really is a God, he replied by citing Bertrand Russell's answer to the same question: "Oh, God, you did not give us enough evidence." It's a curious line of defense because in other places Hitchens rules out the possibility of miracles. In effect he's saying, "You have to give me evidence, but I won't accept the evidence you give to the yokels." One wonders what, other than a miracle, he would find convincing.

You might meditate on the problem of how Christ could have established his message as authoritative in any way other than the one he used. If you were God, what would be the most reasonable thing to do in order to prove your identity while leaving people room for the exercise of faith and free choice? We know that words alone, however eloquent, aren't enough for most of us. On the other hand, cataclysmic miracles—for example, Christ's making himself as large as a mountain and hurling Herod's palace into the sea—would be so overwhelming as to frighten people into acceptance, in which case there would be no merit in their belief. The more you think about it, the more sense it makes that Christ would choose to offer the kind of proofs he did. It looks as though he did find the balance between enough proof and too much proof.

Yet there is more to the Gospels than the miracles. Many of Christ's followers came to believe in him before they had witnessed any miracles, and the vast majority of Christian believers down through the centuries have not personally witnessed miracles. It has to be admitted that Christ's words do pack a lot of power:

> "Do not lay up for yourselves treasures on earth, where moth and rust consume" (Mt 6:19).

> "Judge not, that you be not judged" (Mt 7:1).

> "Beware of false prophets who come to you in sheep's clothing but inwardly are ravenous wolves" (Mt 7:15).

> "Whoever lives and believes in me shall never die" (Jn 11:26).

> "But I say to you, Love your enemies and pray for those who persecute you" (Mt 5:44).

> "As you did it to one of the least of these my brethren, you did it to me" (Mt 25:40).

> "For what will it profit a man, if he gains the whole world and forfeits his life?" (Mt 16:26).

> "I am the good shepherd. The good shepherd lays down his life for the sheep" (Jn 10:11).

> "Greater love has no man than this, that a man lay down his life for his friends" (Jn 15:13).

> "Heaven and earth will pass away, but my words will not pass away" (Lk 21:33).

These passages have penetrated deeply into our culture—so deeply that we sometimes fail to appreciate their revolutionary nature. Imagine how they must have impressed Christ's first hearers. The usual response was along the lines of "No man ever spoke like this" (Jn 7:46). The Gospels say that "the crowds were astonished at his teaching" (Mt 7:28). Even the Pharisees "marveled" at his teaching (Mt 22:22), just as, many years before, the teachers in the Temple were amazed at the twelve-year-old boy whose understanding of Scripture seemed to surpass their own.

It was not simply the words that struck home, but the way they were expressed. The crowds quickly observed that Jesus taught "as one who had authority, and not as their scribes" (Mt 7:29). Jesus often referred to Scripture, but he also based his teaching on his own authority, as in, "I say to you ..." On occasion he boldly revised the teachings of the ancients, as in, "It was said to the ancients ... but I say to you ..." Jesus referred to himself on one occasion as "gentle and lowly in heart" (Mt 11:29), but one can't help noticing that there was nothing meek about his speech. On the contrary, he spoke as though the whole world revolved around him, as though the fate of all men were bound up with his own fate. Occasionally he scored close to zero on the sensitivity scale, as when he called the Pharisees "fools" and "hypocrites".

By whose authority did he say such things? By whose authority did he throw the money changers out of the Temple? By whose authority did he presume to forgive sins? And what gave him the right to exempt his disciples from the rules of the Sabbath, declaring himself to be "lord of the sabbath" (Mt 12:8)? Sometimes he invoked his Father's authority, but he also spoke on his own authority. He apparently thought he had the right to say or do things that no one else dared to say or do. Some of his sayings were hard to take, but he could sometimes adopt a take-it-or-leave-it attitude toward his listeners. The amazing thing is that so many of them took it. In addition to the power and content of his sermons and parables, there must have been something else at work, something that would have been hard for the evangelists to convey in words alone. There must have been power not only in his words but in his voice and in his bearing. At the beginning of Matthew's Gospel and also Luke's, before any miracles had been performed or his ministry commenced, Jesus is walking along the Sea of Galilee when he sees two brothers, Peter and Andrew, casting a net into the water. "And he said to them, 'Follow me, and I will make you fishers of men.' Immediately they left their nets and followed him" (Mt 4:19–20). And the same thing happens shortly afterward with James and John. He sees them in their boats, calls to them, and they follow him.

That's it? "Follow me"? There is evidently a lot unsaid here. Msgr. Ronald Knox, the brilliant English apologist, makes the point this way: "What was the magic of voice or look that drew them away, in those early days when no miracles had yet been done, when the campaign of preaching had not yet been opened?" A lot of what happens in the Gospels can be accounted for only by what Knox describes as "the tremendous impact which his force of character made on people".[3]

Why did those money changers scatter so quickly? Why on several occasions did groups of men try to seize Jesus and fail? Did something about his presence give them second thoughts? Why did his captors in the garden draw back and fall to the ground when he came toward them? Why was Pilate so exceedingly reluctant to prosecute him?

I always thought the makers of the film *Ben-Hur* got it right when they decided not to show Jesus' face but rather the stunned reaction in the faces of those who encountered him. There's one scene in which a Roman soldier is about to bring down a whip on the back of Christ, who is offering water to the fallen Ben-Hur. Christ turns around and looks up at him, and the soldier's face turns to putty. There must have been many such moments of recognition for those who met Jesus.

As variously described in the Gospels, Jesus was followed by "great crowds", "great throngs", "multitudes", and "thousands". He fed them with words, and he fed them with miraculously multiplied loaves and fishes. The force of his words, backed up by the force of his personality, backed up by the power of his miracles must have been a potent combination. And just to make things even clearer, he spelled out the logic of his argument: "If I am not doing the works of my Father, then do not believe me; but if I do them, even though you do not believe me, believe the works" (Jn 10:37–38). I have never liked the reference to Jesus as "the world's greatest salesman", but you can see the point. In his efforts to convert individuals, Christ offered a combination of persuasions that was hard to resist.

What you see in the Gospels is really a multiplicity of proofs—a piling-up of evidence: teachings, backed by miracles, backed by witnesses, all of it mutually reinforcing and all of it culminating in a trial that, despite its outcome, actually serves to prove Christ's innocence.

As final proof of his love and his divinity, Christ offers his life on the Cross, rises from the dead, and—as the apostle Paul recounts—appears afterward to "more than five hundred brethren" (1 Cor 15:6). What's more, all of this layered-up evidence is not just for Christ's contemporaries but for every age to come—for "He came ... that all might believe through him" (cf. John 1:7).

To top it off, there is an abundance of geographical detail in the Gospels. If the whole story of Christ was set in some mythical location, long before the age of recorded history, it would be easier to pass off as a myth. The story takes place, however, not in some vague neverland but in places that can still be visited today—Bethlehem, Nazareth, Jerusalem. Christ doesn't go to some indeterminate wedding feast; he goes to one at Cana. He converses with the Samaritan woman at Jacob's well in the town of Sychar. He cures one man at the pool of Siloam and another at the pool with five porticos. Sidon, Tyre, Caperneum, the Sea of Galilee, the Jordan River, the Mount of Olives, the Garden of Gethsemane, the Praetorium, Herod's Court, Golgotha—there is a real-world specificity that you won't find in mythology.

Moreover, there is a no-nonsense, almost modern reporting style about the Gospels that is hard to reconcile with a sheer fabrication. The Gospel writers record Jesus' travels almost in the way a contemporary reporter might describe a political campaign—something along the lines of "Senator Smith made an appearance at a community center in the Bronx on Wednesday and later in the day gave a talk at the Lincoln Center. On Thursday he visited a home for the elderly in Crown Heights, and on Friday he toured a steel factory in Staten Island. On Sunday Senator Smith attended services at Calvary Baptist Church in upper Harlem."

As to the historical context of the Gospels, you find the same attention to detail. For example, Luke introduces the public ministry of John the Baptist in these words:

> In the fifteenth year of the reign of Tiberius Caesar, Pontius Pilate being governor of Judea, and Herod being tetrarch of Galilee, and his brother Philip tetrarch of the region of Ituraea and Trachonitis ... in the high-priesthood of Annas and Caiaphas, the word of God came to John the son of Zechariah in the wilderness; and he went into all the region about the Jordan, preaching a baptism of repentance for the forgiveness of sins. (Lk 3:1–3).

Clearly, Luke has the intention of writing history, not mythology. In fact, the preface to his Gospel resembles that of a secular historian of the time:

> Inasmuch as many have undertaken to compile a narrative of the things which have been accomplished among us ... it seemed good to me also, having followed all things closely for some time past, to write an orderly account for you, most excellent Theophilus. (Lk 1:1–3)

Does this sort of thing prove the truth of the Gospels? No, but it's one more item in that multiplicity of evidence you find in the New Testament. Luke also wrote the highly detailed Acts of the Apostles, which recounts the experiences of the early Church and provides accounts of more persuasive preaching, more miracles, more witnesses, more confrontations with the authorities, more arrests, more travels, and more of the same kind of attention to the proper names of persons and places: "Go to the street called Straight, and inquire in the house of Judas for a man of Tarsus named Saul" (Acts 9:11).

The New Testament presents an impressive case for the authenticity of its stories about Jesus and his followers. You may not be convinced that these events actually happened, but at least you probably have some familiarity with them. That's not the case, however, with the majority of the world's Muslims, who know very little about Jesus. You can't buy a Bible in most Cairo bookstores, although there are a few Christian bookshops where it can be obtained. You can't even bring your own Bible into Saudi Arabia. If you try to do so, your Bible will be confiscated, and you could be arrested. Most Muslim countries, particularly in the Middle East, offer a number of disincentives to those who might want to familiarize themselves with the life of Christ.

The little that Muslims do know about the life of Jesus comes mainly from Muhammad's account of him—or, if you prefer, the Koranic account. You can't even call it a life of Jesus, because it's mostly a handful of disconnected statements that deny Christ's divinity or claim he was a forerunner to Muhammad. For example, "And of Jesus son of Mary, who said to the Israelites: 'I am sent forth to you from God to confirm the Torah already revealed, and to give news of an apostle that will come after me whose name is Ahmad" (61:6). Christ said nothing of the kind in the Gospels, but the whole point of the Koran's treatment of Christ is to whittle him down in size—to turn him into a messenger instead of a Messiah. Here's another example: "He was but a mortal whom we [Allah] favored and made an example to the Israelites" (43:60). Whenever Jesus is mentioned in the Koran, it's usually a case of special pleading, as in "He was but a mortal." A few of his miracles are mentioned, but with the qualifier that they were "by My [Allah's] Leave" and not from any personal power of Jesus.

Muhammad's purpose in introducing Jesus into the Koran is to discredit the Christian claim that he is divine in order to enhance Muhammad's claim to prophethood. Beyond that, Muhammad seemed to have little interest in Jesus. Here, for example, is the entirety of what the Koran has to say about the Crucifixion: "They declared: 'We have put to death the Messiah, Jesus son of Mary, the apostle of God.' They did not kill him, nor did they crucify him, but they thought they did" (4:157). Muhammad brings up the most important action of Christ— his redemptive death and resurrection—only to deny that it happened. Dan Brown, the author of *The Da Vinci Code*, has a similar theory but at least he concocts a story to support it. No such explanation exists in the Koran. Inquiring minds who might want to know who "they" were, what they did to Jesus, and why they thought they had killed him will be disappointed by the Koran because it does not answer these questions.

Who were "they"? Beyond the fact that "they" were the Jews, Muhammad didn't seem to know any specifics about the actors involved. Or, if he did know, he didn't want his followers to know that there existed an entirely different and far more detailed story of the life of Christ than the one he presents. In the Koran account of Christ's last days on earth, there are no crowds lining the streets of Jerusalem, no Last Supper with his disciples, no agony in the garden, no betrayal by Judas, no trial before the Sanhedrin, no denial by Peter, no Herod, no Pilate, no Cross on Golgotha, and no Mary Magdalen finding an empty tomb on the third day. For that matter, there is no historical context, no geographical location, no setting of any kind. Gertrude Stein once said of Oakland, California: "There's no there, there." That's the feeling you get when you encounter the Jesus portrayed in the Koran.

The Jesus of the Koran exists in a neverland. Set against the Gospel story with all its close attention to persons, places, and events, the Koranic account is vague and vapid—and amazingly brief. If you omit the repetitions, the whole of what the Koran has to say about Jesus can fit on about two pages of typical Bible text. And of that, about half is devoted to denying that he was God's son. The net result is a nullity. In using Jesus for his own ends, Muhammad neglects to give him any personality. The Jesus of the New Testament is a recognizable human being; the Jesus of the Koran is more like a phantom. When did he carry out his ministry? There is not a hint. Where did he live? Again, there is no indication. Where was he born? Under a palm tree. That's about as specific as it gets in the Koran. In short, Muhammad's Jesus is a nebulous figure. He seems to exist neither in time nor in space. In the Gospels, you meet Jesus of Nazareth; in the Koran, you meet someone who can best be described as Jesus of Neverland.

It's curious that with all of his audacious claims to be equal with God, the Jesus of the Gospels is far more believable than the Jesus of the Koran. Not only is it difficult to believe in the few claims that are made for Muhammad's Jesus, it's difficult to believe in his existence. There is just no convincing detail.

On the other hand, whatever you may think of the claims made by the Jesus of the Gospels, it's hard not to believe in his existence. As Dinesh D'Souza puts it in *What's So Great about Christianity*, "Do you believe in the existence of Socrates? Alexander the Great? Julius Caesar? If historicity is established by written records in multiple copies that date originally from near contemporaneous sources, there is far more proof for Christ's existence than for any of theirs."[4] Historical reliability? F. E. Peters, in his book *Harvest of Hellenism*, writes, "The works that make up the New Testament were the most frequently copied and widely circulated books of antiquity."[5] What does that mean? It means that the New Testament survives in some 5,656 partial and complete manuscripts that were copied by hand. And that's in Greek alone. If you add in the Latin vulgate and other early versions, there are more than twenty-five thousand extant manuscript copies of the New Testament.[6] How does that compare with other early histories? Well, there are seven copies of Pliny the Younger's *Natural History*, twenty copies of the *Annals* of Tacitus, twenty copies of Livy's *History of Rome*, ten copies of Caesar's *Gallic Wars*, eight copies each of the histories of Herodotus and Thucydides. Score: Jesus, 25,000; Caesar, 10.[7] When you render unto Caesar the things that are Caesar's in manuscript terms, it doesn't seem to amount to much.

Are there any other factors to take into account? Yes, historians also look at the time gap between the date a book is written and the date of the earliest existing copies. In the case of Caesar's *Gallic Wars*, it's a thousand-year gap; the same for Tacitus. For Livy, the gap is four hundred to a thousand years. For the New Testament, however, there are between 50 and 225 years (the earliest are fragments).[8] That may seem like a lot of years, but it's far less than for any other major document of its time. Of course, that still leaves a gap between the events of Christ's life and the composition of the Gospels several decades later. During this time, the accounts of Jesus' life and sayings were passed on orally, leaving room for the kind of distortions that sometimes occur in oral traditions. In the first half of the twentieth century, some New Testament scholars asserted that the stories of Jesus had been embroidered as they passed from person to person. But few scholars today accept the claim that oral traditions are unreliable. More recent studies show that oral cultures are capable of passing on extended narratives over a long period with a high degree of accuracy.[9]

This claim can sound unlikely, because memorization is not as relied upon as it once was. But even today we don't have to look far to find amazing feats of memorization. Some Muslim apologists have made much of the claim put forward by some New Testament critics that the original words and deeds of Jesus were distorted and corrupted over time, yet Muslims themselves provide plenty of evidence that vast amounts of material can be accurately committed to memory. It's not uncommon for Muslims to memorize the entire Koran, and the estimate of the number who have done so is in the millions.

In addition to the New Testament accounts of Jesus, there are references to him in Tacitus, Suetonius, Pliny the Younger, Josephus, and Thallas, as well as in early Jewish law books and histories. None of these non-Christian writers believed that Jesus was God, but none of them denied his existence. Not many historians do. As Saint Paul said to King Agrippa, "This was not done in a corner" (Acts 26:26).

Nevertheless, there are those who believe that the development of the Christian story *was* done in a "corner", complete with cover-ups, conspiracies, and hidden agendas. Any discussion of the reliability of the Gospels has to contend with what might be called the Da Vinci school of biblical interpretation. *The Da Vinci Code* popularized some ideas that had been circulating for a long time among Bible critics, in particular the claim that the picture of Jesus presented in the Gospels is a legend made up by Christians to promote a political agenda. In the words of Sir Leigh Teabing, *The Da Vinci Code*'s fictional historian, the agenda was "to promote the divinity of the man Jesus and use his influence to solidify their own power base."[10] *The Da Vinci Code* claims that the "original" or "hidden" gospels that depict Jesus only as a man, not as God, were suppressed by the Emperor Constantine and supplanted with the made-up story of a God-man—a story that would have shared similarities with other myths and legends that abounded in the ancient world.[11]

Unfortunately for this thesis, the bulk of historical evidence shows that belief in the God-man was already vibrant two and a half centuries before Constantine came to power. Moreover, the Christ narrative has none of the marks of Graeco-Roman legends and myths. It refers to events that happened in recent history at that time and not in, as is the case with myths and legends, the distant past. In addition, the Christ in the Gospels is not, as a legend might present him, a warrior-hero who goes to war and combats monsters. Moreover, as textual critics point out, the literary form in which the Gospels are composed more closely resembles history and biography than it does mythology. Finally, the story of Christ, the God-man, sprang up not from pagan Romans, among whom such tales were common, but from first-century Jews, who rejected the whole pagan array of multiple gods and demigods. As Gregory Boyd and Paul Rhodes Eddy note in *Lord or Legend?*: "There is no precedent for telling a story of a sup-posedly dying and rising god *in identifiable history*, let alone in *recent* identifiable history, let alone in a *Jewish environment* that was intrinsi-cally hostile to such stories".[12] If, as the authors observe, "first-century Palestinian Jews were naturally going to produce a legend, it seems clear that it would not have looked anything like this one."[13]

Contrary to *The Da Vinci Code*'s claim that all sorts of efforts have been made to cover up the truth, the Gospels have been subjected to an enormous amount of scrutiny right from the start.[14] The historical criteria used to evaluate the Gospels are the same used to evaluate the historical reliability of other ancient documents, and the Gospels have stood up well to the test. As Boyd and Eddy point out, "Clearly, if anyone is going to doubt that the copies of the Gospels we possess today are reasonably close to the originals, they would have to reject outright the textual reliability of virtually every other ancient text."[15]

If you admit the existence of Jesus and the historical reliability of the accounts of his life, the next question is this: What do you make of his claims? Richard Dawkins writes that the "historical evidence that Jesus claimed any sort of divine status is minimal."[16] Dawkins had better stick to studying molecules if he can't do better than that. The fact is, Jesus claimed to be God on numerous occasions in numerous ways: "Before Abraham was, I am" (Jn 8:58); "I and the Father are one" (Jn 10:30); "He who has seen me has seen the Father" (Jn 14:9). His disciples understood his claim and accepted it. The Jewish leaders who rejected the claim clearly understood it nevertheless. They told Jesus they condemned him "because you, being a man, make yourself God" (Jn 10:33).

If Jesus claimed to be God, we are faced with a logical problem—a dilemma that was framed by early Church writers in the phrase *aut Deus, aut homo malus* ("either God or a bad man"). Christ was either God, as he claimed, or else a bad man for misleading people about his identity. In more recent times, C. S. Lewis reframed the argument as a trilemma: Christ has to be a liar, a lunatic, or the Lord. If his claims are true, he is the Lord. If they are false, he either was deliberately misrepresenting himself or was sincerely deluded; that is, he was a liar (who foolishly died for his lie) or else a lunatic.[17]

As Lewis and many other Christian apologists point out, however, it's hard to credit the idea that Jesus was a liar or a lunatic. Unlike a liar, Jesus took pains to back up his words with deeds ("Which is easier, to say, 'Your sins are forgiven,' or to say, 'Rise and walk'?" [Mt 9:5]). In addition he had a habit of speaking out fearlessly against the Pharisees, despite the risks. He was able to tell the woman at the well all that she ever did. He was able to predict the manner of his death and resurrection in detail. And, most significantly, there is nothing in his life to suggest the kind of malevolent character it would take to lead so many people so seriously astray. If he were a liar, then, in a sense, Western culture since the time of Christ is laced with lies because it has been repeating his words and recommending his life as a model of truth and goodness.

A lunatic? Self-deceived? Jesus was not self-absorbed, as madmen are, but rather, full of concern and compassion for others. And unlike the self-deluded, he was a keen judge of human nature—full of understanding and forgiveness when that was needed and demonstrating savvy and shrewdness when they were called for ("All right then, gentlemen, which of you would like to throw the first stone?"). Despite his seemingly crazy claims, Jesus comes across as a model of wisdom and balance.

Jesus, to all appearances, was a good man, the most perfect man who ever lived, yet he said things about himself that a good man—if he were only a man—would never say. As Lewis pointed out, the greater the goodness of a human being, the less he is inclined to claim divinity. The Old Testament prophets—Moses, Isaiah, Jeremiah, Daniel— never claimed to be God; neither did any of the great philosophers or religious figures. Socrates didn't claim to be divine, nor did Buddha, Saint Francis, or Muhammad.

Here's a thought experiment: Imagine how it would sound for any other man, even a great man, to talk about himself the way Christ did. How would it sound if Socrates had said, "Before Abraham came to be, I am"? Or if George Washington had said, "He who lives and believes in me shall never die"? Or if Winston Churchill had said, "Your sins are forgiven you"? The answer? It would sound crazy in the extreme. In today's parlance we would call talk like this a "career killer". The strange thing is that, in the case of Christ, the claims don't seem quite so crazy. In his case, the words do seem to fit the man.

The Jesus presented in the Gospels makes astonishing claims, yet the New Testament provides considerable evidence for believing them. The claims made for Jesus by the Koran are much more modest. Indeed, the author of the Koran seems mainly interested in establishing the point that Jesus "was but a mortal". But even on this point the Koran is not convincing. As presented in the Koran, the figures of Noah, Joseph, and Moses have more substance than Jesus does. In comparison with them, Isa is a blank page. Though poorly drawn, the Old Testament characters are at least recognizable people. The Koranic Jesus is an artifice—a stratagem. He is there for the purpose of proving that Christians are deceived. According to the Koran, the Christians who fail to admit their error and become Muslim will be judged by Jesus when "on the Day of Resurrection he will bear witness against them" (4:159). The prophet Jesus has news for Christians, but it's not good news.

Which is more likely the true account of Jesus? The highly detailed narrative with numerous references to historical and geographical facts, or the rudimentary sketch drawn up by a man trying to supersede him? Which is more believable? An account composed in Arabia some six hundred years after the life of Jesus, or one composed within decades of his death by contemporaries and eyewitnesses?[18]

It doesn't sound like much of a contest. And yet the Muslim faith continues to gain against the Christian one. Until recently the theological differences between Christianity and Islam did not seem terribly relevant to the future course of civilization. If anyone was paying attention at all, the question about whose holy writ has the real Jesus seemed to be something for the interfaith dialogue people to work on while the rest of us got on with our lives. As it turns out, however, the question is becoming one of the main questions of modern times— something you may have to think about as hard as any fifteenth-century European living on the border of an Islamic kingdom; something you may be forced to think about even if you don't want to; something on which you may have to take a stand.

All right then; but it's a question that Muslims need to think about as well. Muslims have developed a policy of placing all the important questions off limits. And in letting them get away with this, we have been acting as enablers. After the violent reactions to Salman Rushdie's novel, to the Muhammad cartoons, to the pope's Regensburg speech, and to numerous other perceived insults, the main concern of many in the non-Muslim West has been to avoid offending Muslims further. But that seems like a failed strategy. It has served only to encourage a tendency on the part of Muslims to avoid asking themselves hard questions about their faith and the faith they reject. Perhaps the most important question both they and we need to ask is the one Christ asked his apostles: "But who do you say that I am?" (Mt 16:15). It's not a question just for his apostles; it's a question for everyone.

What Would Muhammad Do?

One of the most important tasks facing American Christians right now is to clarify their understanding of Islam. By and large, American Christians have focused on the similarities between themselves and Muslims. It seems the time has come for them to understand the differences, particularly since some of these differences now pose a threat to them.

Christians and Muslims have the following four things in common: both trace their faith to Abraham, both profess a reverence for Jesus, both claim to worship the one and only God, and both say they value a moral life. In each of these commonly held assertions, however, lie very important differences. Let's take a look at each of these in turn.

Father Abraham

Many Christians have assumed that since Abraham is the shared ancestor of Jews, Christians, and Muslims, there is some hope that the differences between them can be bridged. Thus, there has been a proliferation of "Abrahamic Faith" conferences throughout the world in recent years, and for some people the term *Judeo-Christian civilization* has been replaced by *Abrahamic civilization*. The trouble is, while Arab Muslims might be the biological descendants of Abraham, their version of the covenant God made with Abraham is very different from the covenant God made with Abraham in the Old Testament. Consequently, when the Catholic Church approaches the subject, it does so with caution. Consider the phrasing in *Nostra Aetate*: "They [Muslims] take pains to submit wholeheartedly to even His inscrutable decrees, just as Abraham, with whom the faith of Islam *takes pleasure in linking itself,* submitted to God" (my emphasis).[1] That's not exactly a ringing endorsement of Islam's claim to Abraham. In the

Catechism of the Catholic Church, the short discussion of the Church's relationship with Muslims takes pains to note that they "*profess* to hold the faith of Abraham" (my emphasis).

While the Koran mentions Abraham, its stories about him sharply diverge from those in the Old Testament. In the Koran, Abraham was a Muslim whom God chose to oppose idolatry and spread the true faith. God asked Abraham to sacrifice his son, but the name of the boy is not mentioned in the Koran. Most Muslim commentators hold that this son was Ishmael, Abraham's firstborn. The Koran says that God was pleased with Abraham's obedience and spared Ishmael, whom he sent to become the prophet and patriarch of the Arab people. Later God made a covenant with Abraham and Ishmael and commanded them to found a major place of worship in Mecca.

In the Bible, however, it was Isaac, the son of God's original promise, whom God asked Abraham to sacrifice. God had made a covenant with Abraham that would continue with his descendants through Isaac. By means of this covenant, God formed a people set apart for him— the Jews. They are the people through whom, Christians believe, God brought Jesus, the Savior, into the world. From the Muslim perspective, Christians and Jews are guilty of distorting and corrupting the story of Abraham. For Jews and Christians, the Koranic version of Abraham negates their understanding of salvation history. If anything, the differing accounts of Abraham contain more potential for divisiveness than for harmony.

Jesus

The second point of supposed commonality between Muslims and Christians is reverence for Jesus. But, as I hope I made clear in the previous chapter, the Jesus of the Koran bears little resemblance to the Jesus of the Gospels. The Isa of the Koran doesn't even qualify as a historical figure. Moreover, the message given by the Koranic Jesus flatly contradicts the claim of Jesus Christ to be the Son of God. In addition, when he returns to earth, Jesus will "bear witness" against Christians who fail to convert to Islam (4:159). According to an oft-quoted hadith, Jesus, upon his return, "will break the cross". At the same time "Allah will perish all religions except Islam."[2] Muslim commentators interpret these actions to mean that Jesus will abolish Christianity and eliminate all religions other than Islam.[3] Although Muslims reverence Jesus, the Jesus they reverence is no friend of Christians. The admonition that Paul delivered to the Corinthians seems especially relevant today:

> But I am afraid that as the serpent deceived Eve by his cunning, your thoughts will be led astray from a sincere and pure devotion to Christ. For if some one comes and preaches another Jesus than the one we preached, or if you receive a different spirit from the one you received, or if you accept a different gospel from the one you accepted, you submit to it readily enough. (2 Cor 11:3–4)

The Same God?

Can we at least say that Christians and Muslims worship the same God? Yes, but only in the broadest sense that there is, after all, only one God. Whether prayer and worship are being offered to our Father in heaven or to Allah or to the Great Spirit, there is only one God who is paying attention. Most Christians assume that if prayers are offered up in the right spirit, God will respond to them even if they are misaddressed. But then we might as well say that we worship the same God together with believers of any faith that acknowledges an omnipotent higher power.

In some ways, the God described in the Koran does resemble the God of the Bible: "He is the Sovereign Lord", "the Giver of Peace", "the Mighty One", "the Most High!" (59:23). It is nevertheless difficult to see how Allah and the God worshipped by Christians are the same. According to the Christian faith, God has revealed that he is a Trinity, a communion of three Persons in one God—Father, Son, and Holy Spirit—and that the Son took flesh and became man in Christ. In the Koran, Allah denies the doctrines of the Trinity and the Incarnation, not once, but repeatedly. For example: "They do blaspheme who say: Allah is one of three in a Trinity" (5:73, trans Yusuf Ali); "The Christians call Christ the son of Allah.... Allah's curse be on them: how they are deluded away from the truth!" (9:30, trans Yusuf Ali).

Allah has no beloved son with whom he is pleased. Rather, he takes pains to assert that Jesus was "but a mortal" (43:60) who was "no more than an apostle" (5:75), and whose reported death on the Cross was "a monstrous falsehood" (4:157). It is impossible to believe that the same God could have revealed such contradictory teachings.

The Moral Life

What about the common belief that Muslims value the moral life? Here again, qualifications need to be made. Do Muslims and Christians subscribe to the same morals, the same standards of conduct? The more we learn about communities ruled by Islamic law, the more we see that Muslims and Christians have different sets of rules. What accounts for the differences? In a word, Muhammad. For many centuries, Islam was known as Mohammedanism. That term is now considered outdated because it implies that Islam revolves around its founder rather than on submission to Allah. But the word *Mohammedanism* is not far off the mark. It reminds us of just how central a role Muhammad plays in Islam.

Even though Muslims don't believe that Muhammad was divine, they do consider him a model of behavior. In Islamic tradition he is considered the perfect man, a paragon of proper conduct. The Sufi philosopher Abu Hamid Muhammad al-Ghazali wrote that "the key to happiness is to follow the sunna and to imitate the Messenger of God in all his coming and going, his movements and rest, in his way of eating, his attitude, his sleep and his talk." [4] Islam hasn't changed in this regard since the time of al-Ghazali. Here's Islamic expert Malcolm Clark on the subject:

> Sura 33:21 says, "You have in the messenger of God [Muhammad] a beautiful pattern". Some Christians say WWJD ("What would Jesus do?") and try to imitate Christ, but this imitation by Christians pales beside the imitation of Muhammad by Muslims. Muslims obey because they accept Muhammad as the chosen one (*mustafa*, one of the most common epithets of Muhammad). To obey means to imitate the actions of the prophet, heed the words of the prophet, and accept as permissible that to which he gave his approval. [5]

Muhammad's role in the lives of Muslims is similar to Christ's role in the lives of Christians. As Christians are supposed to conform their conduct to Christ's, Muslims are expected to conform theirs to Muhammad's. And just as Christians don't question the rightness of Christ's actions, so Muslims don't question the rightness of Muhammad's.

The trouble is, there's a wide divergence between the life of Christ and the life of Muhammad. How divergent? Well, here's a quick quiz: Which of the two had eleven wives? Which one married a nine-year-old girl? Which one married his ex-daughter-in-law? Which one struck off the heads of captives "as they were brought out to him in batches"?[6] Which one ordered his men to gouge out the eyes of a group of captured thieves and to "cut off their hands and legs"?[7] One doesn't need a degree in comparative religion to know that the man in question is not Christ. Critics of Christianity may talk about a moral equivalence between Islam and Christianity, but there is no comparison between the founder of the one faith and the founder of the other. On one occasion, Muhammad ordered the leader of a defeated tribe to be tortured to death and then proceeded to "marry" the man's wife that same evening. Some of Muhammad's behavior was shocking even to his own followers, and on more than one occasion he found it necessary to produce a new revelation from Allah in order to justify his actions.

How do we know about these details of Muhammad's life? Some of them are in the Koran, but others are contained in Islamic sources that are considered almost as authoritative as the Koran—namely, the sira and the hadith. The sira are biographies of Muhammad. The first and most authoritative of these is the one composed by Ibn Ishaq about 130 years after Muhammad's death; it is currently available in an English translation by Alfred Guillaume. The hadith are accounts of the sayings and doings of Muhammad reported by his followers. The most reliable of the hadith were compiled by Muhammad ibn Ismail al-Bukhari (810–70) and by Muslim ibn al-Hajjaj al-Qushayri (821–75), although at least four other collections are considered reliable. The hadith contain far more information about Muhammad than does the Koran. The Bukhari collection alone consists of nine volumes. The main hadith have been translated into English and are accessible online.

The point is, there has never been an effort by Muslims to hide the unsavory side of Muhammad's life. After the initial reservations on the part of some of his followers, a consensus was quickly reached that Muhammad could do no wrong. In Islam, right and wrong are determined not by natural law nor by ethical principles but by what Muhammad did or said. As Gregory M. Davis explains in *Religion of Peace? Islam's War Against the World*, "Because Muhammad is himself the measuring stick of morality, his actions are not judged according to an independent moral standard but rather establish what the proper standard for morality of Muslims is."[8] Thus, in Iran girls can be legally married at nine, and in some Islamic nations the penalty for theft is still amputation.

How does a Muslim follow Allah? By doing what Muhammad did: "Follow him so that you may be rightly guided" (Koran 7:158). For strategic reasons, Islamic apologists speaking to Western audiences sometimes downplay the central place of Muhammad in Islam, but in their tradition he is by far the greatest person who ever lived. His exalted status is made clear in the Koran. Almost every time Allah is mentioned, Muhammad is mentioned in the same breath:

"Believers, have faith in God and His Apostle" (4:136).

"God and His Apostle will watch your actions" (9:94).

"Obey God and the Apostle that you may find mercy" (3:132).

"The spoils belong to God and the Apostle" (8:1).

"God will not forgive them for they have denied God and His Apostle" (9:80).

"Are they not aware that the man who defies God and His Apostle shall abide forever in the fire of Hell?" (9:63).

Words to this effect appear over and over in the pages of the Koran. The greatest sin in Islam is *shirk*—the association of partners with Allah. Yet Muhammad is so closely identified with Allah that it is difficult not to think of him as an associate. Koran 4:150 warns believers not to "draw a line between God and His apostles". *Reliance of the Traveller*, one of the most highly attested manuals of Islamic law, says of Muhammad:

> Allah has favored him above all the other prophets and made him the highest of mankind, rejecting anyone's attesting to the divine oneness by saying "There is no god but Allah", unless they also attest to the Prophet by saying "Muhammad is the Messenger of Allah". He has obliged men and jinn to believe everything the Prophet (Allah bless him and give him peace) has informed us concerning this world and the next.[9]

"What would Muhammad do?" is not an idle question for Muslims. It is the main guide to morality.

Beyond Reason

On examination, the four most commonly cited similarities between Islam and Christianity turn out to be points of major disagreement. Let's look at a few more areas in which the Muslim and Christian faiths diverge.

One of the chief differences concerns the question of whether God is a reasonable being who has created a rational world. Although Christians believe that God acts in accordance with reason, Muslims believe that God is not bound by the rules of reason because that would restrict his freedom. Instead, Muslims believe that God is pure will. And pure will implies arbitrariness. The almost complete reliance on the example of Muhammad partly explains the arbitrary and sometimes cruel nature of Islamic law. But Muhammad was not alone in his capriciousness. In the Koran, Allah himself is not consistent. As a result, Muslims do not expect his actions and his laws to be reasonable, to make sense. Thus, although both Christians and Muslims believe in submitting to God's will, there is a difference. When a Christian says, "It's God's will", he is expressing a belief that what God wills is reasonable, meaning for our ultimate good. When a Muslim says, "It is the will of Allah", he means something like, "God is going to do what he wants to do; it doesn't matter if it makes no sense. We have no right to expect God to be reasonable." In the Islamic view, God has absolute freedom. He is a bit like Nietzsche's "superman", who is above categories such as good and evil, or rational and irrational, and simply exults in exercising his will.

In Islam there is very little sense of an objective rational order and, consequently, little sense that God or God's laws should conform to a rational order. In *The Closing of the Muslim Mind*, Robert Reilly sets out in detail the consequences that follow upon the conception of God as pure will:

> It also means that the "moral" obligations that God sets upon man do not originate in reason.... God can command what is evil to be good, or good to be evil.[10]

> Evil is simply what is forbidden. What is forbidden today could be permitted tomorrow without inconsistency.[11]

> Sheikh Nabhani ... always taught that there was no such thing as morality in Islam; it was simply what God taught. If Allah allowed it, it was moral.[12]

Thus, in Islam, being good is not a result of following your well-formed conscience but only of following the rules. In fact, as Reilly informs us, "There is not an Arabic word for conscience."[13]

Holiness

Also missing from Islam is a duty to strive for personal holiness. Unlike Christianity, which puts the stress on inner purification, Islam stresses external compliance. Christ commanded his followers not to murder, but also not to yield to anger; not to commit adultery, but also not to lust. There is no corresponding call in Islam to clean the inside of the cup. By the standards of Islamic law, a Muslim is clean if he fulfills all of the external duties of sharia, such as praying five times a day, fasting when it is required, abstaining from pork, and so on.

Although sharia demands that Muslims do specified good works, it does not call them to spiritual transformation. By contrast, in the Bible, especially in the New Testament, there is a great emphasis on transformation and sanctification. Christians need to be born again to a new life in Christ; they must "grow up in every way" to be more like Christ (Eph 4:15); they should put off the old self and put on a new self; they should become "a new creation" (2 Cor 5:17); they should be holy as God is holy (1 Pet 1:15–16).

According to the Christian faith, our relationship with God is one of communion with a person who, out of love for us, imprints his own holiness on us. He first makes us in his own image, and then, through baptism, he makes us his children by uniting us to his Son. Thus, "Therefore, be imitators of God, as beloved children" (Eph 5:1). And, "Beloved, we are God's children now; it does not yet appear what we shall be, but we know that when he appears we shall be like him" (1 Jn 3:2).

There is one hadith in which Muhammad is reported to have said that Adam was made in Allah's image, but for the most part, Islamic scripture emphasizes the distance between man and God: Allah is incomparable and utterly transcendent; no one is like him; communion with him is impossible. As theologian Mark Durie points out, "The idea that people should be like Allah, or seek to become like him in any way is regarded as blasphemy."[14] It's not difficult to see, then, why Muslims do not strive to draw near to their Creator in order to be more like him. Rather, the person they strive to imitate is Muhammad.

Heavenly Rewards

The chasm between man and Allah in Islam is also seen in the Muslim conception of heaven. In Christian theology, heaven is the state of being in perfect communion with God. In some accounts, Allah seems to be present in the Islamic paradise, but he is certainly not the main attraction. Rather, the rewards of paradise are largely material—pavilions, fountains, couches, jewels, food and beverage, servants, and shapely companions. In short, you won't be transformed there, but you will be rewarded. There is no need for transformation because heaven is simply a better version of earth. You can end up in paradise (Allah willing) and remain essentially the same person you were before—except now you'll live forever and have a bountiful supply of women and refreshments (the Koran is not clear about what sort of afterlife women will enjoy). There is no notion of a final union with God as there is in Christianity because Allah is too unlike us. There is no possibility of entering into fellowship with him.

The practice of Christianity, on the other hand, is about meeting Christ here on earth so that we can be made ready for an ultimate encounter with the Almighty. The Christian emphasis on spiritual improvement flows from this belief. Why? Because from the Christian perspective, companionship with God requires an amazing amount of development. Transformation in Christ is the necessary antecedent to union with God. Thus writes Saint Paul, "We ... are being changed into his likeness from one degree of glory to another" (2 Cor 3:18). And, "Though our outer man is wasting away, our inner man is being renewed every day ... preparing for us an eternal weight of glory beyond all comparison" (2 Cor 4:16–17). Through Christ, man is offered not only paradise, but also the radical transformation that makes him fit for paradise.

If we are meant to enjoy fellowship with God, it is reasonable to expect that we first need to undergo a process of shaping up. But Christ's promise of transformation seems reasonable in another sense; it corresponds to aspirations that seem to be built into human nature—aspirations of an infinite kind. As C. S. Lewis pointed out, all basic human drives and desires have a corresponding consummation in nature. They point to realities that fulfill them. There is hunger and there is food to satisfy it; there is thirst and there is water to slake it; there is sexual desire and there is sex. So, says Lewis, "If I find in myself a desire which no experience in this world can satisfy, the most prob-able explanation is that I was made for another world." [15]

Lewis suggests that the "inconsolable longing" buried in the human heart and expressed in myth, legend, and literature finds its correlative in the Christian promise. The historical and textual evidence strongly suggests that Christianity is not a legend; nevertheless, it seems to ful-fill the hope that lies at the heart of many myths and stories. The secular belief in things like evolution, progress, and human potential seems to verify this longing. So does the Islamic view of paradise. But since the Islamic paradise is only an extension of worldly satisfactions, it's not a good bet for finding lasting fulfillment. It offers no remedy for our brokenness and no prospect of a better self. Moreover, it falls far short of the desire for an infinite consummation that seems to be built into us. Aside from the question of which is the truer religion, Christianity seems truer to human psychology and aspiration than does Islam. Well, make that "adult psychology". At a certain stage of ado-lescence (and in cases of prolonged adolescence), an eternity of mind-less and impersonal copulation might seem the height of aspiration, but grown-ups yearn for a higher destiny than that.

The problem with Islam's view of human destiny is that it offers a finite solution to an infinite problem. The first hundred years of eter-nity with the devoted virgins may provide some distraction from the eternal questions—but after that? Saint Augustine's observation that "our hearts are restless until they rest in Thee" corresponds with the reality of the inconsolable longing. But the Islamic notion that "our hearts are restless until our sexual appetites are satiated" corresponds only with teenage fantasies.

Muslims value the moral life, but Islam's idea of the moral life is in many crucial respects quite unlike the Christian idea. Muslims believe in an afterlife, but it's a different sort of afterlife from the one for which Christians hope. In addition to searching for commonalities with Islam, it might be wise for Christians to pay attention to some of the differences—as well as to the implications of those differences. Some of those differences pose a significant threat to Christians. For example, one of the consequences of the Islamic view of paradise is that it creates a very real temptation for young men to take a shortcut to get there. Most Christians are not sure if they are quite ready for union with God, but most young men, of whatever religion, are pretty sure they are ready for the rewards offered in the Islamic paradise. So if you live in a society that doesn't offer much in the way of human development or material progress and which, moreover, restricts the supply of available women either through polygamy or through chastity laws, you might be tempted to go to the next life as quickly as possible. According to most interpretations of Islam, the only sure way of getting your reward is through martyrdom—being killed for the sake of Allah, and preferably in the course of killing others.

If many men believe that their violence will be rewarded with a bevy of beauties in paradise, the idea needs to be taken seriously— although not in the sense that multiculturalists accord respect to non-Western ideas. The belief that Allah hates non-Muslims so much that, for killing them, he will reward you with six dozen freshly minted maidens is not just another colorful thread in the rich tapestry of diversity; it's a dangerous idea that needs to be examined and discredited. Of course, it's not much more dangerous than a number of other core Islamic beliefs—that women are inferior to men, that non-Muslims are inferior to Muslims, and that Muslims, by right, should rule over the whole world. It's well past time for Christians to rethink the common-ground approach. There comes a point at which the central tenets of Islam need to be challenged rather than respected.

PART IV

THE CULTURE WAR AND
THE TERROR WAR

Don't Throw Out the Britney
with the Bath Water

As political scientist Samuel Huntington observed, we are in a civilizational struggle with Islam; however, there is a different, intracivilizational struggle underway that may determine the outcome of that global struggle. It's called the culture war. The culture war has many fronts: debates over marriage, abortion, education, the sexualization of children by the entertainment industry, and a dozen other issues. Although the culture war is far from over, it's difficult to avoid the conclusion that Christians have been on the losing side. Moreover, a case can be made that the loss of the culture war will almost inevitably lead to the loss of the struggle against the resurgent Islam that is attacking the West.

In losing ground in the culture war, we've lost ground in defending ourselves against Islamic aggression, but the reason for this is more complex than some think. Before discussing that reason, it's important to address a misleading simplification of the connection between the two conflicts. A common argument—one that many conservative Christians find appealing—contends that Muslim grievances against the West are based almost wholly on our own cultural corruption. There is, of course, plenty wrong with our culture. The trouble with this argument is that it fails to recognize that there is also something wrong with Islam—something that can't be fixed by fixing our own culture. Nevertheless, it has been an influential argument—one that requires a closer look.

The argument is summed up in a discussion that arose a few years ago about pop icon Britney Spears. The debate revolved around what, at first glance, might seem an unusual question: Did Britney cause 9/11? No one, of course, claims that Britney conspired with Muhammad Atta to blow up the Pentagon and the World Trade Center (although in this age of strange conspiracy theories, there might be a few partisans of that view). The argument, rather, is that there is something about American popular culture that provoked the 9/11 attacks. And since "Britney" is shorthand for all that's wrong with American pop culture, let's call it the "Britney thesis".

This is, more or less, the central argument of Dinesh D'Souza's book *The Enemy at Home: The Cultural Left and Its Responsibility for 9/11*. According to D'Souza, the simple answer to the question "Why do they hate us?" is "Because we are decadent." And they (Muslim fundamentalists) fear that we mean to export to their traditional societies our debased values—not just Britney and Eminem and rap music, but also illegitimacy, easy divorce, abortion, and gay "marriage".[1] As proof, D'Souza quotes extensively from Islamic leaders, including Osama bin Laden and Sayyid Qutb, the intellectual father of the modern jihadist movement. For example, in his "Letter to America", bin Laden calls on Americans to "reject the immoral acts of fornication, homosexuality, intoxicants, gambling and trading with interest" and to replace them with "manners, principles, honor and purity".[2] Qutb, who thought American influence was turning the world into a "large brothel", warned what would happen to Muslim countries if, as in America, "free sexual relationships and illegitimate children become the basis of a society".[3] Likewise, the Ayatollah Khomeini claimed that Western freedom is only "freedom of debauchery".[4] Even some Muslim women feel threatened. Masoumeh Ebtekar, a former high-ranking Iranian government official asks, "Must we all conform to Hollywood's view of human nature, which mostly stresses what is base rather than noble in humanity?"[5]

What does America stand for? According to many Muslim opinion makers, it stands for the steady supply of obscenity and vice that America exports to the world. The message hasn't been lost on the Muslim masses. A Pew Research Center Poll reported that nine out of ten Jordanian and Palestinian Muslims feel their religion is threatened by Western secularism, and three-quarters of Lebanese Muslims concur.[6]

So, from the Muslim point of view, there was an American war against Islam going on long before the invasion of Afghanistan. It consisted of America's attack on religion and traditional morality and its attempt to export this to the rest of the world. That, anyway, is D'Souza's thesis, and it accounts, he writes, for the "volcano of anger" that culminated in the 9/11 attack.

D'Souza makes some good points, but there are some problems with this analysis. It doesn't quite explain why radical Muslims attack other traditional people in India or Indonesia or why traditional Sunni Muslims blow up mosques in traditional Shia neighborhoods. Nor is it useful in explaining why Muslims swept out of Arabia in the seventh century and subjugated most of the Middle East, all of North Africa, and most of Spain. Whatever the reason for these conquests, it had nothing to do with outrage over images of scantily clad temptresses beamed via satellite into Muslim societies. There was no Internet porn in eighth-century Spain, but Muhammad's disciples conquered it anyway. D'Souza slides too quickly over the aggressive, expansionistic side of Islam, and he gives too much credit to the notion that the current jihad is motivated solely by fear of cultural subversion. Most Islamic authorities hold that jihad is a duty commanded by Allah in good times and bad.

Naturally enough, D'Souza's book caused outrage on the left for his claim that "without the cultural left, 9/11 would not have happened", but it has drawn the ire of conservative critics as well. For example, Robert Spencer shares D'Souza's concern about Western immorality, but he doesn't buy the decadence argument, and he asserts that the jihad would continue unabated even if "the exportation of American depravity were to end tomorrow".[7] Our cultural degeneracy is a factor in Islam's war against us, but it is not the decisive factor. Muslim aggression in the past never needed the excuse of non-Muslim decadence.

It's possible, however, to overstate the case against D'Souza and risk throwing out the baby with the bath water or, in this case, throwing out the Britney with the bath water—or at least the Britney thesis. Part of the Britney thesis proposed by D'Souza is worth saving—that is, the idea that the culture war and the war with Islamic terrorists are intimately related. It is true that winning the war against decadence would put us in a better position to win against Islamic aggression—although not in the way D'Souza suggests. Unfortunately, Spencer is so incensed by D'Souza's narrow analysis of the reasons for jihad that he comes close to throwing out the whole of the Britney thesis, poking fun at the idea in a blog post he titles "How Britney Spears and I Cause Jihad".[8]

Downplaying the culture war in this fashion carries a risk of its own, because the culture war does matter. No, Britney didn't cause

9/11, but there is a sense in which the outcome of the culture war is related to the outcome of the war Islam has declared on the West.

One of the strategies that is often suggested for defending ourselves against Islamic aggression is to find ways to help moderate Muslims resist radical Muslims. Part of D'Souza's argument is that traditional Americans and traditional Muslims are natural allies because both are religiously and socially conservative and share many of the same values. To keep traditional Muslims from sliding into the radical camp, says D'Souza, we need to show them that there is another America that is not represented by pop stars and those who demand sexual license in the name of civil liberty. D'Souza recommends that traditional Christians and traditional Muslims should unite against moral degeneracy and work together in international forums to block the imposition of abortion on demand and homosexual unions.

D'Souza's argument is flawed because it greatly overstates the similarities between traditional Americans and traditional Muslims. Still, it doesn't make sense to try to win over the "heart and minds" of moderate Muslims if the only face of America you can manage to project is the vacant visage of the latest celebrity. Robert Spencer acknowledges as much in his book *Religion of Peace?*; he agrees that "there is a certain truth" to D'Souza's point about the export of degenerate pop culture: "In Islam, the recurrent view of the West is of a culture of immorality, which is one reason, but by no means the only reason, why the jihadist critique carries such weight."[9] One sure way to lose the war of ideas is to confirm the Muslim world in the belief that Western culture equals pop culture. If that's the best we can do, it makes our claim to speak with moral authority about the deficiencies of Islam seem pretty shallow.

Take the treatment of Muslim women. We point out that in Islamic societies they're treated as commodities and sex objects, but Muslim apologists in turn point to Britney and company and say that we do the same. And our objectification of women is not limited to the entertainment industry. As sociologist George Gilder argued thirty years ago, the American practice of having multiple wives through divorce and remarriage amounts to serial polygamy. As the phenomenon has grown, our case against Muslim polygamy has weakened. Some might say that at least in America women can be as sexually liberated as men and have as many husbands as men have wives. But this is unlikely to convince Muslims of our cultural superiority. As Katharine Boswell puts it in a

review of a book on our sex-obsessed culture, "It is difficult to successfully advocate better conditions for Middle Eastern women when
American women are consistently portrayed as 'sex-hungry floozies'." [10]

Still, it's a mistake to push the comparison too far. There is no
moral equivalence between the enforced subordination of Muslim
women and the voluntary behavior of Americans. Becoming a pop
idol in America is optional; choosing a husband in much of the Islamic
world is not. In America, you're free to make yourself into a sex object,
or not; but in Saudi Arabia, if you're a woman, you're not free to
leave the house without your husband's permission. In America, the
bikini is optional; in some Afghani communities, the burqa is required.
Islamic morality is based on compulsion; Christian morality is based
on freedom. As Spencer points out, despite its deficiencies, the Judeo-
Christian tradition presents a superior vision of God, man, and morality. "Western freedom", he writes, "would be more respected in the
Islamic world if it were presented in this moral context." [11]

But it's a hard sell. There's a big difference between Islamic virtue
and Christian virtue, but from a distance the difference might not be
so apparent. If you're the victim of a tsunami and have been helped by
an American Marine, or if you're a Palestinian who has received compassionate and competent treatment in an Israeli hospital, you can see
that Judeo-Christian morality translates into real charity. Without such
concrete experiences, however, Muslims are apt to base their judgments on media images that portray us as a people soaked in materialism and illicit sex.

It doesn't help to say that Judeo-Christian freedom and virtue are
much better even if they don't look much better. If you live in a
Muslim society, where religious beliefs are very much reflected in daily
life, it's difficult to understand why the supposedly superior religious
beliefs of the West have had so little impact on the moral tone of the
culture. You might draw the conclusion that Christianity is an inef-
fective faith. That was the conclusion reached by Sayyid Qutb, whose
influence on Islamic thinking was boosted by his execution in 1966
for opposing the secular government of Egypt's Gamal Abdel Nasser.
He wrote, "But Christianity ... cannot be reckoned a real force in
opposition to the philosophies of the new materialism; it is an indi-
vidualist, isolationist, negative faith. It has no power to make life grow
under its influence in any permanent positive way ... it has no essential philosophy of actual, practical life." [12]

Qutb's low opinion of Christianity may have been shaped by an incident that occurred while he was a student in America in 1949. While attending a church dance in Greely, Colorado, Qutb was repulsed not only by the "feverish music" and the "dancing naked legs" but also by the minister's willingness to collude in setting the scene by dimming the lights and putting a "seductive song" on the turntable.[13] You can say, as many have, that Qutb was a prude. He was, nevertheless, an extremely influential prude. His critique of Western/ Christian society still resonates with Muslims around the world. And because things have gone considerably downhill since Qutb's visit to America in 1949, his assessment of Western decay must now seem prophetic. There's a point here for Christians to ponder, because the rise of Islamic radicalism has coincided with a decline in personal sexual morality among Christians. While the churches have been fairly effective in raising consciousness about social-justice issues, they've shown little ability or even willingness to address issues of sexual morality. Unless we can do something about our Britneyization problem, we will have a difficult job convincing the Muslim world that we have a better alternative to sharia.

In the final analysis, however, no amount of cultural reform on our part is going to remove the main Muslim motive for attacking us. Islam commands jihad against us not because we are degenerate, but because we are not Muslim. If everyone in the West were suddenly to transform into models of Christian virtue, it would make no difference to those bent on conquering us. According to their tenets, non-Muslims must either convert or submit.

Still, there is a very good reason for Christians to reform themselves and to continue fighting the cultural battles. The most important question to ask about our moral decline is not "What effect does it have on Muslims?" but rather, "What effect does it have on us?" Winning the culture war at home might not convince traditional Muslims to side with us rather than with Islamic radicals, but it might provide us with some moral fiber and give us the will to resist jihad ourselves, whether it comes in the form of bombings or in the form of political and cultural pressure (of the kind that France, England, and Denmark are experiencing right now). One of the effects of moral decline is that people eventually lose the conviction that they have anything worth fighting for. Europe already seems well on its way to losing that conviction, and not surprisingly, it is

Europe that the cultural left in America holds up as a model to emulate. But if Europe has anything to teach us, it's that people who submit to their every desire may soon find themselves in a permanent state of submission.

"Civilizations die from suicide, not murder", wrote the eminent historian Arnold J. Toynbee. Predictions of the suicide of the West have been around now for a long while, but that doesn't mean it's never going to happen. Rome wasn't built in a day, and it didn't fall in a day; but its fall—when it did come—seems to have had something to do with its becoming what we would now call an "entertainment society". As suggested by the protracted decline of the Roman Empire, a society can go on amusing itself to death for quite a while until a determined enemy shows up and administers the final blow. In Rome it took a long while before the old family and martial virtues were finally sapped.

On the other hand, the power and influence of entertainers is now about a thousand times greater than it was in ancient Rome. Round-the-clock entertainment was something only the emperor and a handful of aristocrats could afford; and the worst of Roman decadence didn't reach into farms and villas in the countryside. Nowadays, with the power of the Internet and of cable and satellite television, any American can command more immoral fantasies than the Emperor Nero could have imagined. We don't really know what the effect of this is. We live in an unprecedented historical environment. A television in every home is a phenomenon that goes back only to the late 1950s; two-hundred-channel programming, the Internet, and the iPod are much more recent developments.

Most people understand that entertainment is a distraction from the main business of life, although most appreciate that a little distraction is a healthful thing. But what happens when distraction is the main thing? It's now known that listening to high-decibel rap and rock makes young people prematurely deaf. Could the same sound be making them deaf to the sucking noise of their society going down the drain? It's not just the young who have been sucked in by the endless stream of distraction. How many retirees are glued to their television sets all day? How many working-age Americans waste hours surfing the Internet or playing computer games? How many grown men devote a large chunk of their weekends to the trivial pursuit of determining whether sports team A will defeat sports team B?

In *Casablanca*, when the Nazis enter Paris, Rick Blaine makes note of the time and says, "I'll bet they're asleep in New York. I'll bet they're asleep all over America." America had yet to wake up to the Nazi danger. And no doubt ball games, movies, and concerts served to distract people from weightier matters then, just as they do today. But in the 1940s, the entertainment industry could be easily aroused to dangerous realities because it was still in tune with traditional culture. For the most part, movie makers supported loyalty to family, religion, and country, and after the bombing of Pearl Harbor, Hollywood responded in a remarkably short time with films that helped shape a patriotic consciousness—films such as *Mrs. Miniver*, *To Be or Not to Be* and, of course, *Casablanca*.

It has been eleven years since the September 11 attacks, and nothing remotely comparable has come out of Hollywood on the subject of the war being waged on us by Islamists. Most of what has been produced on the subject seems geared to undermining rather than reinforcing American patriotism—the kind of films you might make thirty years after the war has been won, when you have the peacetime luxury of dwelling on the moral ambivalences of warfare. The reason is that today's movie makers are different from those of the past. By and large, they do not display any loyalty to civic, family, or religious obligations. The movie moguls don't seem to care whether you have any allegiances other than the one you show to their star attractions.

Moreover, current news and entertainment seem to induce a kind of memory loss. To the media, nothing matters but the present. That's why it's so hard to remember September 11, 2001. To an immediate-sensation generation caught up in the hype of the moment, 9/11 already seems like ancient history. By contrast, Islamic fundamentalists remember September 11, 1683. That was the date the Muslim armies advancing into Europe were turned back at the gates of Vienna by the much smaller force of the Christian King Jan Sobieski, thus commencing a three-hundred-year decline of Islamic power.

Individuals think about suicide when their life seems without point or direction, with no connection to a meaningful past or a meaningful future. It's the same with entire peoples. They give up on the effort it takes to survive when they lose their sense of purpose. While pop entertainment can provide lots of intensity, it doesn't help us to make sense of our lives; instead, it distracts us from asking questions about ultimate meaning and, by creating a youth subculture, estranges the young from the people and traditions that might provide the answers to those questions.

Our survival hinges not on generating a succession of momentary sensations, but on finding narratives that tell us who we are, where we have come from, and where we are going. These narratives, however, are increasingly difficult to find. As our pop culture expands, our traditional culture shrinks. And educators, who should be the guardians and transmitters of our heritage, often seem intent on dismissing it. According to a report issued by the National Association of Scholars in 2011, only 2 percent of American colleges offer required courses on Western civilization, though classes in gender or race studies can fulfill needed requirements. When college students do take classes about Western history or heritage, they are often taught to be ashamed of it. Unhappily, people who know little of the good in their civilization's past are likely to care little for its future. During World War II, Frank Capra produced a series of films for the government titled *Why We Fight*. Seventy years later, "Why do we fight?" has become a tough question to answer. We even have difficulty answering the question "Why do we exist?" Our ability to resist aggression—whether cultural or military—depends on the conviction that we have something worth defending: something that ought to be preserved not only for our own sake but also for the sake of those who attack us.

Christianity has a pretty good answer to the question "Why do we exist?" And the answer comes in the form of a story. There's a reason God is called the Author of Salvation and the Gospels are referred to as "the greatest story ever told". It's quite a story—a cosmic drama in which some of the strands come together only in eternity. The story reads in part like realistic fiction and in part like high fantasy. It contains an evil being far more cunning and malevolent than Sauron or Voldemort—a Dark Lord who has more of a hold on people than Sauron has on Frodo or Voldemort on Harry. And the thing—both thrilling and frightening—is that we are written into the story. Christianity maintains that our own life story is connected to this overarching story of Creation, Fall, Struggle, and Redemption. We can throw in our lot with the hero-king and his fellowship and play our own part in weakening the grip of the Dark Lord, or we can succumb to the temptations of the supreme tempter. It's the ultimate, ultimate-stakes thriller, and once you understand its implications, your natural inclination is to decline the invitation in favor of tending to your own affairs. In commenting on Tolkien's *Fellowship of the Ring*, C. S. Lewis nicely captures this strange, otherworldly aspect of our lives and the way it sometimes rudely demands our attention:

> Almost the central theme of the book is the contrast between the Hobbits (or "the Shire") and the appalling destiny to which some of them are called, the terrifying discovery that the humdrum happiness of the Shire, which they had taken for granted as something normal, is in reality a sort of local and temporary accident, that its existence depends on being protected by powers which Hobbits dare not imagine, that any Hobbit may find himself forced out of the Shire and caught up into that high conflict. More strangely still, the event of that conflict between strongest things may come to depend on him, who is almost the weakest.[14]

When you understand the appalling aspects of the Christian salvation story, you can see why most of it focuses on the goodness, compassion, and power of Christ. Otherwise the Hobbit in us might succumb to paralyzing fear. On the other hand, there is also a hero in us. As Lewis says of Tolkien's stories, "One of the main things that the author wants to say is that the real life of men is of that mythical and heroic quality."[15]

In any event, Christianity does answer the question "Why do we exist?" It does provide the narrative that keeps individuals and peoples from giving up in the face of dangers and difficulties. It does provide a story to live by and live for. Moreover, as Chesterton points out in *The Everlasting Man*, it's a story that has met two basic human needs: "It met the mythological search for romance by being a story and the philosophical search for truth by being a true story."[16]

There is a connection between narrative and morale. Likewise, there is a connection between morality and morale. Simply put, societies that lose their sense of morality eventually lose their morale, and for this reason the current disconnect between pop culture and morality hurts us. On that note, consider the following. A Jewish acquaintance who is a strong booster of Israel forwarded to me a YouTube video with the comment: "Too bad our media does not present this normal, vibrant, happy life in Israel!!!" He added, "Not a burqa in sight." The video shows a flash mob of about 150 skimpily clad young people breaking into a semi-erotic dance on an Israeli beach. Of course, a flash-mob exhibition is never a normal, spontaneous event; but aside from that, the disturbing implication of his comment was that this kind of activity is what Israel stands for. In other words, our answer to the burqa is the bikini. A commenter on the YouTube site wrote: "This is why the Arabs/Muslims/Islamists will never be able to wipe out Israel and run them into the sea. Israel will never go down to defeat because God is on their side." This is not only bad theology; it's bad psychology. People who have nothing more to live for than fun in the sun will in all likelihood be on the first plane out if and when the bombs start to fall.

This brings me back to the Britney thesis. Will the Britneys of the world be on the front lines defending freedom, or will they even know or care about anything outside themselves? Whatever its short-term energizing effect, much of pop culture seems to have a long-term demoralizing effect. Britney's own highly publicized breakdown is emblematic of the larger cultural breakdown that her kind of entertainment signifies. The symbolism of it is hard to avoid, yet the media analysts were careful not to make the connection. To the defenders of pop culture, sexual license and moral permissiveness are positive goods and indeed embody the ultimate meaning of freedom. Lacking any larger framework, the media took to describing Spears as "the troubled pop star" as though her life needed to be addressed only in psychological and not in moral terms. The commentators didn't seem concerned with all the troubled teens who suffer through sexually transmitted diseases, pregnancies, abortions, and their own not so highly publicized emotional traumas in part because Britney and others like her have been held up to them as models of ultimate aspirations. Sadly for Britney, her breakdown—by reminding us of what a dead end her lifestyle really is—seems to be the only real service to society that she has ever performed.

Britney is still in the news, but she is no longer the premier pop queen she was a few years ago. That doesn't invalidate the Britney thesis. The Britneyization of the culture will continue whether or not Britney herself is still on the scene because there are plenty of other female stars eager to replace her and plenty of preteen and teen girls eager to idolize them. Pop culture is as powerful as ever and will continue to distract us from the true sources of our culture's strength. That's the real link between the culture war and the war with Islamists, and it's the one part of D'Souza's argument that holds up. So criticize D'Souza for his 9/11 theory—it doesn't stand up to examination—but don't throw out the Britney with the bath water.

The Warrior Code versus the Da Vinci Code

One way to understand how the culture war has weakened us vis-à-vis Islam is to consider the fallout from the battle over gender roles. In the seventies and eighties, feminists sought an expanded role for women. Today, sociologists are worried about the contracting role of men. As a result of feminist victories, some women have become stronger and more independent, but others have found themselves dependent on the government. Moreover, an unforeseen consequence of government paternalism is a general slackening in the willingness of men to shoulder the responsibilities of marriage and family. The irony is that the absence of men from key social roles may pave the way for a form of patriarchy far more restrictive than feminists of the Betty Friedan era could have imagined. As males in the West retreat into self-absorption and self-indulgence, Muslim men are increasingly convinced of their religious right not only to rule over women but to rule over the world. The culture of male sensitivity is in danger of submitting to the culture of male supremacy.

A good way to grasp the situation is to look at the diminishing role of men in Western churches. While we are rightly concerned about the birthrate imbalance between Muslims and non-Muslims, we should also be concerned about another imbalance: church attendance of men as compared with mosque attendance of men. Here's a simple experiment you can perform to establish the point: the next time you're in church, look around you and note the ratio of women to men. Unless you're attending a strict Eastern Orthodox Church, the ratio is likely to be about two to one in favor of the women. For Southern Baptists, it's less than that, but for many mainline denominations such as the Episcopalian and Methodist churches, the ratio is even higher. Kenneth Woodward, *Newsweek*'s religion editor, reported that ratios of three to one are not uncommon in some Protestant churches. Fr. Patrick

Arnold, S.J., observed ratios as high as seven to one in some Catholic parishes. Moreover, women are much more involved than men in church activities. The Notre Dame Study of Catholic Parish Life showed that 80 to 85 percent of those involved in parish ministries or in teaching religion were women.[1]

The preponderance of women in churches is not just an American phenomenon. In Italy, Spain, and South America, men are notoriously poor church attendees.[2] Leon Podles, author of *The Church Impotent: The Feminization of Christianity*, recounts how a friend who stayed for a few weeks in an Italian town was investigated by the local police for the highly unusual behavior—for a man—of attending daily Mass.[3] Likewise, in Spanish-speaking countries, religion is seen as pretty much a woman's business. In Spain, writes Podles, "A man can be a Catholic without disgrace, but to be outwardly religious is incompatible with masculinity."[4]

Islam, however, doesn't have a man-shortage problem. The mosque is mainly a man's province, where women are either entirely prohibited or else segregated from men. The reason all those news clips of Muslims at worship show only men is that Islam is very much a man's religion.

Now put these two demographics together. Birthrates among Muslims are much higher than birthrates among Christians, and religious participation of Muslim men is higher than that of Christian men, who seem, at best, to have only a half-hearted commitment. The situation is not encouraging. On the one hand, you have a growing population of Muslim believers brimming with masculine self-confidence and assertiveness about their faith, and on the other hand, you have a dwindling population of Christians who are long on nurturance and sensitivity but short on manpower. Who seems more likely to prevail?

The triumph of Islam does not require a military victory. Instead of a military confrontation, picture a gradual shift in allegiance as nominal Christian young men begin to notice that there is a more masculine alternative to the feminized Christian churches of their youth. Similar shifts have occurred in the past. During the Nazi period, many German boys transferred their loyalty from church to Hitler Youth. In Communist Russia and Communist China, the Young Pioneers and the Red Guard took the place of the old faiths and loyalties. While participation in these groups was usually mandatory, they were nevertheless quite popular. It's a mistake to underestimate the simple masculine desire to be on the winning side or the side that looks as if it's going to win.

In *The Church Impotent*, Podles observes that there is a kind of natural religion of masculinity that requires boys to separate from their mothers and prove themselves in contests and combats. This helps to explain why "sports are the emotional center of countless men." According to Podles, "Sports provide an initiation into masculinity. . . . Sports are often the way the boy puts away the soft, sheltering world of the mother and her femininity and enters the world of challenge and danger that makes him a man." [5]

The religion of sports is akin to the religion of war and was in times past considered a preparation for war. The Battle of Waterloo was famously said to have been won on the playing fields of Eton. War has a kind of mystical significance for men because it brings together all the elements that are important for establishing their masculinity: initiation, struggle, self-sacrifice, self-transcendence, love of comrades, and brotherhood. The need for these is hardwired into men. For this reason, the jihad doesn't have a recruitment problem: Islam has been highly successful in appealing to basic masculine psychology. Not coincidentally, the progenitor of all the current jihadist groups is called the Muslim Brotherhood.

The natural religion of masculinity can be easily perverted. It can degenerate into worship of power, destruction for its own sake, and love of death. But no society can last without training warriors. As Podles explains, "Any society that faces danger must have an ideology that convinces some to face those dangers voluntarily for the sake of others".[6] Whatever the dangers posed to society by masculine aggression, the greater danger is to be without men who have the inclination to resist aggression.

This brings us back to Christianity's crisis of masculinity. There is a serious problem in Christianity today, but it's the exact opposite of the one presented by the feminist critique of the churches. Reading the works of feminist scholars and theologians, you would think that the main problem with Christianity is that it's too patriarchal: no women in the priesthood, no voice for women, no recognition of the divine feminine. But the reality is the opposite. Women do have a voice in the churches. They run most Christian ministries and basically control the education of Christian youth. As one Catholic writer puts it: "The Roman Catholic Church has a rather rigid division of labor. The men have the priesthood. The women have everything else."[7] In some mainline Protestant denominations, the women have the priesthood too. About 25 percent of Episcopal priests are women, as are about 29 percent of Presbyterian ministers. And the results? Membership of mainline churches is in a state of decline. Episcopalians, Presbyterians, Methodists, and Lutherans accounted for 40 percent of American Protestants as recently as 1960. Today they constitute about 12 percent.[8] If present trends continue, the mainline churches will end up with mostly female clergy preaching to mostly female congregations. Contrary to what liberal Christians think, the feminization of Christianity is not the solution to the problem; it *is* the problem. Christianity is in trouble not because it's perceived as too masculine but because it's perceived as too feminine.

Of the men who do go to church, a good many are there because of their wives. Many men, especially young single men, stay away from church because they consider it unmanly. They feel that religion, and particularly Christianity, is somehow feminine and that men who are attracted to religion are somewhat effeminate. A study conducted by Lewis M. Terman and Catherine Cox Miles in the mid-1930s showed that clergy and seminarians tended to score low on a masculinity scale, whereas men who scored high showed little or no interest in religion.[9] One can only imagine how Christian clergy would score on the scale today.

Does it matter—the feminization of Christianity? Well, yes, it matters very much. When Islam, history's most hypermasculine religion, is experiencing a worldwide revival and is looking to recruit more young men, it might not be the best time for the Church to emphasize its feminine side. In light of current realities, it seems slightly suicidal to indulge in feminist fantasies such as *The Da Vinci Code*, which promotes the theory that Christianity was meant to be a revival of goddess worship. If the so-called gospel of the divine feminine were to catch on even more than it already has, it could transform Christianity into the kind of religion that has little chance to counter the attractions of the Muslim faith. An emasculated Christianity—the kind favored by *Da Vinci Code* devotees—is an invitation to disaster.

Though *The Da Vinci Code* is a work of fiction, it has popularized the feminist critique of Christianity as too patriarchal. But, if anything, our churches and the society they built need to get back to their patriarchal roots. Podles explains why: "Patriarchy, we can easily

forget, was and is a great achievement in the face of the male tendency to promiscuity and alienation from children and the women
who bear them." [10] Patriarchy, in short, puts family responsibility at
the center of a man's life.

And matriarchy? Well, in its modern form, that's a society in which
children are angry at their mothers all the time because Daddy keeps
canceling his scheduled visitations; or worse, children don't even know
who their father is and don't know anyone else who is growing up
with a father in the house—a common state of affairs in many American cities. A matriarchy is full of momma's boys, and ironically a momma's boy is one of the greatest dangers to a society. Why? Because one
way or another, boys have to establish their masculinity, and if they
can't establish it in a socially beneficial way, they'll establish it at the
expense of society. Without a father at home to provide a mature
model of masculinity, boys often turn to extreme and overly aggressive models of masculinity. Father absence, as it turns out, is the factor
that correlates most highly with juvenile and adult crime. About 70 percent of violent criminals grew up without a father.

So, replacing patriarchy with matriarchy might please some feminist
factions, but it will not establish stable families or a stable social order.
Boys already know that mothers are, on the whole, faithful and responsible. But mothers are not enough to keep them in line. A patriarchal
society, when it's operating the way it should, expects fathers to guide
their sons and expects sons to obey their fathers and the rules of society. Our patriarchal faith teaches sons that even if their earthly fathers
fail them, they have a loving and authoritative Father in heaven who
expects much of them.

The irony is that the absence of patriarchy threatens women most
of all. The initial stages of a society's feminization may bring with it
an increased sensitivity toward women and an expanded role for them.
But eventually, it means masculine abdication of responsibility and an
abundance of fatherless boys inclined toward violence and hypermasculine ideologies and groups. As men drift away from fatherhood, children need to find substitute father figures. They might find them in
the YMCA, the Boys Scouts, or sports teams if they're lucky—or they
might find them in a street gang. Or they might find them—as is
increasingly the case around the world—in Islam.

Islam claims to be the "natural religion" of mankind, and there is
something to be said for that claim because Islamic culture is essentially

an honor culture—that is, a culture in which a great premium is placed on men earning and maintaining the respect of other men through acts of strength and courage. To get a better idea of what an honor culture looks like, conjure up an image of a street gang in which young men with little opportunity for personal success in the larger society attempt to achieve some level of status among themselves.

You may have noticed that there are considerably more gangs now that there are fewer intact families. According to the FBI, there are more than thirty-three thousand gangs, comprising approximately 1.4 million active gang members, in the United States, the District of Columbia, and Puerto Rico. This represents a 40-percent increase from an estimated one million gang members in 2009.[11] It used to be a "West Side Story"; now it's East Side, West Side, all around the town, and in Little Rock, Phoenix, and Falls Church, Virginia. The increase in gangs is another of those demographic trends that favors Islam, because, as an honor culture/religion, it has a certain advantage when it comes to appealing to gang psychology. There are a lot of "old boys" in the Muslim world—sheiks, imams, and mullahs—but Islam is really a young man's club. It operates according to the code of young male warriors or warrior hopefuls. And this is one of the chief reasons Muslims have been extremely successful in recruiting prisoners to Islam both in this country and in Europe. In the United States, roughly 80 percent of inmates who find faith during their incarceration choose Islam. Many of these men are in prison in the first place because they were attracted to the masculine world of gangs. Now they're being offered the chance to join the biggest, most powerful "gang" in the world. We're seeing the beginning of a trend in the West: fatherless boys joining gangs, then ending up in prison, then coming out of prison as converts to Islam and the jihad.

Simply put, father absence paves the way for distorted masculine ideologies. For a historical example of what can go wrong when fathers aren't around, consider that the Nazi rise to power took advantage of the fact that a whole generation of German fathers had been lost in the First World War. Fatherless boys and young men growing up in the twenties and early thirties would have had a natural attraction to the masculine ideology and trappings of the Nazi party. Hitler understood this and presented the Fatherland, the Nazi Party, and himself as the substitute for what they had lost. Anyone who has seen Leni Riefenstahl's *Triumph of the Will*, the film documentary of the 1934 Nazi

Party Congress at Nuremburg, will understand the point. The games, the fireworks, the group singing, the torchlight parades, and the camaraderie convey the atmosphere of a gigantic Boy Scout jamboree.

Today it's not war but the breakdown of marriage that's creating generations of fatherless boys. Divorce and out-of-wedlock births are proving as effective as artillery and rifle fire in removing fathers from the field. The illegitimacy rate for the United States as a whole is about 41 percent. It's about 55 percent for Hispanics and about 70 percent for blacks, and up to 90 percent for blacks in some inner-city areas.[12] These figures mean that there are a lot of fatherless boys and young men looking for father substitutes. They're going to be particularly vulnerable to the masculine appeal of Islam.

Fatherless boys are a problem in any society. They're prone to violent, destructive behavior. It's precisely this type of behavior that patriarchy was "designed" to prevent. What's the illegitimacy rate among Orthodox Jews? It's pretty close to zero. What is the delinquency rate for Orthodox boys? Again, close to zero. Whatever the drawbacks of living in an Orthodox Jewish community, being mugged by your neighbor's teenage son is not one of them.

How about Christianity? Although it exalts womanhood, Christianity is solidly in the patriarchal tradition. Christ was a Jew, and his mission is to return mankind to the God of the patriarchs, whom he reveals as our Father. Christ comes to do the Father's will, and he is obedient to the Father even unto death. The Father, in turn, takes pride in the Son: "This is my beloved Son, with whom I am well pleased" (Mt 3:17). Christianity presents a model for earthly fathers and sons to emulate. The Son, who knows he can turn to his Father for strength, dedicates himself to doing his Father's work. On several occasions, he makes a point of distancing himself from his mother for the sake of his mission. He loves his mother, but he is not a momma's boy.

Forget for the moment the sentimental holy cards featuring the Jesus of the long lashes, and concentrate instead on the picture that emerges in the Gospels. The Gospel narratives are much closer to the heroic themes of *The Odyssey* and *The Aeneid* than to today's Hallmark-card depictions of Jesus. Jesus entered the world as someone who had a job to do. He came to win back what belonged to his Father, and he battled death and the devil to accomplish his destiny. In the ancient world, the model for men was the hero. It is unlikely that men bred on *The Iliad* and *Beowulf*-like sagas would have gone over to Christianity unless they recognized the heroic nature of Christ.

Although he disregarded the Jewish restrictions on contact with women and had many women disciples, Christ gathered a band of men around him. These men were not just his followers but his friends. He was willing to lay down his life for them, and he expected them to be willing to lay down their lives for one another. The closest analogy is not that of a teacher and his pupils—as in Plato and his students—but that of military comradeship. The apostles shared dangers and hardships with Christ and became, in effect, blood-brothers with him. Before his death he commissioned them to continue his mission: "As the Father has sent me, even so I send you" (Jn 20:21). His was and is the kind of life that men can understand. As Podles puts it, "Men are made for brotherly love. It is the escape from the prison of self in which all human beings are locked but afflicts men even more deeply because they flee from the connectedness of the feminine world precisely to live and die for others, including women." He continues, "Those who suffer together become brothers.... A man who has suffered with Christ becomes his brother."[13]

While Christianity is a patriarchy, it is a new kind of patriarchy. Christ treated women as equal to men in dignity and, in his teaching against divorce and remarriage, set a new standard for the relationship between men and women. Christ didn't abrogate the differences between the sexes, but he did bring a new understanding of what it means to be a man or a woman. He taught his apostles that to rule was to serve—a concept alien to the warrior-heroes extolled by the Greeks and the Romans. In other words, both patriarchy and masculinity need to be redeemed through Christ. Unfortunately, feminists and feminist theologians have attempted to introduce a radical egalitarianism into society and the Church that is based neither on Christ nor on the facts of life. The resulting climate of confusion is a large part of the reason men now play a diminished role both in their families and in their churches.

But Islam has a masculinity problem of its own. Again, it's not quite what it seems. As is well known, the Koran treats women as clearly inferior and therefore not worthy of a great deal of consideration. You could chalk up this condescending attitude toward women as being typical of patriarchal religions, but then you're faced with a problem:

in the most elemental sense of the word, Islam is not really a patriarchal religion. True, in Islam the men rule. And it's also true that Islam traces its origins to the Hebrew Patriarchs—Abraham, Isaac (Muslims also include his half-brother, Ishmael), and Jacob. But, on the other hand, the central element in patriarchy is missing.

As the French scholar Alain Besancon points out: "Although Muslims like to enumerate the 99 names of God, missing from the list, but central to the Jewish and even more so to the Christian concept of God, is 'Father'—i.e. a personal God capable of a reciprocal and loving relationship with men".[14]

In other words, Allah cannot be a model of loving and responsible fatherhood because he is not a father. He doesn't have sons. He doesn't have a son. He is eternally alone and aloof. If he is a model of anything, he is a model of absolute and arbitrary authority. The trouble with Islam is not that it's a patriarchy, but that it lacks the essential warrant for patriarchy—a loving God whom we can call our Father.

One result is that although Islam looks to be a man's religion, its ideal of manhood appears immature by Judeo-Christian standards. The natural arc of masculinity is separation, initiation, and reconnection; that is, separation from one's mother and the world of the feminine, initiation into the masculine world (whether through education, rites of passage, or warfare), and then reconnection with the world of women by becoming a responsible husband and father. Jewish and Christian teachings reinforce this natural arc by sanctifying the married state and by emphasizing the importance of marital fidelity. Christianity goes further and draws a parallel between the love a husband ought to have for his wife and the love of Christ for his Church: "Husbands, love your wives, as Christ loved the church and gave himself up for her" (Eph 5:25). The result of the struggle to attain manhood should be that a man becomes mature enough to relate to his wife as an equal made in the image of God, rather than as a possession or a plaything. Men in Christian societies may often fail to live up to this ideal, but in Islam the ideal is not even there.

What is the ideal in Islam? Well, pretty much what the ideal is for most seventeen-year-old boys: plenty of impersonal and uncommitted sex. The final reward for being a good Muslim male is a heavenly garden of carnal delights—food, drink, and seventy-two eternally young virgins: "Theirs shall be gardens and vineyards and high-bosomed maidens for companions" (78:31–33). There are numerous passages like this in the Koran, and the hadith contain similar assurances concerning the exquisite physical proportions of the young "houris" in heaven. Meanwhile, contemporary Islamic scholars debate the burning issue of whether a man's state of arousal in the next world is "perpetual" or merely "protracted".[15]

This is an invitation for men not to grow up but to remain in a state of perpetual adolescence. As Roy Schoeman writes, "Heaven, by definition, entails the greatest state of perfection that God can give man; it represents the ultimate meaning and goal of man's existence."[16] He continues, "The effect on moral development from teaching that the highest good that God can offer to man is sexual gratification is obvious".[17] Well, in case it's not obvious, it means that women are not regarded as important in themselves: their purpose is to serve and service men—just the way the average teenage boy would like to have it. In Islam, in other words, you don't have to complete the arc of masculinity: you needn't develop a mature understanding of masculinity. Individual Muslims do, of course, rise above this level and commit themselves in a mature way to their wives and families, but institutional Islam with its allowance for polygamy, "pleasure marriages", and easy divorce for men doesn't give them much support. As Darwish observes, "A man may decide to be faithful to one woman, and never marry another, but in the back of his mind he always knows that his faithfulness is not required by God."[18]

While it's true that Christian cultures currently have a masculinity problem, that problem is not intrinsic to Christianity. True Christianity offers a fulfillment and a perfection of masculinity. By contrast, Islam has a much more serious and more intrinsic masculinity problem. While it has the trappings of masculinity, it is in essence a boy's religion based on immature dreams of endless physical pleasure. Those seventy-two houris are not there to offer intellectual or spiritual companionship.

Keep in mind, though, that the trappings of masculinity are still appealing to a boy or young man who is looking to establish his own masculine identity. He's still a long way from a mature understanding of what it means to be a man, and without a good grounding in the Judeo-Christian ideal, radical Islam's simplistic view of manhood might seem like the real thing. Christians had better address the feminization and emasculation of their churches and their societies in a serious way if they hope to counter the attractions of Islam. That means they can no longer afford to let modern theologians sympathetic to feminism, pacifism, and homosexuality shape the perception of what it means to be a Christian. It also means that Christians who are inclined to sentimentalize their faith will have to do some rethinking.

During the period of conquest that Muslims look back upon as the Heroic Age of Islam, Islam appeared as an unstoppable masculine force. Many Muslims today want to revive the spirit of that age, while in the West the masculine spirit looks more like a ghost. In the *Suicide of Reason*, Lee Harris puts the matter in stark biological terms: "While we in America are drugging our alpha boys with Ritalin, the Muslims are doing everything in their power to encourage their alpha boys to be tough, aggressive, and ruthless." He continues:

> To rid your society of high-testosterone alpha males may bring peace and quiet; but if you have an enemy that is building up an army of alpha boys trained to hate you fanatically and who have vowed to destroy you, you will be committing suicide.[19]

It sounds as if Harris is talking war, but in reality his book is more about cultural conflict than armed conflict. War isn't necessary if the males of one culture can cow and intimidate into submission those of another culture. Our culture derives much of its strength from its Christian faith, but Christian societies without strong men willing to defend them won't be able to stop Islam's cultural jihad. The question is not so much how to turn altar boys into aggressive alpha boys, but rather how to convince them that some things are worth fighting for and that cultural appeasement and cowardly concessions do not become a man.

There are many possible answers to that question, but here is a cautionary tale that might provoke some thought. On December 6, 1989, a young Muslim man walked into a classroom at the École Polytechnique in Montreal and murdered fourteen female students. Before doing so, he first ordered the professors and male students out of the room. The incident, which is known as the Montreal massacre, is emblematic of the West's masculinity problem. Here's Mark Steyn's comment on the incident:

> The defining image of contemporary Canadian maleness is not M Lépine/Gharbi but the professors and the men in that classroom, who, ordered to leave by the lone gunman, meekly did so, and abandoned

their female classmates to their fate—an act of abdication that would have been unthinkable in almost any other culture throughout human history. The "men" stood outside in the corridor and, even as they heard the first shots, they did nothing. And, when it was over and Gharbi walked out of the room and past them, they still did nothing.[20]

Consider the incident as a metaphor for a larger problem that we face today—or, rather, fail to face. Right now, women and girls all over the world are being abused and often murdered in the name of Islam. Today, men in Western societies say nothing about the abuse because they are paralyzed by the fear of offending against multiculturalist dogmas. They lack the manly courage to stand up and speak out because they have been cowed by Islam on the one hand and by our self-imposed sensitivity codes on the other.

The trouble is, the sensitive males of the West reserve all their sensitivities for the Muslim bluebeards and the system that enables them and almost none for the female victims. Somewhere on the periphery of his consciousness, the average Western male is aware that under Islamic law a woman is basically the property of a man, that a Muslim woman may be forced to share her husband with other wives, and that eight- and nine-year-old girls can be married off to pay a debt. Maybe he's read about the frequent occurrence of wife beating, the stonings, the genital mutilations, the burning of girls' schools, and the acid attacks on females who fail to cover up properly. It's too bad, of course, but, judging by the tepid response, none of it seems to weigh heavily in the scales against the sacrosanct value of cultural diversity.

Diversity, it seems, covers a multitude of sins. The French have a saying: "To understand all is to forgive all." These days all we need to understand about a malefactor is that he lives in a different culture, and then we are ready to forgive him all his sins in advance. More than that, we won't even call them sins; rather, they are just "cultural variations". But the multiculturalist excuse is beginning to wear thin. When the sensitivity is so one-sided, when the feelings of the oppressor take precedence over the feelings of the oppressed, you have to wonder if cultural sensitivity is not simply a cover for cowardice.

Cowardice is suggested by the fact that many of these "other culture" practices are now being planted in our own culture, and the response has been little more than a shrug. Muslims want the right to practice sharia in the West, and some Western governments are allowing it—if not *de jure* at least *de facto*. So, in England, France, the Netherlands, and Sweden, Muslim women are—as in Muslim countries—little more than the property of their fathers or husbands.

The trouble with the West's reluctance to impose Western standards on the Muslim enclaves in its midst is that this hands-off policy more or less guarantees that Muslim culture won't remain a subculture for long. The Muslim subcultures in Europe have already begun to impose their values on the ever-obliging "dominant" cultures, as exemplified by the non-Muslim women who have changed their habits and dress in deference to Islam. In 2001, when it was reported that the majority of rapes in Norway were committed by members of the small Muslim minority, a prominent Norwegian academic opined that "Norwegian women must take their share of responsibility for these rapes. . . . Norwegian women must realize that we live in a multicultural society and adapt to it." [21] In Norway, apparently, the way to adapt to a multicultural society is to dress as the Muslims do.

Thankfully, some brave souls have another take on who needs to do the adjusting. Ayaan Hirsi Ali says it is Islam that needs to transform itself in order to be compatible with Western standards. "We in the West", she writes, "would be wrong to prolong the pain of that transition unnecessarily, by elevating cultures full of bigotry and hatred toward women to the stature of respectable alternative ways of life." [22]

But Hirsi Ali is an exception and, like most of the other exceptional people who are criticizing Islam's treatment of women, is herself a woman. Few men have been as forceful in their condemnation of Islamic abuse as have Hirsi Ali, Nonie Darwish, Brigitte Gabriel, Phyllis Chesler, and others. Edmund Burke once said, "The only thing necessary for the triumph of evil is for good men to do nothing." For our time it might be said, "The only thing necessary for the triumph of evil is for complacent men to stand around with their hands in their pockets and say things like, 'Well, you can't really judge another culture.' "

The multiculturalist code is essentially an emasculating code. It has the effect of paralyzing the normal masculine response of coming to the protection of those in danger. It's understandable that the male students at the École Polytechnique were not able to find the courage to go up against a well-armed assailant. It's less understandable that European and North American men can't find the courage to speak up against what Canadian author Kathy Shaidle calls "the tyranny of nice".

Once again, let's remind ourselves that *Islam* does not mean "peace"; it means "submission". It shouldn't take much insight to realize that an overly feminized culture puts itself at a decided disadvantage against those who are more interested in subjugation than in sensitivity. Feminization, with its attendant emasculation, is not just a problem for Christians but also for the culture as a whole. Christians nevertheless bear a certain amount of responsibility for the spread of the cult of sensitivity and thus for the predicament in which we find ourselves. And since Christians bear some of the responsibility, they have a special obligation to reestablish the healthy balance between masculine and feminine that Christianity brought into the world. There are a lot of young men in our world who are uncertain about whether to follow the sign of the crescent moon or the sign of the Cross, but it's a good bet that none of them will be interested in following the "yield" sign that some overly accommodating Christians raise whenever there is a hint of conflict.

"Onward Christian Soldiers" is a fine old hymn that conveys some of the spirit that needs to be recaptured. You may be familiar with it from the 1942 Academy Award–winning movie *Mrs. Miniver*. Winston Churchill said that Greer Garson, for her role as Mrs. Miniver, was worth six divisions in the war against Hitler. The film and the rousing hymn that caps it express the unconquerable resolve that England displayed in its "finest hour". But it's unlikely you would hear it sung in any English or American church today. It has been dropped from most hymn books for reasons of political correctness. Although the lyrics clearly refer only to the battle with Satan, even that is considered too warlike for today's sensitive souls.

> Onward, Christian soldiers, marching as to war,
> With the Cross of Jesus going on before.
> Like a mighty army, moves the church of God;
> Brothers, we are treading where the saints have trod.[23]

It might not be a bad idea for Christians to regain some of this spirit of brothers-in-arms ready to fight the good fight; otherwise all the young men might start marching over to the other side.

PART V

THE COLD WAR WITH ISLAM

The Moderate-Muslim Strategy

In a speech to the World Affairs Council on March 26, 2008, Senator John McCain said, "Our goal must be to win the 'hearts and minds' of the vast majority of moderate Muslims who do not want their future controlled by a minority of violent extremists." [1] In May of the same year, the Homeland Security chief, Michael Chertoff, expressed a similar sentiment. He said Muslim communities "have seen their religion hijacked by a group of ideologues." [2] In May 2010, John Brennan, the president's counterterrorism advisor, said that "violent extremists" should not be described in "religious terms". *Minority of violent extremists, majority of moderates, hijacked*—these have become the favored expressions for explaining events in the Muslim world. And so, since 9/11, a good deal of energy has been expended in devising strategies to enlist moderate Muslims, who are presumed to be the vast majority, against Muslim radicals, who are presumed to be a small minority.

According to proponents of this strategy, an essential first step in this direction is to avoid offensive words or actions that might drive the moderates into the radical camp. In *The Enemy at Home*, Dinesh D'Souza argues that attempts to demonize Islam are having that very effect. This apparently is also the reasoning behind the Homeland Security Department's guidelines for talking about terror. To wit: we should not use words and phrases such as *jihadist, Islamic terrorist, Islamist,* and *holy warrior*. The guidelines warn that such terms might offend mainstream Muslims by implying a connection between Islam and terror. [3]

But just how helpful are terms such as *mainstream* and *moderate* in discussing or understanding Muslims? Before we can answer that question, we need to know what is meant by the terms. Only in the broadest sense can the majority of Muslims be described as moderate. If you define moderate as "not violent", then most Muslims are moderates. Most people everywhere, whatever their creed, are moderate in the sense that they want to go about their daily business, don't want to put their lives at risk, and don't want bombs exploding in their neighborhoods.

Moderates of this sort cannot be relied upon to keep well-organized and violently inclined minorities in check. During Hitler's rise to power, the majority of Germans were moderate in the sense that they did not participate in Nazi thuggery. The same undoubtedly applied to the majority of Russians with respect to the Bolsheviks during the Russian Revolution. Most people prefer the certainty of daily bread and drink to the uncertainty of violent upheavals. What's more, this kind of moderation is arguably an aid to the radical elements: they know they can count on the silent majority to remain silent while they go about their bloody business.

When Westerners pin their hopes on moderate Muslims becoming an effective force in the Islamic world they must have in mind some higher definition of *moderate*—something like, "characterized by a strong commitment to equal rights for all, the rule of law, separation of church and state, checks and balances, freedom of speech, freedom of religion, freedom of inquiry"—in other words, a distinctively Western understanding of *moderate*. So, in expecting Muslims to be moderate, we are, in effect, expecting them to become Westerners. There are, of course, Muslims who meet this definition of *moderate*, but for the most part, they are Muslims who have already become Westernized or secularized.

And there's a further problem. Hoping that the majority of Muslims will embrace a Western ideal of moderation is already expecting a lot, but it's an even bigger stretch to imagine that they are going to risk their necks for it, which is what you're asking when you ask them to resist the radicals. When you consider what radical Muslims have done to moderate Muslims in Pakistan, Palestine, Iran, Lebanon, and Afghanistan, you'll realize just how much it is to ask.

Even in America there are substantial risks for Muslims who stand up to the radical agenda. Moderates such as Tawfik Hamid, Mand Ervin, and Zuhdi Jasser have exposed themselves to repeated threats for supporting efforts to spread a Western understanding of human rights and to contain the spread of sharia-compliant Islam. Their efforts are all the more admirable when we consider that relatively few Westerners themselves seem willing to make the sacrifices needed to defend Western values. Are European and Canadian leaders fighting hard to preserve the Western heritage of free inquiry, free press, and women's rights? Or are these values being bargained away piecemeal for the sake of some illusory harmony? If it's doubtful that Westerners are willing to fight and die for Western values, why should Westernized Muslims? And why should we expect Muslims in Iran or Afghanistan to step up to the plate?

The expectation that moderates in the Muslim world will save the day also ignores the fact that many moderate Muslims are not particularly moderate by Western standards. Dinesh D'Souza is enlightening on this point. He writes, "Another common illusion, held across the American political spectrum, is that the Muslim world is divided into 'liberals' and 'fundamentalists.'" But according to D'Souza, "There are virtually no liberals in the Muslim world." [4] Moreover, by our definition of *fundamentalist* "all Muslims are 'fundamentalists' because all Muslims believe that the Koran is the literal, unadulterated word of God.... If you don't believe these things, you're not a Muslim." [5] This is quite telling when you consider that D'Souza is extremely sympathetic to traditional Muslims and even envisions an alliance between traditional Muslims and traditional Americans. When someone who has been accused of being a Muslim apologist and a dhimmi by fellow conservatives insists that the majority of Muslims should be called traditional Muslims but not moderates, it may be time to reappraise the term *moderate Muslim*.[6]

Are there any moderate Muslims? Yes, there are—even in the Western sense of the term—but D'Souza is hitting close to the mark when he asserts that the majority of believing, practicing Muslims are not moderates. Of course, this doesn't mean that they can't be good, decent, and honorable people, but it does complicate the task of separating the "moderates" from the "radicals". D'Souza asks, "What are the theological differences between traditional Islam and radical Islam?" He answers: "On the fundamental religious questions, there are none. What are the political differences? In general, there are few. Remarkable though it seems, traditional Muslims and radical Muslims agree on the threats faced by Islam, on where those threats come from, and even on the general solution." [7]

D'Souza's division of the Muslim world into traditional and radical is oversimplified, but it seems to be a much more accurate way of describing the situation than to divide the Muslim world into a vast majority of moderates and a small minority of radicals. While the majority of traditional Muslims may not resort to violence, they can hardly be considered moderate by Western standards. In fact, a traditional Muslim can believe things that are beyond the pale in Western societies and still be well within the mainstream of Muslim culture. Consider some of the evidence:

- A 2010 Pew opinion survey of Egyptians found that 77 percent support whipping and amputation for thieves, 82 percent support the execution of adulterers, and 84 percent support the execution of apostates.

- When the Pakistani governor of Punjab was assassinated in January 2011 because he opposed the blasphemy law, a group of five hundred leading Muslim scholars, representing what the Associated Press called the "mainstream religious organizations", praised the assassin as a *ghazi* (Muslim warrior) and warned that no one should mourn the dead governor or pray for him.

- In Iran, when hard-liners and moderates debate the issue of flogging for adulterous women, the debate is not over whether flogging is an appropriate punishment, but whether it should be administered in public or in private.[8]

- A prominent, pro-Western physician in Gaza explains his position on suicide bombings this way: "Martyrs are at the level of prophets. They are untouchable. I can denounce suicide bombings, which I have many times, but not the martyrs themselves, because they are like saints. . . . I don't believe in religion myself, but I cannot say that martyrs are wrong. If you do that, you will discredit yourself completely."[9]

- The one Muslim sect that comes closest to the Western definition of *moderate* is the Ahmadiyya community. The Ahmadiyyas believe in the spiritual unity of mankind, that the Muslim scriptures should be interpreted in a symbolic rather than literal way, that hell is a place of temporary cleansing, and that tolerance should be extended to all. They are regarded as heretical by many Muslims, and in Pakistan, where they are most numerous, they have been the victims of frequent persecutions. Recently, in Indonesia the government ordered the Ahmadiyyas to return to orthodox Islam or face up to five years in prison for insulting Islam.[10]

■ Contrary to expectations, popular elections in the Middle East often strengthen extremist groups. This has been the case in Gaza, Egypt, Kuwait, Lebanon, Tunisia, and Turkey. Given a free electoral choice, Muslims do not necessarily choose moderates.

■ In July 2008, the government of Lebanon closed all offices and declared a national day of celebration to greet jihadist prisoners just released by Israel. These "heroes of freedom" were headed by the "great" Samir Kuntar, who in 1979 burst into an Israeli apartment, shot Danny Haran in the head in front of his four-year-old daughter, then bludgeoned the girl to death with his rifle butt. Kuntar was greeted not only by terrorist leader Hassan Nasrallah but by Lebanese President Michel Suleiman, Prime Minister Fouad Siniora, and Speaker of Parliament Nabih Berri, along with tens of thousands of cheering Lebanese. The moderate leader of the Palestinian Authority, Mahmoud Abbas, sent "blessings" to Kuntar's family.[11]

Despite a mountain of evidence, Islamic apologists keep insisting that the overwhelming majority of Muslims are moderate. Take, for example, a study conducted by John Esposito (of Georgetown University's Prince Alwaleed Bin Talal Center), and Dalia Mogahed (director of the Gallup Center for Muslim Studies). Their book, *Who Speaks for Islam?: What a Billion Muslims Really Think*, contends that only 7 percent of Muslims are "politically radicalized" while "about nine in ten Muslims are moderate". The authors reached the 7-percent figure by adding up the number of Muslims (in a three-continent poll) who agreed that the 9/11 attacks were "completely justified". But if you include those who think 9/11 was "largely justified", the percentage of the radicalized jumps to 13.5 percent, or 169 million. And the full data from the 9/11 question reveals that another 23.1 percent of respondents felt that the attacks were "somewhat justified".[12] So, in total, about 37 percent of Muslims, or the equivalent of 469 million, thought the 9/11 attacks were either "somewhat", "largely", or "completely" justified. But when it came time to write their book, Esposito and Mogahed narrowed the definition of radical to the point where it would generate only the 7-percent figure. Esposito and Mogahed reassure us that 93 percent of Muslims are "moderates", and then define a moderate as anyone who entertains doubts about the legitimacy of blowing up three thousand innocent men, women, and children. The Esposito/ Mogahed book is, to say the least, highly misleading. The spontaneous worldwide jubilation in Muslim streets following 9/11 probably gives us a much better picture of Muslim sentiment about that event than this highly manipulated survey. Unfortunately, the book is the basis for the film *Inside Islam: What a Billion Muslims Think*, which is widely shown to church groups to help them "better understand" Islam. Like the study, the film massages the polling data to make it appear that Islam is a predominantly peaceful religion.

There's another, more revealing way of approaching the question of moderation. Instead of asking whether there are moderate Muslims, let's ask the question we are not supposed to ask: Is there a moderate Islam? We can begin to answer the question by looking at those Muslims who claim to be moderates or are widely considered to be moderates. In a recent book, Tarek Fatah, founder of the Muslim Canadian Congress, makes the familiar argument that "Islam has been hijacked by radicals who falsely invoke the Koran and name of their prophet." A real Muslim, on the other hand, "uses Islam as a moral compass for his own betterment and betterment of his family." [13] From the viewpoint of most Islamic authorities, however, one doesn't "use" Islam; one submits to it. Not surprisingly, Fatah is much more interested in the "spirit of Islam" than in institutional Islam. In fact, he upbraids former Canadian Prime Minister Paul Martin for meeting only with "heads of mosques and imams, most in full mosque regalia" [14] after the London terrorist bombings in 2005. Fatah points out that 90 percent of Muslims in Canada "are not associated members of any mosque or a Muslim organization". The figure seems doubtful, but his point seems to be that moderate Muslims don't go to mosque. His Muslim Canadian Congress is a secular organization; and as Fatah admits, the MCC doesn't claim "to represent the Muslim community, as we just represent our 300-odd members". [15] In any event, if you read between the lines, you'll find that one inescapable message of the book is that moderate Muslims tend not to be orthodox Muslims.

Mark Steyn makes a similar point by going through a list of "moderate Muslims" and concluding, "What the West calls 'moderate Muslims,' Islam regards as apostates." [16] Magdi Allam was considered a moderate Muslim until he converted to Christianity. Ayaan Hirsi Ali has very progressive and enlightened views, but she's now an atheist, not a Muslim. Irshad Manji is a keen critic of Islamic extremism, "but she is not a 'moderate Muslim': she is a lesbian and, thus, to almost all her co-religionists cannot be any kind of Muslim." [17] Dr. Wafa Sultan, a California psychiatrist and an advocate for a more moderate Islam, describes herself as a secularist "who does not believe in the super-natural".[18] We could add several more to Steyn's list: for example, Ibn Warraq, another former moderate Muslim who is no longer a Muslim at all, or Nonie Darwish, the Egyptian-born author who wishes for a more moderate Islam but who has become a Christian.

How about those moderate Muslims who still identify themselves as Muslim? Iraq's Grand Ayatollah Ali al-Sistani has long been considered an example of moderation for his refusal to take sides in the Iraqi conflict and for his strong support of democratic elections. On the other hand, Sistani's religious beliefs are hardly an advertisement for moderation. He does not meet with non-Muslims, whom he considers unclean, and he has asserted that gays and lesbians should be "killed in the worst manner possible".[19] Another example of a not-so-moderate moderate is the globe-trotting scholar Sheik Yusuf-al-Qaradawi, who has been praised by many (including Georgetown's John Esposito and London's former mayor Ken Livingstone) for his reformist stance. Among his reforms is this: "It is permissible [for a husband] to beat [a disobedient wife] lightly with his hands, avoiding her face and other sensitive parts."[20] Qaradawi is not so sensitive, however, about the treatment of non-Muslims, and he has publicly endorsed suicide bombings against Jewish civilians. Moreover, in a 2009 speech, he called the Holocaust a "divine punishment" of Jews: "The last punishment was carried out by Hitler. . . . Allah willing, the next time will be at the hands of the believers."[21] The Swiss scholar Tariq Ramadan, who has encouraged European Muslims to integrate more fully into European culture, has also been seen as a moderate. Yet Ramadan favors the death of the "Zionist entity", and rather than declaring his opposition to the stoning of adulteresses when requested to by Nicholas Sarkozy, he suggested instead "a moratorium" on stoning.[22]

Other Muslim spokesmen are much less circumspect. In May 2008, Sheik Ali Al-Faqir, Jordan's former religion minister, boasted that Islam "will conquer Rome" and take back Spain, suggesting that the end is near for America and Europe. He added, "We will rule the world, as has been said by the Prophet Muhammad."[23] Jordan is usually considered one of the more moderate nations, so one might assume that its minister of religious endowment would be in the mainstream rather than on the fringes.

One might assume the same about the late Muhammad Sayyid Tantawi, who was the most respected cleric among Sunni Muslims and in
some respects a moderate. He opposed extremists and suicide bombers (but praised Yasser Arafat and "martyrdom operations" against Israel),
and he spoke out against the practice of female genital mutilation. Yet
Tantawi also wrote a seven-hundred-page treatise rationalizing the
Koran's depiction of Jews as "degenerate", "corrupting", and "lascivi-
ous". In a 2002 sermon, he described Jews as "enemies of Allah, descendants of apes and pigs".[24] As Andrew Bostom, an authority on Islamic
anti-Semitism, points out, "Tantawi embodies how such hatred remains
firmly rooted in mainstream, orthodox Islamic teachings, not some
aberrant 'radical Islam.' "[25]

Are there moderate Muslims? Yes. Is there a moderate Islam to provide institutional reinforcement for them? The second question is much
more problematic. As Bostom's book *The Legacy of Islamic Anti-
Semitism* shows, hatred of Jews is imbedded not only in Islamic history, but also in the Koran, the hadith, and the biography of Muhammad.
Likewise, the notion that Islam should inherit the earth is thoroughly
grounded in Islam itself; it is not the invention of al-Qaeda. The imper-
ative to wage war against unbelievers to establish the reign of Allah on
earth is asserted over and over in the Koran. Take for example:

"Fighting is obligatory for you, much as you dislike it" (2:216).

"Believers, make war on the infidels who dwell around you" (9:123).

"Prophet, make war on the unbelievers and the hypocrites and deal
rigorously with them. Hell shall be their home: an evil fate" (9:73).

"If you do not go to war, He will punish you sternly and will
replace you with other men" (9:39).

Some Muslim apologists make a distinction between the "lesser jihad"
(fighting one's enemy) and the "greater jihad" (fighting one's ego),
but there is only one passage in the hadith that supports this reversal
of meaning, and it is considered by many Muslim authorities to be an
unreliable transmission. The Koran, on the other hand, makes it quite
clear which is the greater jihad: "Do you pretend that he who gives a
drink to the pilgrims and pays a visit to the Sacred Mosque is as worthy as the man who believes in God and the Last Day, and fights for
God's cause? These are not held equal by God.... Those that have

embraced the Faith, and left their homes, and fought for God's cause with their wealth and with their persons, are held in higher regard by God. It is they who shall triumph" (9:19, 9:20). And, if that's not clear enough, how about this: "The believers who stay at home ... are not the equals of those who fight for the cause of God with their goods and their persons. God has exalted the men who fight with their goods and their persons above those who stay at home" (4:95).

Muslim apologists contend that these verses have to be taken in context and that they are balanced by peaceful verses. For example, "It is unlawful for a believer to kill another believer, accidents excepted" (4:92). But this passage extends only to other Muslims, as do the many injunctions to be charitable to orphans and widows. There is, however, one verse that seems to have universal applicability, and it is often cited as proof that Islam is a genuine religion of peace: "That was why we laid it down for the Israelites that whoever killed a human being, except as punishment for murder or other villainy in the land, shall be regarded as having killed all mankind; and that whoever saved a human life shall be regarded as having saved all mankind" (5:32).

But the take-it-in-context argument often overlooks the very next verse: "Those that make war against God and His Apostle and spread disorder in the land shall be slain or crucified or have their hands and feet cut off on alternate sides, or be banished from the land" (5:33). Unless Muhammad is speaking strictly in terms of self-defense, the second verse seems to cancel the first. But when the Koran refers to the legitimacy of slaying "those that make war against God and His Apostle", it is not necessarily referring to Muslims' defending themselves against acts of aggression. Muhammad considered people who rejected his message as villains in rebellion against God and therefore subject to conquest or extermination. For some more context, consider another verse that appears a few passages later: "As for the man or woman who is guilty of theft, cut off their hands to punish them for their crimes. That is the punishment enjoined by God" (5:38).

So, in context, the Koran's poster passage for peace is less promising than it initially appears. If you broaden the context further to include the life of Muhammad and the actions of his immediate successors, the notion that Islam was intended to be a religion of peace becomes even less credible. Jesus is quoted in Matthew's Gospel as saying, "Do not think that I have come to bring peace on earth; I have not come to bring peace, but a sword" (Mt 10:34). But it is clear that, taken in the context of Christ's life, this passage is not a call to any literal violence. In fact, when Peter does takes up a sword in the Garden of Gethsemane, Christ makes him put it away.

With Muhammad, however, the situation is quite different. It's difficult to put a symbolic interpretation on the many Koranic passages urging Muslims to kill the unbelievers, because that literally is what Muhammad did. During the last ten years of his life, Muhammad participated in twenty-seven battles, almost all of which he initiated. In some cases, the defeated were enslaved. In some cases, they were executed, and in some of these instances, Muhammad himself performed the executions. After the flight to Medina in 622, fighting and killing for Allah was almost the chief preoccupation of the prophet. After his death in 632, the caliphs who succeeded him carried on in the same tradition. In 635 Damascus was captured; in 636 al-Basrah in Iraq. In 637 Antioch fell. In 638 Jerusalem was taken. In 639 the invasion of Egypt had begun. By the end of 642, Alexandria was in Muslim hands. And so on.

The spread of Islam by conquest continued until the decisive Christian victory at Vienna in 1683. And Muslim conquests involved far more territory and far more loss of life than is generally realized in the West. The Muslim empire stretched not just around the Mediterranean but into what we now call Iran, Afghanistan, Pakistan, India, and beyond. Recall that India's most famous landmark, the Taj Mahal, was built by a Muslim ruler.

The numbers killed as a result of Islamic aggression are hard to estimate, but it is probable that they exceed one hundred million. Bill Warner, the director of the Center for the Study of Political Islam, estimates that over a fourteen-hundred-year period the total killed is about 270 million—"the biggest single-source killing in the history of the world".[26]

The Muslim conquests didn't stop because the caliphs decided to turn over a new leaf or because the *ulema* (Islamic scholars) developed a new, more peaceful interpretation of Islam. They stopped because the Muslim world ran out of steam and was no longer able to compete with the West, militarily, technologically, or economically. In short, Islamic expansion stopped, not because Islam was no longer willing to expand, but because it was no longer able. This is a key point to understand because it provides an important clue for determining those policies and strategies that will actually ensure a more moderate Muslim world. The relative moderation of Islam in the nineteenth and much of the twentieth century is the kind of moderation that takes place when someone does not have any other options. Since the martial injunctions of the Koran and the hadith could not be practiced, they tended to be neglected, forgotten, or ignored. Attitudes change and readjust as circumstances change, and the changing fortunes of the Islamic world forced the militant nature of Islam into the background. But militant Islam is not an aberration. If anything, the more peaceful Islam of the recent past is the aberration. And now that Muslim population growth and Middle East oil money have reshifted the geopolitical balance, militant Islam has resurfaced.

Ever since the formation of the Muslim Brotherhood in Egypt in the 1920s, Muslim activists have been busy trying to call their coreligionists back to the full observance of their faith, and that includes "the forgotten obligation"—jihad. In recent years Islamists have been quite successful in persuading otherwise peaceful Muslims that militant Islam is the "pure Islam". How does one account for their success? In a word, facts. The militant Muslims have the facts on their side. They can make an excellent case that warfare against unbelievers is an integral part of the Koran, the hadith, the life of Muhammad, the life of his successors, and all four schools of Islamic jurisprudence. As Robert Spencer puts it, "Modern mujahedin do not believe they are 'hijacking' Islam. They believe they are restoring its proper interpretation—and they are successfully convincing peaceful Muslims around the world that they are correct." [27]

If we want to encourage a more moderate Muslim world, we need to understand the elements that make for peace and moderation. For Islam, as a whole, one of those elements, and perhaps the chief one, is political and military weakness. If, in recent centuries, Islamic tribes and nations haven't waged jihad as strenuously as in the past, it's because they haven't been able to.

Individual Muslims have differing reasons for not embracing violent jihad, but one reason is simply ignorance of Islam. Just as many Christians have only a vague notion of what Christians are supposed to believe, so too with Muslim believers. As Spencer points out, "Many who call themselves Muslims know or care little about what the mainstream authorities of the religion actually teach. Some who are quite devout have only a glancing familiarity, at best, with ... jihad warfare." In addition, "Most Muslims worldwide today are not Arabs, and do not speak Arabic—especially the Qur'an's difficult seventh-century Arabic. Yet all the sects and schools of Islam mandate that prayers must be said and the Qur'an recited in Arabic—making this for many merely an exercise in formalism, involving the repetition of syllables they do not understand." [28]

This is not to suggest that traditional or peaceful Muslims comprise only those who pay lip service to their religion. Just as there are devout and fervent Catholics with little knowledge of Catholic theology, there are devout Muslims who find consolation in submitting themselves to the will of Allah, but who may be unfamiliar with the "sword verses" in the Koran or with the bloody exploits of Muhammad. But while the devout Catholic who goes on to study Catholic theology in depth is not likely to accept the warfare as a good way to spread his faith, the Muslim who follows a similar path may very well end up in the same spiritual camp as the mujahedin. That is why increased education in the Muslim world does not necessarily lead to increased moderation. Many militant Muslim leaders are well educated, often with professional backgrounds, as in the case of al-Qaeda's current leader, Dr. Ayman al-Zawahiri. Like-wise, militant Islamic groups have had a high degree of success in recruiting university students. The young man who acquaints himself with the fullness of the Catholic faith is unlikely to develop an interest in bomb-making, but the young man who learns the fullness of Islamic teaching may begin to realize he has obligations he hadn't thought of before.

A final element in Muslim peacefulness is the one mentioned at the start of this chapter. Although most people are capable of violence, most people are not disposed to round-the-clock, 365-days-a-year violence. Even the Koran acknowledges as much when it says, "Fighting is obligatory for you, *much as you dislike it*" (2:216, emphasis added). Many passages in the Koran suggest that not all of the prophet's followers were eager for the fray. The exception to this rule is young men. They are more naturally inclined to combat and risk-taking than the general population, and one of the problems of the Muslim world in this respect is that the normal inclination to avoid violence is offset by the youthfulness of Muslim populations. The next time you see a news video of Palestinians celebrating the latest suicide-bombing success, recall that the average age for a resident of the Gaza Strip is about fifteen.

If many individual Muslims manage, for whatever reason, to be peaceful, that does not make Islam a peaceful religion. There are peaceful passages in the Koran, but taken as a whole, and in context, Islam is not a peaceful religion. From an Islamic perspective, true peace will be established only when all people are subject to Islam. Consequently, it's a mistake to base policy on the assumption that there is a moderate form of Islam and an immoderate version and that the trick is to nudge Muslims in the direction of the moderate version. A moderate Islam would have to be an extremely watered-down one. Large chunks of the Koran, the hadith, and the biographies of Muhammad would have to be ignored, forgotten, or explained away. While such a moderating process is possible, it is unlikely. By now, with the help of modern communications networks, most Muslims will have picked up on the fact that militant Islam is much closer to the essence of Islam as it was practiced for centuries than any mild expression of the faith. It will be difficult to put that genie back in the bottle.

This doesn't mean that respecting the militant aspect of Islam necessarily implies supporting terrorism. Many Muslims prefer that Islam be spread through cultural jihad rather than armed jihad, but they do believe it should be spread. This is what D'Souza, Spencer, Andrew McCarthy, and numerous other commentators mean when they say that there is little fundamental difference between radical Islamists and traditional Muslims about aims. As McCarthy puts it, "There are about 1.4 billion Muslims in the world and the majority of them would not come close to committing a terrorist act. But the rejection of jihadist *methods* is not an en masse rejection of jihadist *goals*."[29]

For a devout Muslim, it's a duty to spread the faith. As for cultural Muslims who are less religiously inclined, it's well to remember that culture is still a powerful force. There's a little bit of "my culture, right or wrong" in all of us—a natural disposition to side with one's family, one's tribe, one's culture against forces that seem to be at odds with them. So even if, in the best scenario, there are large numbers of religiously lax, cultural Muslims, their natural inclination will be to go with their culture, not ours. And since a large part of their culture is orthodox Islam, that is where their sympathies will tend to lie. They may be sitting on the fence, but their inclination will be to favor the familiar side of the fence.

"Sitting on the fence"; "seeing which way the wind is blowing": these may sound like overly simplistic ways of describing complex situations, but sometimes the simple formulation is the most helpful.

Here's another simple formulation, courtesy of Osama Bin Laden: "When people see a strong horse and a weak horse, by nature they will like the strong horse." Simple or not, it seems to be a pretty realistic assessment of human nature. Right now militant Islam is perceived more and more to be the strong horse, and militant Islam includes much more than al-Qaeda. Al-Qaeda may be on the run, but there are dozens of organizations with similar designs on the world; and some of them, such as Hezbollah, are better trained and equipped. In truth, the vision of militant Islam transcends the activities of armed jihadists—rather, it is the vision of Islam triumphant: the long-awaited and well-deserved victory of the supreme religion, a victory that might be achieved militarily or might be accomplished by other means.

One way to create moderation in the Muslim world is to demonstrate that there is no future for this supremacist vision, to show that those who are betting on it are betting on the wrong horse. The obvious first step in this direction is to fight and defeat armed jihadist groups like al-Qaeda wherever and whenever possible and to isolate Islamic terror states like Iran. One of the main lessons of fourteen hundred years of Islamic history is that Islam ceases to wage jihad when it is unable to.

But since this is not a book on warfare, and since I have no expertise in military strategies, I can offer only that broad observation. The concern of this book is cultural jihad and how to defend ourselves against it. Of course, there is an overlap between cultural jihad and physical jihad. A few well-timed and well-placed bombs can have an enormous cultural impact, as was demonstrated by the Madrid train bombings. But whether we are talking about bombs or threats or lawsuits or school textbooks, the same principle applies. The way to convince fence-sitters to come over to the right side of the fence is to persuade them that there is no future for any form of jihad.

In a way, cultural jihadists are harder to resist than militant ones. They are even harder to identify because they wear business suits rather than bomb vests and prefer lawfare to warfare. The official face of Islam in the United States is organizations such as the Council on American Islamic Relations (CAIR), the Islamic Society of North America (ISNA), the Muslim Public Affairs Council (MPAC), and the Muslim American Society (MAS). They present themselves as moderate Muslims and are accepted as such by the media and by government.

Nevertheless, they are deeply involved in cultural subversion. To resist cultural jihad is to resist these mainstream representatives of Islam.

CAIR, for example, is an outgrowth of the Islamic Association for Palestine (IAP), which functioned as the public-relations and recruitment arm for Hamas in the United States. Several former CAIR directors and board members have been convicted of supporting terrorist groups. CAIR has also been at the forefront of attempts to hinder domestic counterterrorism efforts. It worked to repeal the Patriot Act, fought successfully to block a 2010 Oklahoma law that would have banned sharia-based court decisions, and called for an investigation of the NYPD's antiterrorism program. Although CAIR claims to be mainstream and moderate, many American Muslims disagree. Kamal Nawash of the Free Muslim Coalition Against Terrorism says that CAIR and groups like it "condemn terrorism on the surface while endorsing an ideology that helps foster extremism". According to Tashbih Sayyed of the Council for Democracy and Tolerance, CAIR is "the most accomplished fifth column" in the United States. Islam scholar Stephen Suleyman Schwartz asserts that "CAIR should be considered a foreign-based subversive organization, comparable . . . to the Soviet-controlled Communist Party USA."[30]

American Muslims do not seem to have much confidence in the leaders who supposedly represent them. A recent Pew survey showed that 81 percent of American Muslims reject violence against civilians in order to defend Islam and 60 percent are concerned about a possible rise of Islamic extremism in the United States. Forty-eight percent agreed that US Muslim leaders had not done enough to speak out against extremists. Of those born in America, 59 percent said that Muslim leaders had not done enough.[31]

But if the Muslim leadership in the United States is not representative of mainstream American Muslims, it does accurately reflect the supremacist agenda of traditional Islam—an agenda that is widely approved in the Muslim world. Measured by the standards of most Muslim societies, the American leadership groups *are* in the mainstream. And even if they are not in the mainstream in America, they are nevertheless in control. Their campaign of stealth jihad has gone largely unopposed. Thus, it's a mistake to think that the only threat to Western culture is from violently inclined radicals. Many of Islam's mainstream representatives pose an equal threat. It's also a mistake to think that the goal of the cultural jihadists is to impose radical Islam. Their goal, rather, is to impose Islam.

Does this mean we are at war with Islam? No, not necessarily. Although we are in a war against Islamic terrorists, we are not officially at war with Islam. But we are in a struggle with Islam—a civilizational struggle that will determine the kind of society we will live in. The best analogy is the struggle with Soviet Communists. At no point were we directly at war with them, but no one can deny that we were engaged in an ideological struggle with them. One of the turning points in that struggle—one that is applicable to today's situation—was the formulation of the policy of containment. Beginning with the Truman administration, strong measures were taken to halt the spread of communism and Communist Party influence. Communists proclaimed themselves to be the wave of the future, and for a while it looked as though history was on their side. That proved to be false, but only because the United States and its allies were clear-eyed enough to realize that they were indeed caught up in a high-stakes ideological struggle.

In our struggle with Islam, we have yet to reach that point of realization, and the myth of a moderate Islam is one of the main reasons why. The promotion of the moderate myth is counterproductive because it misleads the West into thinking that its problem is only with a small slice of Islam and because it strengthens the hand of traditional Islam, which is the source of radicalism, not the solution to it. The more perfectly one practices traditional Islam, the more radical one is likely to become. A more perfect practice of the faith is exactly what the jihadists have been calling for. Is that the call we want Muslims living in the West to answer?

Westerners have assumed that by accomodating the requests of mainstream Muslim leaders they would win over the supposedly moderate majority. But the policy hasn't resulted in increased satisfaction on the part of traditional Muslims, only in increased appetite. I believe the applicable cliché is "give them an inch, and they'll take a mile"—another one of those simplistic sayings that happens to be true much of the time. A good deal of accumulated experience now suggests that capitulating to Muslim demands is not going to make them more moderate; it's going to make them more convinced that Islam has the right to rule. The cumulative effect of all those double-standard rulings and reactions whereby Islamic sensitivities are deemed to count for more than the sensitivities of other groups and, for that matter, to count for more than free speech or a free press, is to send a message that, yes, we infidels concede there is something very special about this religion and the usual rules don't apply to it. So every time you jail a Protestant pastor for merely criticizing homosexuals, while giving a free pass to an imam who calls for killing them; every time you send multiple welfare checks to a polygamous Muslim household; and every time you suggest that sharia is an acceptable alternative to the civil law of the land—as a Catholic bishop in the Philippines recently urged—you are feeding into a preexisting sense of superiority and entitlement. In short, you don't make moderates by consistently demonstrating that immoderate demands will be applauded and rewarded.

Here's an item that helps to put the problem in perspective. After a US soldier in Iraq used a Koran for target practice, Maj. Gen. Jeffrey Hammond, the commander of US forces in Baghdad at the time, apologized to tribal leaders in the area. So far, so good. Outright provocations are not a good way to win friends and influence Sunni militiamen. There's no sense in alienating the people you want to win over. An apology of some sort was appropriate. What is interesting is the nature of the apology:

> "I come before you here seeking your forgiveness," Hammond said to tribal leaders and others at the apology ceremony. "In the most humble manner I look in your eyes today and I say please forgive me and my soldiers."
>
> Another military official kissed a Quran and presented it as "a humble gift" to the tribal leaders.[32]

Did the Muslim tribal leaders respond in kind? Not quite. In a speech on behalf of all tribal sheiks of Radhwaniya, Sheik Hamadi al-Qirtani called the shooting incident "aggression against the entire Islamic world". Other tribal leaders said that the apology was not enough and demanded a harsher punishment for the soldier who committed the "crime". (He was relieved of his duties and reassigned.) As Robert Spencer points out, such abject apologies only play into the mentality that proclaims, "We are the greatest!"

> Major General Hammond is anxious to show that the U.S. is not at war with Islam. Fine. But to kiss the Qur'an and to beg for forgiveness are signs that one accepts its authority and the authority of those before whom one is begging. Coming from non-Muslims, it is likely that they will be interpreted as gestures of submission, and the submission of non-Muslims to Muslims is a significant concept in Islamic law.[33]

Submission is not just a significant concept in Islam; it's the main concept. And Western leaders still seem unable to understand that the more the West submits, the more submission will be required. In February 2012, after several Korans were mistakenly burned at NATO's Bagram Air Base in Afghanistan, violent protests resulted in twelve deaths, including the murder of two American soldiers. In response, President Obama sent a letter to Afghan President Hamid Karzai expressing his "sincere apologies" for the desecration of the Koran. In Washington, a senior Pentagon official apologized to Washington-area Muslims for the Koran burning.[34] No apologies were requested or given for the murder of the two American soldiers. Despite the apologies, the rioting continued for several weeks, resulting in the deaths of several more American soldiers and dozens of Afghans. For some perspective, it's instructive to note that in May 2009 at the same air base, the US military deliberately burned a shipment of Bibles printed in the Pashto and Dari languages that had been donated by a church in America. US commanders were afraid the Bibles would be used to convert Afghans.[35] Meanwhile, in Saudi Arabia, confiscated Bibles, along with crosses and rosaries, are regularly burned by the government.

When bin Laden talked about a "strong horse" and a "weak horse", the strong horse he was talking about was not al-Qaeda but Islam. Every time Westerners accomodate traditional Islamic practice, they inadvertently make Islam look like the stronger horse. Many Muslims may disapprove of bin Laden's tactics for advancing the cause of Islam, but they can't very well disagree with his theology since it is well within the traditional mainstream. The argument that the jihadist's Islam isn't the real Islam doesn't hold up to examination. When a fence-sitting Muslim goes to the sources, he'll find the same thing bin Laden found: the obligation to bring the world under the rule of Allah. And this necessarily implies the imposition of sharia. By endorsing moderate Islam, we are simply legitimizing a slower and less bloody form of jihad.

If we are in a cultural struggle with Islam, why would we want to shore up Islam in this way? Why would we want to promote a wider observance of a religion that has world domination as its goal? Why would we show special favors to a religion that sanctions intolerance, the oppression of women, and the killing of apostates? Wouldn't it be more in our interests—and also in the interest of many Muslims—if we gave more Muslims the opportunity to live in a sharia-free society? And what about giving Muslims the opportunity to question their religion? Instead of considering moderate Islam as the only alternative to radical Islam, shouldn't Muslims be encouraged to consider alternatives to Islam itself?

Here's an interesting observation by Theodore Dalrymple:

> Shrillness and intolerance are not signs of strength, but of weakness; fundamentalism is a response to an awareness that, if the methods of intellectual inquiry that were used to challenge Christianity were permitted in the Muslim world, Islam would soon fall apart.[36]

If Islam is inherently weak, so weak that it has to be maintained by force or coercion, why is it desirable to prop it up? The Cold War policy of containment was based on the assumption that communism was so inherently flawed that it would eventually collapse if it could be kept from spreading. We didn't suggest to the people living in East Germany, Poland, and Czechoslovakia at the time that there was a moderate or positive form of communism worthy of their allegiance. We maintained instead that there was a far better alternative to communism, and we set out to show that our system of government worked and theirs didn't. Eventually, communism began to be perceived as the weak horse, and eventually it crumbled.

Instead of a constant yielding to Islamic sensitivities, it may be time for some containment. Sharia flies in the face of Western concepts of law and human dignity. It should not be allowed to spread through Western societies. Many moderate Muslims realize this. Many of them immigrated to Western nations in order to flee the mandates of sharia. The last thing they want is to see sharia established in the West. Several of these moderates have joined with groups like ACT! for America to curb the spread of sharia in the United States. Thanks in part to their testimony, several states have passed laws to keep sharia law out of their courts, and more than twenty other states are considering similar laws. ACT! for America provides an example of what an effective moderate-Muslim strategy should be: enlisting genuine moderates to convince politicians and lawmakers about the threat from sharia-compliant Islam. Instead, Western leaders have foolishly bestowed their seal of approval on the leaders of Muslim Brotherhood–controlled groups whom they mistake for moderates. The expectation that these Muslim Brotherhood surrogates will be a moderating influence is wishful thinking. In order to prevent Islamization, Western people need to challenge and resist Islamic beliefs and practices that run counter to Western values. At the head of the list should be the most egregious violations: honor killings, forced marriages, polygamy, and spousal abuse. Next on the list should be attempts by Muslims to censor and criminalize free speech in the West. And after that, there's a whole litany of special exceptions and double standards that need to be addressed—the hookah parlors, the public footbaths, the segregated taxi cabs and swimming pools. The message should be: no more special treatment, no more double standards, no more nonsense. "No." "Sorry." "I'm afraid we can't comply." "We don't do that here." The refusals should be courteous but firm. The underlying message? Islam will not prevail. The West will not yield. You must accommodate to our values and way of life if you choose to live among us.

Law can be used as a way to Westernize Muslims. The US government turned polygamous Mormons into monogamous Mormons in the late 1800s by outlawing polygamy. And once the Supreme Court upheld the law, the Mormons got the message. In a similar way the British helped Hindus in India change their position on *suttee*—the practice of burning a widow on her husband's funeral pyre. Here's the way Mark Steyn tells it:

> General Sir Charles Napier was impeccably multicultural: "You say that it is your custom to burn widows. Very well. We also have a custom: when men burn a woman alive, we tie a rope around their necks and we hang them. Build your funeral pyres; beside it, my carpenters will build a gallows. You may follow your custom. And then we will follow ours." [37]

Such use of law may seem harsh, even immoderate, when judged by our new, highly evolved standards of sensitivity. But as Lee Harris points out in *The Suicide of Reason*, moderation is not necessarily a virtue at all times or in all situations. For example, when someone is trying to kill you, it is immoderate to react in a moderate way. This, says Harris, is the situation we are in regarding Islam. He believes that because we are so accustomed to living in a reasonable society, we grossly underestimate the "sheer power of Islamic fanaticism", which is not merely an isolated phenomenon but a "collective fanaticism" shared by an entire society. Contrary to our belief that "life-and-death struggles between cultures and civilizations are a thing of the past", they are a constant of history, says Harris. And when those confrontations come, moderation, especially when combined with a lack of cultural confidence, can be suicidal, even for a society with military superiority. How do you prevail in such a situation? The solution, says Harris, is not to drop our commitment to tolerance, but to realize that in some situations other virtues are more important.

> In order to secure a tolerant society, you must teach the young that there are times when they have a civic duty to be intolerant, namely, when dealing with those who refuse to play by the rules that are necessary for the creation of a tolerant society.[38]

In other words, in order to preserve a culture of freedom, tolerance, and reason, you must be willing to defend it at all costs, to fight for it, and to die for it. And, paradoxically, to the extent that you can convince your adversary that is what you will do, the less likely it will come to that. One of the great tragedies of English history is that the English failed, prior to the Second World War, to convince the Nazis that they would fight. By the time the Nazis found out that the British would fight, it was too late to prevent the enormous casualties suffered by both sides.

Harris relates a story about Joseph Goebbels that sums up the paradox. Late in the war, Goebbels was upset by a joke that "he feared would have a terrible effect on German fighting morale if it spread". The joke, which was already widespread in the Reich, went like this: "The English are even more stubborn than we Germans are." The joke meant that the Germans were coming to the realization that it was futile to continue the war. The English would not be conquered.[39]

If there is one point that we ought to be conveying both to "radical Islam" and to "mainstream Islam", it is not that we are a tolerant and open society that wishes to give no offense but that there are certain core beliefs on which we will never yield. Moderate Muslims? We'll know the tide has turned in that direction when there's a new joke sweeping through the Muslim world: "The Westerners are even more stubborn than we are."

14

Is Islam Too Big to Fail?

The atheist detractors of Christianity seized on 9/11 as an opportunity to portray Islam and Christianity as evil twin brothers. And, thanks to being absolved by multiculturalists from having to know anything about any religion, a lot of Americans don't know enough about either Christianity or Islam to be able to tell whether the comparison is true.

Aside from surface similarities, however, the differences between Christianity and Islam are striking. For one thing, Islam is not just a religion; it's also a political system. For example, there is a fifty-seven-country voting bloc in the United Nations called the Organization of the Islamic Cooperation. As the name suggests, there is little separation between mosque and state in the Islamic world. Many Muslim religious and civic leaders desire that there be little or no distinction between civil law and Islamic law. In many Muslim countries, religious law—that is, sharia—is the basis of law.

One of the major Western miscalculations about Islam is to assume that Islam is simply a religion—in the same way that Christianity, Buddhism, and Hinduism are religions. Islam is also a political ideology and a political movement. Christ's kingdom may not be of this world, but the Islamic *umma*—the worldwide community of believers—definitely is. Until November 2003, the Islamic Affairs Department of the Saudi Arabian embassy in Washington carried this statement on its website: "The Muslims are required to raise the banner of Jihad in order to make the Word of Allah supreme in this world." [1] Sayyid Abul A'la Maududi, who is considered one of the most important theorists of jihad, had this to say: "Islam requires the earth—not just a portion, but the whole planet." [2]

Several critics of Islam suggest that it closely resembles totalitarian ideologies such as communism and Nazism in its ambitions. And

Maududi seems to bear this out: "The truth is that Islam is not the name of a 'Religion,' nor is 'Muslim' the title of a 'Nation.' In reality Islam is a revolutionary ideology and programme which seeks to alter the social order of the whole world and rebuild it in conformity with its own tenets and ideals."[3]

This non-religious aspect of Islam is hard for Westerners to grasp because it's so different from the not-of-this-world religions with which the West is most familiar. Gregory M. Davis, who produced and directed a documentary on Islam, suggests that Westerners need to reorient completely their thinking about Islam:

> The first task for the West must be to reclassify Islam as a political system with religious aspects rather than a religion with political aspects. Islam is an alternative form of government in competition with Western governments that seeks to weaken and, ultimately, replace them.[4]

So perhaps the basic mistake the West makes in regard to Islam is to think of it as comparable to Christianity, with Muhammad being in the same general category as Jesus. But, in fact, this is an enormous category error. To understand Islam, you have to realize that Muhammad belongs to a completely different line of "prophets". Instead of thinking Abraham, Moses, and Jesus, think Lenin, Stalin, and Mao Zedong. That, essentially, is the historical grouping to which the prophet belongs, and the failure to understand this is the reason much of the political and religious dialogue with Islam is doomed to failure. Like the Communists, Islamic leaders have their own peculiar understanding of words such as *peace, justice, freedom,* and *equality.*

Some writers, such as Davis, think that Islam is a more formidable enemy to the West than communism was. This is partly because Islam has more followers (billions as opposed to millions) and a more extensive propaganda reach. Imagine a worldwide Communist or Nazi Party movement that openly operated recruitment and indoctrination centers in almost every large and medium-size city in the world. Mosques and madrassas are everywhere, and they continue to spread. That is an advantage that Nazis and Communists never had.

Many people think of a mosque as the equivalent of a Christian church, as a place of worship. But according to Bernard Lewis, one of the leading scholars of the Middle East, it is "seriously misleading" to think of the mosque as a Muslim church.[5] It's much more than that. Fr. Samir Khalil Samir, S.J., an expert on Islam, concurs. The mosque cannot be likened to a Christian church, he says, because it "represents something absolutely and radically different".[6] A mosque is a place for prayer but also a place for dealing authoritatively with social, cultural, and political issues. Thus, on Fridays in many Muslim countries, the mosques are supervised by police. Father Samir explains, "There is a simple reason for this: many political decisions start from the mosque during the Friday *khutba* (sermon). Historians of Islam know that many riots and revolutions were launched from the mosques and that *jihad* is often proclaimed during the *khutba*."[7] Indeed, many of the 2011 Arab Spring demonstrations were set in motion from mosques following Friday prayers. Christians assume that a mosque is simply a house of prayer, but in the minds of activist Muslims it is also a staging area. As a popular Muslim poem puts it, "The mosques are our barracks, the domes our helmets, the minarets our bayonets and the faithful our soldiers."

Politicization of mosques is not just a Middle East phenomenon. Between 1998 and 2011, four independent studies of mosques in the United States came to the same conclusion: approximately 80 percent of mosques in America conveyed a supremacist vision and provided their members with anti-Semitic, anti-Christian, pro-sharia, and pro-jihad literature.[8] In January 1999, Muslim Sheik Muhammad Hisham Kabbani, who had visited 114 mosques, testified before a State Department open forum that 80 percent of American mosques promoted an "extremist ideology".[9]

It's difficult to know where the religious component of Islam ends and the political component begins. One thing, however, is certain: political expansion is very much on the Islamic agenda. Al-Azhar University in Cairo is considered the foremost center of religious authority for Sunni Muslims, and in 1991 a manual certified by Al-Azhar reiterated one of Islam's ancient laws: "The caliph . . . makes war upon Jews, Christians, and Zoroastrians . . . until they become Muslim or else pay the non-Muslim poll tax."[10]

Islam mandates the subjugation of unbelievers. Will it happen through riots and revolutions? Through open war? In America, probably not. Jihadists are politically astute, and they realize that violence in America could be counterproductive. As Robert Spencer puts it, "This is one of the lessons that some jihadists learned from September 11: attack America, and it tends to strike back; but quietly undermine America from within, and there's a lot less resistance. In fact, people tend not even to notice."[11]

While groups like al-Qaeda are inclined toward violent jihad, other groups—such as the much larger and more influential Muslim Brotherhood—prefer to employ what Spencer terms "stealth jihad". In the words of Mohamed Akram, a top Brotherhood leader, the Muslim Brotherhood "must understand that their work in America is a kind of grand jihad in eliminating and destroying the Western civilization from within and 'sabotaging' its miserable house by their hands and the hands of the believers so that it is eliminated and Allah's religion is made victorious over all other religions." [12]

Unrealistic dreams of glory? Unfortunately, no. The Muslim Brotherhood and its various front groups have already made significant progress in paving the way for the eventual establishment of sharia in America. Here are some examples of stealth jihad:

- In many public colleges and universities Muslim student groups have pressured administrators into establishing separate Muslims-only prayer rooms. Elsewhere university facilities meant for all faiths have been taken over by Muslims for their exclusive use. At the University of California in Irvine, Jewish students avoid wearing clothing or symbols that might identify them as Jewish out of fear of Muslim intimidation and attacks. [13]

- In 2008 the American Textbook Council reported that ten of the most widely used high school and middle school history texts had a clear bias in favor of Islam and against Christianity: "While seventh-grade textbooks describe Islam in glowing language, they portray Christianity in a harsh light. Students encounter a startling contrast. Islam is featured as a model of interfaith tolerance; Christians wage wars of aggression and kill Jews. Islam provides models of harmony and civilization. Anti-Semitism, the Inquisition, and wars of religion bespot the Christian record." [14]

- A state judge in Pennsylvania, a convert to Islam, dismissed assault charges against a Muslim man who attacked an atheist dressed like Muhammad for a Halloween parade. The judge ruled that the Muslim was obligated by his religion to attack the man. He then lectured the atheist for insulting Islam. [15]

- A voluminous set of documents released in early 2012 by the Department of Justice Civil Rights Division revealed a high degree of cooperation and collaboration between the DOJ and various Muslim Brotherhood groups. Pamela Geller, the director of the American Freedom Defense Initiative who reviewed hundreds of documents and e-mails, was struck by "the casual familiarity of ISNA [Islamic Society of North America], the ADC [American-Arab Anti-Discrimination Committee], and senior officials of the Department of Justice". Among the documents is a request from ADC to have the NYPD investigated for anti-Muslim bias. Another request dated October 11, 2011, calls for an investigation of FBI training materials.[16]

- In October 2011, in compliance with Muslim requests, the deputy US attorney general ordered the FBI and other national-security organizations to eliminate from their training materials all references to Islam that suggest a tendency to violence.[17]

- In January 2012, not long after the complaint to the DOJ, the New York Police Department withdrew the film *The Third Jihad* from its training program. The film, narrated by Zuhdi Jasser, a physician with a reputation as a moderate Muslim, was branded as Islamophobic. Muslim activist groups also called for the resignation of the police commissioner.[18]

- In 2010 the DOJ sued a small school district in Illinois on behalf of a Muslim teacher who was denied a three-week leave to make a pilgrimage to Mecca. The unusual lawsuit alleged that the school had violated the teacher's religious rights.[19]

- In December 2011 the State Department hosted a three-day conference in Washington, DC, entitled "Combating Intolerance, Negative Stereotyping and Stigmatization of, and Discrimination, Incitement to Violence and Violence against, Persons Based on Religion or Belief". The largest group at the conference was the Organization of the Islamic Cooperation. Critics of the meeting see it as a step by the State Department toward helping the OIC achieve its long-standing objective of silencing speech critical of Islam.[20]

- Despite its professed concern over violence against religion, the State Department refused a request from the US Commission on International Religious Freedom to put Egypt on a list of states that violate religious freedom following the participation of the Egyptian military in the murder of twenty-five Christian Copts.[21]

Ever since the McCarthy investigations, many Americans consider it bad form to talk about the subversion of our social and governmental institutions. Yet, as the release of the Venona Project papers revealed, there was quite a bit of subversion going on during the Cold War.[22] Our institutions seem even riper for subversion now, having created an elaborate set of tools for their own undoing. Unless a cultural jihadist sports a "death to the infidel" placard on his desk, he can use diversity policies to rise quickly through the ranks in most institutions. When he wants to introduce a Muslim tradition into the workplace or stifle discussion of Islamic goals, he needs merely to play the "race card" or the "Islamophobia card" and, lo, all the other hands will fold.

Muslim activists, in other words, quickly learned to game the multiculturalist system. Muslim Brotherhood organizations such as the Islamic Society of North America (ISNA), the Council on American-Islamic Relations (CAIR), and the Muslim Public Affairs Council (MPAC) found that by framing an issue in terms of civil rights or diversity, they could overcome almost any resistance. For example, the Muslim Student Association, an affiliate of the Muslim Brotherhood, advises Muslim students to present their demands to university officials within a framework of civil rights grievances—even though, as Spencer points out, their request for *separate* eating, exercise, and prayer facilities runs counter to the original spirit of the civil rights movement.[23]

Muslim activists around the world have mastered the art of political maneuvering, but political maneuvering by itself isn't enough to explain their success. Islam has also been the beneficiary of numerous positive interventions by the West. Think of them as "bailouts".

On many occasions over the last several years, we have heard that various giant companies had to be bailed out by the federal government because they were "too big to fail". AIG, Fannie Mae, Merrill Lynch, Citigroup, GM—all were considered as having too large a share of the US economy to be allowed to go bankrupt. Although some argued that it might be a healthful thing to let underperforming companies fail, the consensus among policy makers was that these companies had to be propped up or else the entire global economy would collapse with them.

There seems to be a similar, although unspoken, assumption about Islam—that it also is too big to fail; that somehow it is in the interest of us all to keep it going, to prop it up, to bail it out. Ever since 9/11, Western elites—government officials, the media, academicians, even Jewish and Christian clergy—have been providing bailouts to Islam. Thus, immediately after 9/11, several Western leaders, including President Bush, made it a priority to visit local mosques to assure one and all of their belief in the peacefulness of Islam—a phenomenon that Mark Steyn dubbed the "get me to the mosque on time" syndrome. The next bailout was provided in the form of a quickly devised and widely adopted formula: Islam was a great religion that had been hijacked by a handful of radicals. There was nothing to fear from the true Islam.

More bailouts followed. History books for American schoolchildren were rewritten to present Islam as a model of interfaith tolerance; those who were troubled by Islamic aggressiveness were labeled "Islamaphobes"; and the word *jihad* was put through the political-correctness translation machine and came out as an "interior spiritual struggle".

Eleven years and eighteen thousand terrorist attacks later, Western leaders are still intent on portraying Islam as a great religion with which we share much in common. That was the thrust of President Obama's Cairo speech in June 2009, and even Pope Benedict seemed to lend legitimacy to Islam in his speech to Muslim leaders at the Dome of the Rock in Jerusalem. "Here", said the pope, "the paths of the world's three great monotheistic religions meet, reminding us what they share in common."[24] Whenever its capital reserves of trust and goodwill run low, Islam can always count on a prelate, a president, or a prime minister to provide a new infusion of capital in the form of reassurances that it is a great religion with which we share plenty of common ground.

Sometimes the bailouts are like those to which we have recently become accustomed: direct financial support. The United States sends large amounts of foreign aid to Muslim states; and depending on how you look at it, that may or may not be the prudential thing to do. But beyond foreign aid, most of the major Western financial institutions have now established sharia-compliant finance regulations, which are intended to bring financial practices in line with Islamic norms. In addition to lending legitimacy to sharia, these initiatives also have the effect of giving Islamic interests increased leverage over Western markets. One of the stipulations of sharia finance is that companies establish sharia advisory boards composed of Islamic clerics and scholars. Another rule requires that 2.5 percent per year of portfolio funds goes to charities. Who decides which charities will benefit? Answer: the Islamic scholars and clerics. What organizations do they favor? In a nutshell, those that promote the spread of traditional Islam.

Perhaps the biggest and most ill-considered bailout that the West has given Islam is its willingness to go along with the Muslim project of stifling all criticism of Islam. As we have seen, individuals as diverse as Mark Steyn, Oriana Fallaci, and Brigitte Bardot have already been tried on charges of defaming Islam—and not in places like Tehran or Lahore, but in places like Vancouver and Milan. Numerous others have had books or speeches canceled on the grounds that Muslims might be offended. Increasingly, Islam is off limits to critical examination. In the world of bailouts, this puts Islam in a class by itself. At least in the case of the AIG bailout, government auditors were allowed to look at the books.

Is Islam too big to fail? That seems to be the working assumption behind the various forms of life support provided for it. How do you account for this assumption? There seems to be two answers. First, Islam is a religion—a big religion. And religion is generally considered to be a good thing because it is thought to be a stabilizing force in society. Even nonbelievers tend to subscribe to a belief in the beneficial effects of religion. It's widely recognized that churches encourage believers to be hardworking, family-oriented, and law-abiding; so even those who doubt the truthfulness of religion are often willing to concede its usefulness. The question is, if religion equals stability, what would happen if one of the largest religions were to collapse? Apparently the answer is, let's not think about it. Let's just give Islam whatever help it needs.

The second reason for thinking Islam is too big to fail is really a tautology. Islam is too big to fail because it's too big. Most people have a hard time coming to terms with the disappearance of a big familiar fixture in the social environment, especially one that has been around for so long that it seems to have become permanent. If you have difficulty imagining a world without Fannie Mae or General Motors, try to imagine a world without its second-biggest religion. Something of that size and longevity eventually acquires a fixed status. And since we can't imagine anything other than its continued existence, we can only imagine strategies for coming to terms with it.

But consider that many in the West had the same attitude toward Soviet-bloc communism. It also seemed permanent, something that was too big to fail—and therefore something with which we had to come to terms. Yet it did fail. And it failed in large part because the West removed the ideological life-support apparatus and began to challenge communism.

In his recent book, *Defeating Political Islam*, political analyst Moorthy Muthuswamy contends that the West needs to confront and challenge Islamic ideology in the same manner that the West confronted Soviet ideology.[25] In short, he is calling for the West to engage Islam in an ideological cold war, and that means going after the religious foundations of Islam. Like many other observers, Muthuswamy thinks Islam is more a political ideology than a religion, but he admits that the theology can't really be separated from the ideology. After all, as he points out, the chief distribution centers for radical Islamic ideology are not urban apartments or mountain caves but mainstream mosques, madrassas, and seminaries.

It seems, then, that if we are to halt the spread of Islam, there is no choice other than to discredit Islam's theological underpinnings. Instead of propping up Islam, it's in our interest to expose the shaky foundations upon which it is built. At one time, Soviet communism had an air of inevitability about it. But once America dropped the let's-not-do-anything-to-upset-the-Soviets policy of the Carter era, the collapse of communism in Eastern Europe and the Soviet Union came with surprising speed. We might be similarly surprised at how quickly Islam loses credibility once the bailouts cease and the tough questioning begins.

Like communism, Islam may prove to be more fragile than it appears. The rigid exoskeleton of rules and penalties conceals a weak core. As I've suggested in previous chapters, the most striking testimony to the hollowness of the ideology can be found in the Koran, which is the reason more Westerners need to acquaint themselves with it. Raising questions about the Koran is a ticklish business, but some questions simply beg to be answered. For example, the Jesus of the Koran doesn't look anything like the Jesus of the Gospels. For that matter, he doesn't look anything like an actual human being. Which is the real Jesus? In a normal world, this is the kind of historical question that might be expected to generate some curiosity. Yet few seem inclined to consider it.

Avoiding the question is another bailout of Islam. The Jesus of the Koran is not very convincing. Like the Koran itself, it's unlikely he would survive any serious critical/historical inquiry. And so, with the exception of a few Christians and former Muslims, the inquiry is never made. The Western media engage in endless speculation about the Christian revelation—for example, cover stories about the "real" Jesus of the Gospels have become a *Newsweek* holiday tradition. But the Islamic version of Jesus is given a free ride.

Ordinarily one keeps one's reservations about another's religion to oneself. But if we are in a fight to the death with Islamic ideology/ theology, why wouldn't we want to examine it more carefully? Why wouldn't we want to call into question the revelation on which it is all based? And, further, why not seek ways to disillusion and demoralize the proponents of that ideology? In short, why shouldn't we want Islam to fail?

Is Islam too big to fail? Soviet-bloc communism was a big thing at one time, but it eventually failed, thanks in part to the willingness of a few Western intellectuals to break ranks with their politically correct colleagues and tell the truth about communism. The world is better off without Soviet communism. It's also a better place without the child-sacrificing religion of Moloch or the human sacrifices of the Aztecs. Religion is not always and everywhere a good thing. It's time for the West to reconsider its excessive deference to Islam and start thinking instead of ways to create a future in which, to quote Winston Churchill's seldom quoted wish, "the faith of Islam has ceased to be a great power among men".[26]

Let's pause here to anticipate an objection. Is imagining a world without Islam just the mirror image of President Ahmadinejad's call for imagining a world without Israel? No, it's not. There's a big difference between wanting to eradicate a people and a nation, as Mr. Ahmadinejad does, and wanting to discredit a belief system. Just as a world without communism does not mean a world without Russians or Ukrainians or Georgians, a world without Islam does not mean a world without Egyptians or Saudis or Iranians. It would, however, be a world in which the Egyptians, the Saudis, and the Iranians would have to make a lot of adjustments, but perhaps, for a change, it's time for them to start making the adjustments.

Another likely objection is that Islam is too deeply rooted to fail. But deeply held beliefs are not always as deeply rooted as they seem.

For example, in the space of about a dozen years, the civil rights movement managed to overturn what were thought to be deeply held racial prejudices. In the twenties, fascism was an enormously popular worldwide movement; by the late thirties, it was almost totally discredited. Thirty-five years ago, it would have been non-controversial to say that the Catholic faith was deeply rooted in Ireland, but if you said it today, you would be going out on a limb. More to the point, the deeply held beliefs of millions of Muslims were tightly constrained under the secular regimes of Atatürk in Turkey, Nasser in Egypt, and Hussein in Iraq. The discrediting or delegitimizing of widely held and firmly held beliefs is not a rare phenomenon in history.

Deeply held beliefs? Consider the following passage from an article for the *Chronicle of Higher Education* by Ali A. Allawi, a former Iraqi cabinet minister:

> I was born into a mildly observant Muslim family in Iraq. At that time, the 1950s, secularism was ascendant among the political, cultural, and intellectual elites of the Middle East. It appeared to be only a matter of time before Islam would lose whatever hold it still had on the Muslim world. Even that term—"Muslim world"—was unusual, as Muslims were more likely to identify themselves by their national, ethnic, or ideological affinities than by their religion.
>
> To an impressionable child, it was clear that society was decoupling from Islam. Though religion was a mandatory course in school, nobody taught us the rules of prayer or expected us to fast during Ramadan. We memorized the shorter verses of the Koran, but the holy book itself was kept on the shelf or in drawers, mostly unread.[27]

The hold that Islam exerts over believers has waxed and waned over the years. Sixty years ago, Islam seemed on the way out in much of the Middle East. It would be a mistake to assume that its current comeback in that region is now permanently fixed. It would be an even bigger mistake to think that Islam's momentum in the West is irreversible.

Last year's pro-democracy rallies in the Middle East and North Africa inspired hopes that new regimes would bring moderation to those countries. But there have been many regime changes in the Muslim Middle East and little moderation to show for it. It's true that many Muslim nations have been more moderate—if not more democratic—in the past, but the evidence suggests that Muslim societies become more moderate to the degree that they are able to move away from Islam. Moderation seems possible only in those places where the power of Islam is weakened or restricted or where people look upon Islam as a traditional folk religion and ignore its harsher mandates. Yet even in these situations, radical Islam—that is, the Islam handed down by Muhammad—always manages to reemerge. Muslims surely deserve better regimes, but as long as Islam remains the ruling spirit in Muslim lands, it's unlikely that regime change will ever be enough.

Meanwhile, while we fret about the fate of the Middle East, stealth jihad continues apace in the West. In Holland, where they've had a bit more experience with Islamic aggressiveness, some people are having second thoughts about coming to terms with Islam. Geert Wilders, who has been living under police protection for the last few years, recently referred to Islam as "an ideology that is threatening our way of life".[28] What's the Muslim population of Holland? About 6 percent. Yet at least two Dutch civic leaders have needed police protection from Islamists who want to kill them, and the middle class is leaving the country in record numbers. What's the Muslim population of Britain? If you consider the size of the proposed megamosque, the pressure on Catholic schools to stop teaching the Catholic view on polygamy, and the banning of piglet knickknacks from workers' desks, you might think it was closing on 50 percent. But the fact is, it's less than 5 percent. How about Italy—the country with the biggest mosque in Europe and from which Oriana Fallaci was forced to flee to avoid a prison sentence for insulting Islam? About 1.6 percent. In France, where the Muslim population is a respectable 10 percent, it took police three weeks to put an end to Muslim rioting in over three hundred cities. The logical question is, what's going to happen when the Muslim population of Europe is 15 or 20 percent?

And do we in America want to wait to find out? There's no need to wait. The political nature of Islam demands that it eats up territories and cultures until the whole world dwells under *dar al-Islam*, "the House of Islam". Whether that goal is achieved by military conquest or by cultural jihad is a secondary concern.

We are told that Islam has a long-time horizon, that it's willing to wait for what it wants. True enough, but sometimes Islam moves with surprising speed—as it did in the middle of the seventh century. If history is any guide, Islam prefers to be on the move. It has never prospered when its imperialistic ambitions have been thwarted. Swift conquest is much more in line with the original spirit of the faith. When Islam waits, those periods of dazzling conquest are what it is waiting for. Given the absence of resistance they have so far encountered, Muslims have good reason to believe that this may be one of those times.

The War of Ideas

How do you fight an ideological cold war? There are two answers: with conviction and with a determination to win. In past ideological struggles we wisely sought ideological victory—the discrediting of the belief system that inspired our enemies. But in the past we had a stronger sense that our cause was just, and equally important, we actually believed in the existence of enemies. Although there are many warnings about "enemies" in the Bible, in a therapeutic society the concept of "enemy" seems somehow unsophisticated and outdated. But the sophisticated view of things is now beginning to unravel. The sooner we can revise our thinking in this and other areas, the better.

A world dominated by Islam would be a nightmare beyond the imagining of most Americans. Yet the future may well belong to Muslims unless Westerners wake up and realize that they are in the midst of an ideological struggle with Islam. But waking up is not enough. As the Dracula-like return of communist ideology demonstrates, an ideological war must be fought to complete victory. The enemy ideology should be so thoroughly discredited that no one—not even its former staunchest defenders, not even the most doctrinaire college professor—will want to be associated with it.

In regard to Islam, then, our aim should go beyond simply resisting jihad; it should be the defeat of Islam as an idea. But, aside from inflicting crushing military defeats on Islamic powers, how do we accomplish that? The answer lies in the fact that, despite its power and momentum, Islam is ideologically weak. Jihad is fueled by faith, but that faith rests on a surprisingly flimsy foundation. If the West hopes to survive, it must expose the lies upon which Islam is built.

On Christmas Day 2009, Umar Abdulmutallab, the "underwear bomber", nearly succeeded in killing 270 passengers on Northwest flight 253. There are many more like him in the United States and in numerous other countries waiting for their chance at martyrdom. How can they be stopped? There is much that can be done in the way of improved intelligence and security, but the flow of jihadists will continue unless we can shut off the tap from which they flow. It's important to take out the terrorist, but in the long run it's more important to take down the terrorist's ideology.

"Believers, make war on the infidels who dwell around you" (9:123). "Make war on them until idolatry shall cease and Allah's religion shall reign supreme" (8:34). One of the principle themes of the Koran is that Allah hates unbelievers and wants them to be punished. As Muhammad said, "I have been commanded to fight against people, till they testify that there is no god but Allah." Islam is, in effect, an open-ended declaration of war against non-Muslims. Consequently it's not just Muslim terrorists who need to be feared, but also Muslim theorists and theologians. The attacks won't stop until the belief system that inspires the terrorists is undermined and dismantled. If the idea of fighting an ideological cold war sounds extreme, consider a couple of the alternatives: a hot war possibly involving nuclear weapons or a slow capitulation to Islam. You fight a cold war to avoid the alternatives. The West's victory in the Cold War against Soviet communism demonstrates that a willingness to fight an ideological war does not necessarily lead to a shooting war. Rather, it may be the best way to prevent one.

Much of the momentum behind Islam's current push for world domination comes from a renewed conviction that Islam has God on its side. A policy of ideological appeasement, just like a policy of political appeasement, only fuels the conviction that Islam is destined to overcome. On the other hand, by undercutting that certitude, you also undermine the will to fight. In the long run, a war of ideas offers the best hope for a peaceful resolution to the growing conflict.

What role should Christians play in this struggle? Because the current conflict is in large part a spiritual struggle, it follows that Christians ought to play a leading role. Islam claims to be a true account of the universe; thus, any effective resistance to it must address that claim. The usual appeals to the practical benefits of Western culture won't cut it with those who have their eyes on a higher prize. We have democracy, freedom, and an abundance of choices, but we can't make the case that those things will move anyone any closer to paradise. Claims to truth cannot be met with claims to five-hundred-channel broadcasting.

Christians are better positioned to occasion a Muslim rethinking because Christians also make truth claims. To the extent that Christians are serious about the truth of their faith, Muslims will take them seriously. To the extent that Christians merely ape the secular accommodationist response to Islam, they only strengthen the Muslim conviction that Islam is the superior religion and culture. Right now, the Islamic world seems fairly secure in that conviction. One doesn't often hear of Islamic leaders voicing their "great respect for Christianity".

Because Muslim confidence is religion-based, the only way to shake Muslims' conviction is by engaging Islam on religious grounds. If Islam's claims are true, then Muslims are right to be annoyed by our blindness. If Allah is as he is described in the Koran, if he is the Creator and Lord of the Universe (and thus knows more than we do), and if he wants us to submit to his law, then, out of respect for truth, that is what we ought to do. By the same token, Muslims are under a corresponding obligation to reflect on the facts of their faith. We can help them do this, not by telling them we have deep respect for their religion, but by telling them we have deep suspicions about it.

Contrary to what Islamic apologists say, Muslims are not used to having elements of their faith questioned or criticized. They should get used to it. Those who are interested in resisting cultural jihad ought to take every opportunity to question the truth claims of Islam. As long as jihadists are kept secure in the illusion that their faith is unassailable, they will continue the jihad by whatever means seem most expedient. They won't question their faith—and neither will the majority of Muslims—unless they get used to the fact that it can be questioned and criticized.

We are told that reforming Islam is something only Muslims can do. But it's beginning to look as if they could use some help. I'm suggesting, however, that something more radical than reform is needed—which means they will need considerable help. One way to help is by casting doubts—by asking the hard questions about Islam that are seldom asked. But these challenges should be coupled with a positive presentation of the Christian faith. We can help Muslims to rethink their faith by taking pains to inform them that there are spiritual alternatives they might consider. The fact is, the average Muslim knows very little about Christianity beyond some simple caricatures. And for their part, Christian churches do little to fill in the picture for them. During one Catholic-Muslim forum, the Muslim delegation's coleader, Seyyed Hossein Nasr, complained of "aggressive proselytizing" by Christians in Muslim-majority states. But the facts are otherwise: the historic Christian churches in the Middle East don't proselytize; and because of the risks involved, they even discourage potential converts to Christianity.[1] Of course, you can't blame them. But it's another matter when Christians in the West fail to get their message across while they still have the freedom to do so. Too many Christians are still locked into the accommodation-at-any-price mode—such as the Catholic bishops of England and Wales who want to have Muslim prayer rooms created in every Roman Catholic school, along with special toilet facilities. For many Christians, devotion to diversity is the new measure of faith. We now tend to deplore the older triumphalist Catholic attitude that announced the truth of the faith unapologetically; but it gave others something to think about, and it kept the Church from falling into the category of religions that are, as one Egyptian cleric recently put it, "utterly humiliated"—and thus of utterly no interest to Muslims.

The evidence is mounting that Christian reticence doesn't make the world a safer place; it makes it more dangerous. This dhimmi posture only feeds into the conviction, widespread in the Muslim world, that Christians have nothing to teach them, that Christian silence is a tacit acknowledgment of the superiority of Islam and of its right to rule over others. In short, by creating a perception of weakness and irresolution, Christians are inviting continued jihad. If Muslims are ever going to rethink the truth claims of Islam, they need to know about other standards of truth—let's even say a higher standard. Thanks in part to Christian reticence, most Muslims know very little about the alternative.

In a totalitarian society, silent resistance may be the only choice. Otherwise, silence is not a virtue—at least not when it comes to preserving your beliefs and values. Historian James Hitchcock once wrote an article for the *American Scholar* on "The Dynamics of Popular Intellectual Change" that seems pertinent here. "Ideas and movements", wrote Hitchcock, "are either in the ascendancy or in the decline". He cautioned that one way of ensuring that your movement is in decline is to keep your beliefs to yourself or else to speak about them tentatively or apologetically.[2]

Hitchcock observed, "There is perhaps no surer sign of a group's imminent decline than the unwillingness of its spokesmen to talk

confidently and aggressively in public about its purposes and beliefs." [3]
On the other hand, rising groups are confident and self-assured, and
their representatives are able to speak compellingly about their beliefs
and goals: "Rising groups succeed precisely because they claim to have
the truth and are able to convince significant numbers of people that
they do." [4]

Hitchcock wrote this in 1976, long before Islam began flexing its
muscles, but it's clear that his list of the characteristics of rising movements fits Islam like a glove, while his corresponding list of the characteristics of declining movements seems to describe the condition of
the West. Take this observation:

> Groups that become diffident about their beliefs in the public forum,
> that renounce the desire to make converts, that profess to see broad
> areas of agreement between themselves and other groups and admit
> there are many roads to the same destination, that acknowledge the
> dogmatism and rigidity of their past—these are usually groups that have
> begun to doubt their own legitimacy at some profound level. [5]

That could be a description of a typical public-school curriculum committee trying to decide how best to apologize for Western history, or
it could be a description of a conference of bishops debating whether
missionary work is offensive to native populations. Thanks to the work
of multiculturalists, it's difficult to find many bold spokesmen for either
Western civilization or the Church.

But fortune favors the bold; so if Western Christianity is again to
become a rising religion, it needs to recover some boldness. The
churches need boldness in the first place to re-inspire or reassure
their own members, and in the second, to attract potential converts.
Those converts ought to include Muslims. Conversions are a game
changer, not just because they shift the numbers balance, but also
because they speak volumes about the side converts are defecting
away from. That's why the Communists in Eastern Europe went to
great lengths—miles of walls, barbed wire, and guard posts—to prevent defections. That's also why the West ought to make a lot of
noise about the sharia death penalty for apostates. The complete discrediting of that practice would be the religious equivalent of tearing
down the Berlin Wall. In addition to that, Christians and non-
Christians in the West ought to keep up a steady barrage on a whole
range of Islamic beliefs and practices.

Ordinarily it's not a good idea to go around questioning other people's firmly held beliefs. But these are not ordinary times, and Islam is no ordinary religion. Under sharia, the beliefs of non-Muslims are of little consequence: other religions are considered inferior and are treated as such. The rules of dhimmitude specifically require the humiliation of Christians and Jews. Just ask a Coptic Christian or a Chaldean Christian—if you can find one who's not afraid to speak up. So, by reason of its supremacist claims, Islam deserves scrutiny. Those who declare their religion to be the only acceptable one should be prepared to answer a few questions.

For instance, what's the evidence that Muhammad actually received a revelation from God? Unless you accept military conquest alone as proof of a divine mandate, there's not much to go on; as Christians long ago pointed out, making conquest by itself a sign of divine favor would put Genghis Khan and Attila the Hun in line for prophethood. Here are two more questions: If Muhammad's revelations were from God, why did so many of them work directly to Muhammad's personal advantage and to the disadvantage of others? And if the Koran is the dictated word of God, why is the Koran, despite its flashes of poetic brilliance, put together like a Soviet-era automobile?

Asking Muslims such questions may seem uncharitable, but there is no charity without clarity; and right now clarity is in short supply. Many Muslims seem to labor under the impression that the West's failure to respond to its theological claims is a sign of the speechless awe that Islamic truth justly inspires. The West, for its part, insists on chivalrously shielding Islam from the kind of scrutiny that the West reserves for its own institutions and traditions. And with good reason. Because it's generally understood, though rarely said, that Muhammad's claims would not meet the tests of critical reason and historical evidence that we apply to the Judeo-Christian revelation. The much-revered Sufi theologian al-Ghazali wrote, "The dhimmi is obliged not to mention Allah or His Prophet".[6] You can see why. Curiosity didn't kill Christianity, but curiosity would almost certainly kill the caliphate— or, in our times, the hope for a resurrected caliphate.

Obliged not to mention the prophet? Given the threat Islam poses to the world and to Muslims themselves, it's beginning to look as though the obligation runs the other way. To paraphrase another prophet, "There is a time for politeness, and a time for frankness." If the time for politeness is not entirely past, it is, at the least, certainly time for a polite frankness. Fr. Zakaria Botros, a Coptic priest who broadcasts a program in Arabic for *Life TV* provides an example of the kind of questions that need to be asked about him-who-must-not-be-mentioned. During one program, Father Botros focused on the hallmarks of "prophethood", and he began by asking: "Was Muhammad the prophet a moral man—the most upright man, worthy of being emulated by the world?" Before proceeding, Father Botros asked his Muslim audience to keep in mind the question: "Is this the prophet I follow?" Then, reading from hadith and other well-attested Islamic sources, he went through a catalogue of Muhammad's sexual habits. These included descriptions of the prophet's homosexual tendencies, his transvestite tendencies, and his sexual attraction to children. After reading the Islamic sources in all their painful detail, Father Botros repeated his initial question: "Is this the prophet I follow? . . . Are these the activities of the man described in the Koran as being the pinnacle of moral perfection?"

Father Botros then interrupted himself to apologize to the Muslims in his audience who might find these revelations disturbing. His cohost, an ex-Muslim, reassured him, "It's not your fault, Father, but rather the fault of those Muslims recording these vile incidences. Either way, Muslims must know. More please." [7]

Yes, that says it rather succinctly: "Muslims must know. More please."

And it wouldn't hurt if non-Muslims knew and understood more. For example, how many know about the "revelations of convenience"— revelations that seem tailored to get Muhammad out of a jam or to resolve a dispute in his favor? Once, when there was a dispute over the division of spoils after the Battle of Badr, Muhammad received a revelation that one-fifth of the spoils belonged to God and his apostle (8:41). On another occasion, he received a revelation allowing him to marry his daughter-in-law (33:37). Another revelation allowed Muhammad to marry as many wives as he desired, though other Muslim men were limited to four (33:50). In another revelation, Allah freed Muhammad from his oath to one of his wives that he would stay away from his concubine Mary (66:1–4). Muhammad's ability to produce self-serving revelations should give pause to those who think the Koran is divinely inspired. Even his young wife Aisha was amazed. After one of the convenient revelations, she sceptically remarked, "Truly thy Lord makes haste to do thy bidding." The prophet is Islam's main prop. If he is discredited, Islam is discredited—hence the mighty efforts to make it a crime to blaspheme the prophet. The fact that many Christians seem inclined to go along with these anti-blasphemy and anti-defamation initiatives is an indication of how naïve some of us have become. Currently, our whole society is in danger of ending up in dhimmitude because there are many aspects of Islam we decline to examine out of a misplaced sense of sensitivity.

"Is this the prophet I follow?" It's a good question to pose to the members of an honor culture because, with all its faults, an honor culture is still based on a sense of honor. But if the prophet you follow turns out to be a dishonorable man, what then? Eventually your own honor as a man is at stake. If it turns out that the prophet was not only a sexual deviant but also a habitual hypocrite, it's a reflection on your own character if you continue to follow him. That's why it's important to insist, as Father Botros does, that Muslims confront the full truth about Muhammad. Would such questioning of the prophet's character provoke anger among Muslims? Undoubtedly, yes. The first time a Muslim hears the moral flaws of the prophet exposed, he might well be angry at the exposer. But how about the third time? The tenth time? The twentieth time? What initially provokes anger might eventually provoke doubts. According to a piece by Islamic scholar Raymond Ibrahim, "The outrage [over Father Botros] appears to be subsiding." Ibrahim contends that Life TV "has conditioned its Muslim viewers to accept that exposure and criticism of their prophet is here to stay." [8]

Islam may be a seventh-century ideology, but Muslims can't quite get away from the fact that they live in the twenty-first century. They can't help but be aware that much of the world lives by, or at least professes, a set of standards different from those established by Muhammad, and this knowledge is bound to create some cognitive dissonance. It's in the interest of the civilized world to increase that dissonance. The best way to do that is for those who have been shaped by Western/Christian standards to honor those standards and stop apologizing for them. At the same time, they need to call Islam to task for failing to meet those standards. Would this make Muslims feel uncomfortable? Hopefully, it would. That's the point. We should want them to be uncomfortable with their faith—uncomfortable to the point at which more and more Muslims come to the conclusion reached by Kemal Atatürk, the founder of the Turkish secular state, who once described Islam as the "theology of an immoral Arab".

Father Botros's sceptical approach toward Islam might seem to some like a violation of the sensitivity code: "With all our sins, what right have we to take another faith to task?" That's one way to look at it. But on the other hand, the sins of Christians are not modeled for them by the founder of their religion. Most Muslims don't know the full story about their faith or its founder. If the majority of Muslims really are moderately inclined, they deserve some help in better understanding the immoderate and immoral system in which they are caught up. Therein lies a more genuine kind of sensitivity toward Muslims.

The point of a propaganda war is to sow the seeds of doubt in the minds of your opponents. It does not necessarily involve spreading falsehoods, but it does involve spreading information. One might add that, to break down resistance, an information campaign must be conducted in a somewhat relentless fashion. Father Botros' effectiveness is due to the factual, checkable nature of his presentations, to his lack of hesitation in saying what ought to be said, and to his saying it over and over. His success in conditioning his audience to accept criticism brings us back to James Hitchcock's discussion of rising groups and their ability to speak confidently about their beliefs and goals. One could make the case that the formula for success is even simpler than that. It almost boils down to "Just keep talking." Islam is based on falsehoods, but the propaganda campaign carried out by Islamic apologists has been largely successful because they have not been reluctant to make their case.

This kind of persistence also characterizes one of the most successful propaganda programs of recent times—the campaign to normalize homosexuality. In a 1987 article and later in a book, homosexual activists Marshall Kirk and Hunter Madsen outlined a strategy for ensuring public acceptance of homosexuality. Their basic recommendation was simply to bring the discussion out into the open and keep it there. They argued that the "fastest way to convince straights that homosexuality is commonplace is to get a lot of people talking about the subject in a neutral or supportive way. Open, frank talk makes gayness seem less furtive." Their goal, they said, was to get the public to the "shoulder-shrug stage".[9] In a way, that is what Father Botros has accomplished with his Muslim audience. He has conditioned them to listen to a message they would ordinarily refuse to hear.

A Christian's first priority should be to tell the truth; but on the principle that Christians sometimes need to be "as wise as serpents", it might be wise to take a page from the Kirk/Madsen playbook and make every effort to keep the conversation alive by putting forth the case for Christianity in an unabashed way. The case for Christianity is quite strong. The claim that the Koran is an authentic revelation has little basis in reality. Just as we pressed the Cold War case that communism was an unrealistic and unworkable system maintained only by deception, Christians should take advantage of Islam's many weaknesses and press the far more compelling case for Christianity—while we still can.

Unless you believe in the myth that the problem we face is some tiny splinter group called radical Islam rather than Islam itself, then the logical response to Islam's aggressiveness is to do everything we can to force Islam to question its faith in itself. Why? Because, as Mark Steyn observed, "There's no market for a faith that has no faith in itself." [10] He was speaking, of course, of the more mushy versions of Western Christianity. But it's a good point to keep in mind, because, unless I'm wide of the mark, loss of faith is the fate we should wish for Islam. Or, to come at it from a different direction, just what are the arguments for a strong and confident Islam? Offhand I can't think of any. There are undoubtedly some Islamic experts who still think in Marxist categories and assume that the Islamic faith will act as an opiate on the masses instead of as a stimulant. This just goes to show that some experts can't tell their opiates from their amphetamines.

That's not to say Muslims don't derive consolation from their faith in God and from their prayers. Many undoubtedly do. God hears all prayers and answers them in appropriate ways. Along with the consolations of religion, however, many Muslims, especially Muslim women, suffer from the feeling of being trapped in a fourteen-hundred-year nightmare, with no way out. One indication of their desperation is that women in Islamic societies have high rates of mental illness and suicide. For example, Iran has the third-highest rate of suicide in the world, and most of those who take their own lives are women. According to Ibn Warraq "In Ilam, a western province of Iran ... about 70 percent of those who commit suicide are reported to be women, most of them between seventeen and thirty-five years old". [11]

Muslims who have left Islam don't generally talk in terms of reforming Islam, but rather in terms of freeing themselves and other Muslims from its bondage. On the Internet one can read countless testimonials from former Muslims, describing the various types of physical and psychological coercion aimed at controlling their thoughts and actions and keeping them within the confines of Islam. In her book *Allah is Dead*, Rebecca Bynum maintains that Islam creates in its adherents a powerful inner "thought police" that reduces them to spiritual slavery. Therefore, Bynum contends, the best way to serve our Muslim brethren is to help free them from the "totalitarian thought-system" in which they are ensnared:

> We seek only to free them from this tyranny and allay the deep spiritual suffering caused by Islam, and we do this from the most altruistic of motives, that of love and concern for Muslims as human beings; human beings who are trapped, through no fault of their own, in a totalitarian system of physical, mental and spiritual repression.[12]

It's difficult to see any convincing argument for propping up a system that oppresses so many people. On the contrary, it seems almost a duty to undermine that system and call it into question at every turn. So yes, let's take every opportunity to give Muslims second thoughts about their faith. After all, in our own culture we consider it a salutary thing to shake up someone's faith—especially if his faith is in Christianity or the American way. If done in the right spirit, asking people to question their faith *is* a reasonable thing to do. Everyone should make sure his faith has some basis in facts and is not simply wish fulfillment or a dangerous delusion. But that rule ought to apply to Muslims and atheists as well as to Christians. One purpose of this book is to encourage Muslims and atheists to reexamine their beliefs. But they're not likely to do that if Christians don't present the alternative in an unapologetic way. To repeat Steyn's observation, "There's no market for a faith that has no faith in itself".

16

What Christians Should Do

If you get your information mainly from the mainstream media, you may gain the impression that all is fairly quiet on the Western front, that having killed some important leaders of al-Qaeda and foiled some terrorist plots, we are safe from Islamist aggression. But if you dig a little deeper, you will gain a different impression—namely, that the West is on a collision course with Islam. How did we get to this point? Let's recap the argument so far:

- Islam poses a serious threat to Western culture, to Christians and Jews, in fact, to all non-Muslim religions and cultures. Whether the threat comes from "jihadists", "Islamists", "radical Islam", or Islam itself seems increasingly to be an academic question. There are certainly plenty of moderate Muslims in the world, but it's difficult to make the case that Islam is the cause of that moderation. Until the Iranian Revolution ushered in a trend reversal, many Muslim countries—Egypt, Iran, Pakistan— were more moderate than they are today. But could it be that the moderate Muslims were the ones who "hijacked" Islam by ignoring its harsher mandates? And could it be that the radicals are the ones who are restoring their religion to its pure form?

- Multiculturalists in the West have aided and abetted Islamic aggression by sapping cultural confidence and by making it nearly impossible to discuss and debate the dangers of a resurgent Islam. As Mark Steyn puts it, "It's hard to deliver a wake-up call for a civilization so determined to smother the alarm clock in the soft, fluffy pillow of multiculturalism." [1]

- In Europe, the rise of militant Islam has coincided with a loss of Christian faith. Bruce Bawer, the author of *While Europe Slept*, left America because he wanted to distance himself from Christian fundamentalists and evangelicals. But after a few years in de-Christianized Europe, he had second thoughts: "I was beginning to see that when Christian faith had departed, it had taken with it a sense of ultimate meaning and purpose—and left the continent vulnerable to conquest by people with deeper faith and stronger convictions." [2]

■ If the loss of Christian faith is a large part of the problem, a revival of Christianity is the best hope of regaining that "sense of ultimate meaning and purpose" necessary to resist Islamization. In *Decline and Fall*, Bruce Thornton observes that "Europe's slow motion suicide" results from "the lack of a unifying belief and set of values that can substitute for an abandoned Christianity".[3] But what if there is no substitute for Christianity? It's becoming increasingly apparent that there is none.

What's the next step? The logical answer to the Islamic threat is a Christian rethinking and renewal. We can't expect Muslims to rethink their faith if we don't rekindle our own. The ideological struggle with Islam is in large part a spiritual struggle. It will be won by those with the deepest faith and strongest sense of purpose. Many Christians, of course, have lost their sense of purpose. How might they recover it?

The first, most important step is simply to sound the alarm. Like others in the West, Christians need to wake up to the dangers of Islamic expansion. More to the point, they need to wake up in time. We are not at the beginning of a civilizational war with Islam; the war is already at least two-thirds over. Who is winning?—naturally enough, the side that fully realizes they are at war. Something similar happened with the culture wars. The forces of militant secularism had been waging war against Christian values for decades before Christians—some of them, at least—finally woke up and noticed they were under fire. This belated recognition on the part of Christians led to victory after victory for the secularists. Although Christians have had occasional successes in blocking pro-abortion initiatives, other fronts have been almost totally lost. For example, Christians in this country may soon face legal penalties if they dare to stand up to secular doctrines about homosexuality.

As tough as the culture wars have been, the civilizational struggle to resist Islamization will be much more difficult. It will require Christians to stand up not only to jihadists, but also to the enablers of jihad, both Christian and secular. In addition it will require them to overcome the effects of a decades-long disinformation campaign engineered by Muslim organizations and obligingly transmitted by the mainstream media. Finally, it will require an effort to overcome a long-standing inclination on the part of Christians to think well of all religions.

Whatever the causes of Christian complacency, it's urgent that Christians start informing themselves about the nature and extent of the Islamic threat. Most Christians in America simply don't know about the massacres of Christians in Africa, the full mosques and empty churches in Europe, or the worldwide reach of Saudi-funded indoctrination. Why is awareness the most important step? Because once Christians realize the seriousness of the situation, other things will begin to fall into place. It will be easier to see what's important and what isn't. What was it that Samuel Johnson said? "When a man knows he is to be hanged in a fortnight, it concentrates his mind wonderully."

Christians also need to wake up to the fact that Christianity is not in good shape in the West, not even in the United States. America is much further away from the falls than Europe; but as recent polls suggest, America is becoming less Christian, more secular, and thus more prone to the kind of anomie that has enfeebled Europe. Furthermore, of those who count themselves as Christians, many seem to prefer watered-down versions of the faith. To a large extent, American religion has been secularized and desacralized. Churches borrow so freely from the worlds of therapy, entertainment, business, and advertising that it's often difficult to see the difference between the Church and the world. This informal, we're-just-folks style might be good for getting people inside the church doors, but not necessarily for keeping them there. American Christians are notorious church hoppers, and often they're shopping for a better emotional or therapeutic experience rather than for an increase in sanctity. In order to combat the pull of secularism, Christians need to work to recover the sense of the sacred.

Traditionally, the Christian life has involved a slow reshaping of our lives—partly our own work and mostly God's—to become more like Christ. Christ accomplished his work through the mystery of his suffering, and so it seems likely that much of Christian growth will take place in the same way. It looks as if we are heading into an era of prolonged struggle, suffering, and sacrifice that will demand much of Christians and will be difficult to comprehend in secular or therapeutic terms. Early Christians understood that their lives might be required for their faith. Christians in the West today have their own personal struggles concerning health, family, and finances, but few have had to think in terms of suffering for their faith. That time may be coming. And it will require Christians to think as much about the worldwide community of believers as they do about their personal walk with Jesus.

Christian renewal also depends on family renewal. That requires a reemphasis on sexual morality, on the sanctity of marriage, and on the rewards and duties of family life. America doesn't lack for children the way Europe does, but a lot of those children aren't growing up in stable circumstances. The marriage rate has plunged 50 percent since 1970; the nation's divorce rate is the world's highest; and out-of-wedlock births have soared sevenfold since 1960.[4] So our population picture is not as pretty as a simple birthrate figure would suggest. Children who are coping with highly unstable home environments could see Islam as a solution rather than as a problem.

In addition to taking marriage more seriously in their own lives, Christians need to do a better job of resisting attempts to alter the meaning of marriage. The push for alternative forms of marriage not only undercuts the special status of marriage, but also paves the way for legalized polygamy. The biggest beneficiaries of the gay-marriage movement will be polygamous Muslim men. Polygamy, in turn, accelerates the birthrate imbalance, which, in turn, makes the eventual recognition of sharia that much more likely. This is one of the patterns now unfolding in Europe. The bottom line is this: homeland-security measures are important, but they don't matter nearly as much as making American homes more secure places for raising children. And the best way to achieve that is to recover the sense of marriage as a sacred vocation.

What other elements are necessary for a Christian revival? Neither family renewal nor Christian renewal will get very far without a reemphasis on the masculine nature of Christianity. In one sense, the feminization of Christianity simply means that there are more women in church than men; in another sense, it means that Christianity is perceived as something weak and unmanly. The masculine spirit of the band of brothers who first launched Christianity needs to be recaptured to attract more men to Christianity and also to counter the masculine appeal of Islam.

If the masculine side of Christianity needs to be reemphasized, so also does the masculine nature of Christ. The power and authority of Christ is a central element in the Gospels, yet our therapeutic culture prefers to picture Christ as mild and sensitive. But if the squishy portrayal of Christ hasn't gone over particularly well with the males of the therapeutic society, what are the chances of its exciting the imaginations of males in a totally non-therapeutic culture? We hear a lot about how important it is to understand things from the perspective of another culture and to respond in kind. Well, in Islamic culture, the truth of a religion is judged mainly in terms of power. Power, in fact, is the proof of Islam's legitimacy. Muhammad didn't produce any miracles, but his conquests and those of his successors constitute a miracle in the eyes of many Muslims. And as the Muslim population grows younger, the argument from strength grows more appealing. If Christians want to speak to Muslim concerns, they should address this concern with power. Leaving aside the desire to subdue others, power is, of course, a perfectly legitimate religious category. After all, God is by definition supremely powerful.

So, in addition to proclaiming the loving side of Christianity, it makes sense to present the powerful side as well. Not to put too fine a point on it, but who wants to be loved by a weakling? The Christ portrayed in the Gospels is hardly that. He subdues chain-bursting demoniacs, commands storms, and, in the end, defeats death and the powers of hell. Christ's kingdom is not of this world, but he made it known that he did have a kingdom, and that it was within his power to summon legions of angels.

We hear a lot these days about the "hidden gospels": the Gospel of Bartholomew, the Gospel of Mary, and the Gospel of the Egyptians. Well, if you've ever read the hidden gospels, you can see why they went into hiding. They make for fairly drowsy reading. There is, however, a "hidden" gospel that's well worth reading. The theme of Christ's power and authority practically dominates the four Gospels, but it might as well be hidden for all the emphasis it gets— which is too bad because, at least from the point of view of a boy or a young man, that is the most interesting theme. The power of Christ is one of the initial attractions that Christianity has for the young. It impressed me as a boy in Catholic school, and I suspect it impressed others of my age. The sentiment I felt could be summed up along the lines of, "Wow! He could really do that!" Christ could not only feel pity for the blind and the crippled; he could actually do something about it.

Unlike the unimpressive Jesus of the Koran, Christ is a man of action. Read the first few pages of Mark's Gospel. Almost all of it is taken up with displays of Christ's power: his recruitment of the fishermen, the exorcism of a man possessed by an unclean spirit, the curing of Peter's mother-in-law, the healing of numerous people who had gathered around Peter's house, the cleansing of a leper, the curing of a paralytic, the announcement that he also had the power to forgive sins, the recruitment of Levi, and the healing of the man with a withered hand. When it comes to fighting evil and coming to the aid of people in trouble, Christ's schedule is as busy as Spiderman's.

The point is, the Muslim obsession with power is not altogether misguided. After all, without it, words are just words. What makes the Christian conception of power different from Islam's is that it is not an arbitrary power, but power that is inseparable from love and truth, justice and mercy. Islam spread by the power of the sword, Christianity spread because of its powerful message of sacrificial love. It is an immensely comforting message, of course—this story of Christ's suffering and dying to redeem our lives—but it's comforting only if Jesus was not a hapless victim but the Son of God who indeed possessed the power to accomplish his mission. On that score he left little doubt. Consider these words from the Gospel of John: "I lay down my life, that I may take it again. No one takes it from me, but I lay it down of my own accord. I have power to lay it down, and I have power to take it again" (Jn 10:17–18).

What's more, Christ's power extends to the power of final judgment, the power to separate the sheep from the goats: "For the Son of man is to come with his angels in the glory of his Father, and then he will repay every man for what he has done" (Mt 16:27). Repay every man for what he has done? Muslims seem unimpressed with assurances by trendy Christians that we are truly openminded and non-judgmental. The possibility that Christ will judge all mankind when he comes again might make a deeper impression.

Christ's standard of judgment (what one does to the weakest is done to him) is a reason Christianity has been a defender of human dignity and rights. Perhaps it is time for Christians to champion those who are most oppressed in Muslim societies. Amnesty International reported in 2011 that throughout predominately Muslim North Africa and the

Middle East "virtually all women" are at risk of "gender-based violence".[5] Abusive treatment of women is also prevalent among Muslim
immigrants living in Europe, though estimates of such behavior vary.
An editor for the German Turkish newspaper *Hurriyet* guessed that 50
percent of Muslim women living in Germany have been the victims
of domestic violence.[6] In 2011, the German Federal Ministry of the
Family reported 3,443 forced marriages in a single year. Seventy percent of the victims were physically abused to convince them to marry.
Since the report was based only on women who sought help at coun-
seling centers, the real number of coerced marriages is likely much
higher.[7] Britain also is experiencing an epidemic of forced marriages,
as well as of other practices that were once thought confined to backward societies. According to an article in the *Telegraph*, up to one
hundred thousand women in Britain have undergone genital mutilation.[8]

For Christians not to speak out about wife-beating, forced marriages, genital mutilation, and honor killings is a failure of charity, as
well as a failure of courage. Christians are supposed to stand up for
the downtrodden, the oppressed, and the abused. Some Christians might
object that it's none of their business to comment on the practices of
other cultures or religions, but that's a contemporary cultural-diversity
defense, not a Christian one. Christianity, like Islam, makes universal
claims, not culturally specific ones. Christians can accommodate plenty
of cultural differences, but they can't pretend that honor killings are
legitimate cultural variations.

What else should Christians do in the face of Islamic assertiveness?
I've offered several broad proposals, and at this point it is customary,
and usually prudent, to say something along the lines of "more detailed
recommendations are beyond the scope of this study". But the current crisis is so acute that there simply isn't time to wait for the definitive book of recommendations to hit the bookstores. So here are a
few additional and more detailed suggestions for resisting Islamization.

Christians should not sign on to the anti-blasphemy campaign. In
the long run it will only have the effect of silencing Christians. It has
that effect in the short run, too. In Pakistan, a Christian woman is
under sentence of death for insulting the prophet Muhammad. When
the pope called for her release, thousands demonstrated in Karachi to
denounce the pope and to support the blasphemy laws. Shortly after,
two prominent Pakistani government officials who opposed the blasphemy laws were killed. But the blasphemy laws don't just apply to

Christians living in Muslim lands; they apply to Christians everywhere. Non-Muslims all over Western Europe have been subject to heresy trials for defaming the prophet and his religion, and the reach of the blasphemy laws now extends to the United States.

Molly Norris, a cartoonist at the *Seattle Weekly*, had to give up her job, change her identity, and go into hiding as a result of a fatwa issued against her by Anwar al-Awlaki in 2010. Norris started the idea of Everybody Draw Muhammad Day and quickly apologized once she understood the ramifications. But by that time, al-Awklaki had decided that her "proper abode is hellfire". Molly Norris? Perhaps the name doesn't ring a bell. Most of her colleagues in the media didn't have much to say about the matter. When asked for a statement about Norris, both the American Society of News Editors and the Society of Professional Journalists declined to comment. We've all heard about the "Unsinkable Molly Brown", but Molly Norris seems to have sunk out of sight without a trace. She failed to grasp in time the new rules of the game: Islam must be free from insult.[9]

The Organization of the Islamic Cooperation (OIC), which represents fifty-seven member states, has been pushing the United Nations to enforce universal blasphemy laws. The defamation of a prophet would then be a criminal offense in Europe and the United States as it is in Pakistan and Saudi Arabia. Muslims want Christians to join them in their "stop defamation" campaign, and it is, of course, a great temptation to Christians. Who wants to have their religion defamed? Still, it is a temptation to be avoided. The defamation laws are aimed at strangling legitimate criticisms of Islam, including criticisms that Christians may feel duty-bound to make. If you have no plans to defame any religion, you may think you have nothing to worry about, but think again. Christianity itself is inherently a criticism of Islam's claim to have the final revelation. Simply to assert the divinity of Christ is a blasphemy of the highest order by Islamic standards. If you are a believing Christian, you are already a blasphemer in the eyes of Islam. Those who think that anti-hate, anti-defamation, and anti-blasphemy laws will somehow protect the interests of all religions haven't quite grasped the big picture.

The OIC's anti-blasphemy campaign is one part of a larger worldwide movement to suppress free speech. It may well be the most important front in the civilizational struggle with Islam. Freedom of speech is, of course, a prerequisite for the freedom to know. If the West is not allowed to know the truth about Islam's aggressive designs, the extent of stealth jihad, or the goals of the Muslim Brotherhood, it can't very well defend itself. Take, for example, the trial of Elisabeth Sabaditsch-Wolff—a pivotal event in modern European jurisprudence. In effect, the verdict placed the principles of sharia above the right to freedom of expression. Not since the disgraceful show trial of Cardinal Mindszenty in 1949 have Europeans witnessed a greater travesty of justice. Yet Americans knew about the Mindszenty trial, while no one who relies exclusively on the mainstream media for news would know about the trial of Sabaditsch-Wolff. As Bruce Bawer writes:

> With the exception of a syndicated Diana West column entitled "A New Silent Night Descends on Austria", a series of Google searches didn't turn up a single report on Sabaditsch-Wolff's appeals verdict in any newspaper in the Western world—certainly not any major one. A search on the *New York Times* website for any mention of Sabaditsch-Wolff since 1981 yielded the following strangely chilling sentence: "Your search for Elisabeth Sabaditsch-Wolff in all fields returned 0 results".[10]

Judging by the heresy trials in Europe and the self-censorship of the press in the United States, we are losing badly on the free-speech front.

Viewed in terms of multiculturalist manners, it may be that critics of Islam such as Wilders, Steyn, and Sabaditsch-Wolff have gone too far. They violated the code of sensitivity. But viewed in terms of a struggle for survival, they have done the rest of us a great service. If you must fight a war, the time to fight it is when you can still win, especially if it looks as if your enemy will develop an overwhelmingly superior force. The same applies to a war of ideas. The time to fight such a war is when you are still free to express your ideas. Unless you prefer being a martyr to your beliefs, the best time to speak out is while contrary beliefs can still be openly considered and debated. If, out of politeness, political correctness, or simply fear, you put off making your case, you may never get the chance to make it. The preemptive attempts to silence Geert Wilders, Elizabeth Sabaditsch-Wolff, and many others suggest that Europeans are dangerously close to the point of having waited too long.

The average Christian won't have many opportunities to vote on UN laws restricting free speech, but he can speak up in his own parish or congregation. In many churches, the full story about Islam is being suppressed by Islam's well-meaning Christian enablers. This is a challenge that the ordinary Christian in the pew can take on if he prepares properly. Christians need solid and accurate information about Islam, not seminars in sophistry. Instead of inviting trained Muslim apologists, skilled in the art of taqiyya, to explain Islam to unwary parishioners, churches should be urged to invite ex-Muslims who have converted to Christianity. A short list would include Walid Shoebat, Nonie Darwish, Kamal Saleen, and Mark Gabriel. These are people who are in a position to understand both faiths and to explain Islam accurately. There are also a good number of cradle Christians who can impart solid teaching about Islam. Brigitte Gabriel's group ACT! for America has local chapters all over the country that can provide lists of speakers. Church groups can also make use of a number of good documentaries on Islam. The Clarion Fund has produced three: *Obsession: Radical Islam's War against the West; The Third Jihad: Radical Islam's Vision for America;* and *Iranium,* a film whose title is self-explanatory. Coral Ridge Ministries also has produced informative documentaries on Islam. These include *Radical Islam on the March* and *Islam: Religion of Peace?*

Of course, one of the best ways for the individual Christian to bring himself up to speed on Islam is by reading. Christians ought to familiarize themselves with the Koran, but because it is such a confusing book, they might want to supplement it with Robert Spencer's *Complete Infidel's Guide to the Koran* or something similar. Beyond that, there are a number of recent books on Islam from which to choose. Among the most reliable authors are Robert Spencer, Brigitte Gabriel, Nonie Darwish, Melanie Phillips, Mark Durie, Andrew McCarthy, Fr. Samir Khalil Samir, Mark Steyn, Bruce Thornton, Joel Richardson, Walid Shoebat, Wafa Sultan, and Serge Trifkovic. Those of a more scholarly bent might want to look into the works of Bat Ye'or or Andrew Bostom. For a look at the link between radical Islam and the radical left, read Jamie Glazov's *United in Hate.* For a better understanding of sharia, the book to read is *Shariah, the Threat to America,* published by the Center for Security Policy. Those who are interested in keeping up with daily news and commentary on Islam might visit on the Internet *Jihad Watch* or *FrontPage* although there are dozens of other fine websites from which to choose. One of the initial benefits of consulting the Web is the realization that much of the news about Islam is either ignored or slanted by the mainstream media.

In his First Letter to the Corinthians, Saint Paul asks, "And if the bugle gives an indistinct sound, who will get ready for battle?" (1 Cor 14:8). By and large, the churches have not provided a clear message on the subject of Islam. The sound given out by church leaders is an uncertain sound, to say the least. What are Christians supposed to believe about Islam? It's difficult to say. Official Catholic Church pronouncements on Islam are short on content. One way the Catholic Church could remedy the situation would be to issue a new document on Islam to supplement the inadequate treatment in *Nostra Aetate* and in the *Catechism of the Catholic Church*. The purpose of *Nostra Aetate* was to promote "unity and love among men" and to consider "what men have in common and what draws them to fellowship". The purpose of the short section on Muslims was not so much to instruct Catholics about Islam as to provide the beginning basis for dialogue and mutual understanding between the two faiths. Likewise, the short statement in the *Catechism* is simply not sufficient for any adequate understanding of Islam.

What is needed now is a full discussion of Islam that compares and contrasts it with Christianity. It would serve not as a stepping stone for outreach to Muslims, but as an informational guide for Catholics and other Christians to help them better understand what is now the fastest-growing religion in the West. In the meantime, Christian leaders should reconsider just how much their flocks have in common with Islam and whether it is wise to keep referring to Islam as an "Abrahamic faith". This approach has served as a source of confusion to many and as a source of complacency to others. Thanks to the work of a number of capable scholars, we now know much more about Islam than we did when these concepts were introduced. As George Weigel writes, "To speak of Judaism, Christianity, and Islam as the 'three Abrahamic faiths,' the 'three religions of the Book,' or the 'three monotheisms' obscures rather than illuminates. These familiar tropes ought to be retired." [11]

In some respects, the churches have been behind the curve when it comes to addressing the expansion of Islam; in other respects, they have been far ahead of the curve. If all followers of Christ had remained faithful to traditional Christian teaching on contraception and abortion, there would not have been a population vacuum for Islam to expand into. The march of events is making a lot of the modern notions about population control seem suddenly outdated. A rediscovery of the traditional Christian reverence for marriage and children would contribute far more to the survival of Western societies than all the hand-wringing about global warming or homophobia.

Europeans are facing extinction, not because they are insufficiently sensitive to matters of race, gender, and ecology, but because of a baby gap that resulted from being insufficiently attentive to traditional Christian teachings. What secularists have taught for the last forty years—do your own thing, easy divorce, contraception, sterilization, abortion, cultural relativism—now seems like a recipe for societal suicide. This is a good opportunity for the Catholic Church to remind the world why the "culture of death" is so named. In other words, the Catholic Church should not be shy about showing the connection between the contraceptive mindset and the demise of European culture.

Up to this point, I've outlined some steps that Christians should take to address the inadequate response to Islam within their own faith. But what can Christians do in their role as citizens? For example, what are they supposed to think about the proposed Ground Zero mosque or about sharia in America? What are they supposed to do?

Once again, the first order of business is simply to wake up. And, once again, this is not nearly as simple as it sounds, because waking up entails a radical revision of our thinking. Pre-9/11 patterns of thought will be of little help in resisting Islam. Many of our cherished assumptions will need to be reexamined and revised. For example, because much of Islam's radical agenda has been advanced under the banner of religious freedom, we may have to think far more deeply about the concept of freedom of religion than we have needed to in the past. Islam is a hybrid that doesn't fit into the usual categories; consequently, the solutions for dealing with it will not be of the beaten-path variety. Some of the recommendations for halting Islamization that are now being offered by security experts are certainly a departure from the well-trodden ways. They may strike some readers as unfair, un-American, uncharitable, and even un-Christian. Nevertheless, they deserve serious consideration.

Before looking at some of those recommendations, it's important to understand the overall complexity of the problem presented by stealth jihad. A secret twenty-page document written in 1991 by a member of the Board of Directors of the Muslim Brotherhood in North America sets forth the mission of the Brotherhood as a "settlement process" entailing a "grand jihad in eliminating and destroying the Western

civilization from within".[12] But the document goes beyond grand generalities. It lists eighteen departments within the overall organization,
each with its own particular jihad mission. These include the Dawa
and Educational Organization; the Political Organization; the Media
and Art Organization; the Economic Organization; the Scientific, Educational, and Professional Organization; the Cultural and Intellectual
Organization; the Social-Charitable Organization; the Youth Organization; the Women Organization; the Administrative Organization; the
Security Organization; and the Legal Organization. Needless to say,
each of these organizations is composed of several sub-divisions.[13] News
analysts often observe that the Muslim Brotherhood is the best organized political group in Egypt. You can see why.

The Muslim Brotherhood's plan is to infiltrate and influence almost
every area of public life. It follows that an effective resistance to
Islamization must also address a broad range of organizations: government, media, the courts, businesses, arts, entertainment, public
schools, and universities. A moment's thought will reveal that even
to begin to reverse Islam's march through these institutions will be
an enormous undertaking. How easy would it be to convince large
corporations to drop lucrative sharia-compliant financial units? How
easy would it be to convince textbook companies to rewrite their
books to reflect more accurate views of Islam and Christianity? How
easy would it be to convince educators to reverse their decades-old
multicultural policies? How about the universities? Considering their
built-in anti-American bias and their steady supply of Saudi money,
how easy would it be to convince them to present a balanced view
of Islam? (It's no coincidence that the universities were one of the
first targets of the Muslim Brotherhood. The Muslim Student Associations, which are offshoots of the Muslim Brotherhood, were first
introduced into American universities in the early 1960s.) Finally,
how easy would it be to convince the mainstream media to stop
covering up the extent of stealth jihad in our society? And while
we're on that topic, why is it that we are just now hearing about the
Muslim Brotherhood—and why only in connection with the revolution in Egypt?

None of these changes will be accomplished without a major shift
in thinking. Up to now, the ruling belief has been that all differences
can be accommodated and all cultural practices can peacefully coexist.
Our society casually accepts the notion that married couples may have

irreconcilable differences, but it can't countenance the possibility that irreconcilable differences may exist between cultures and ideologies. Consequently we balk at making the kind of choices that are now called for.

As an example of either/or thinking, consider some of the recommendations recently offered by Team B, a group of high-ranking security and intelligence experts:

- "Practices that promote shariah ... are incompatible with the Constitution and the freedoms it enshrines and must be proscribed."

- "To the extent that imams and mosques are being used to advocate shariah in America, they are promoting seditious activity and should be warned that they will be subject to investigation and prosecution."

- "Immigration of those who adhere to shariah must be precluded, as was previously done with adherents to the seditious ideology of communism." [14]

The main plank in the Team B platform is the outlawing of sharia on the grounds that it is not only unconstitutional but also anticonstitutional. According to the Team B report, the obligations of sharia "must be seen as an illegal effort to supplant our Constitution with another legal code". [15]

In line with this thinking, a number of states have recently proposed legislation that would, in effect, prevent sharia from gaining a foothold in their territory. During the November 2010 election, 70 percent of Oklahomans voted for a state constitutional amendment to prohibit Oklahoma courts from considering Islamic law in their deliberations. A federal district court judge then blocked the amendment on the grounds that it would favor one religion over another—a violation, she said, of the First Amendment. Following suit (so to speak), the liberal American Bar Association established a task force to prevent twenty-eight other states from banning sharia. Like the Oklahoma judge, the ABA invoked the First Amendment.

The judge and the ABA are insisting that we follow the beaten path—even if the path may lead us over the precipice. They are not alone. Any attempt to put limits on Islam's growth in this country is met with the standard argument that the First Amendment guarantees the free exercise of religion. During the debate over the proposed

Ground Zero mosque, many argued that the First Amendment guarantees that all religions be treated equally. Therefore, they said, if you would allow evangelical Christians to build a church near Ground Zero, you must allow Muslims to build their mosque and community center—otherwise, you would be guilty of employing a double standard. The Team B response to this contention is to draw a distinction between Islam and "sharia Islam": Muslims in the United States should have the right to worship Allah but not to practice sharia. The trouble is that the two are not so easily separated. Many Muslims consider sharia and Islam to be inextricable. The constitutions of most Islamic states enshrine sharia as the main source of law. In addition, the Pew Survey of Muslim attitudes found high support for sharia in the Muslim world, with two-thirds of Jordanians, Palestinians, and Egyptians agreeing that sharia must be the only source of legislation. Support for sharia is probably much lower among American Muslims; as in the Catholic Church, however, matters of doctrine are not decided by popular vote in Islam. Islamic scholars do not consider sharia to be manmade; they look upon it as divinely ordained. Thus, the dictates of sharia are no more optional for Muslims than are the Ten Commandments for Christians. In this regard, it's telling that the man behind the Ground Zero mosque—Imam Feisal Abdul Rauf—has made the advancement of sharia his main project. Although the media portrayed Rauf as a model of Muslim moderation, he, like most imams, is well aware of the obligatory nature of sharia. In a 2009 *Huffington Post* essay entitled "What Shariah Law Is All About", Rauf wrote, "What Muslims want is a judiciary that ensures that the laws are not in conflict with the Qur'an and the Hadith."[16] What he advocates, in short, is a sharia-compliant America.

One way to reply to the First Amendment argument is to say that while the religious aspect of Islam is protected, the legal aspect (sharia) is not. Another way is to assert that Islam doesn't qualify as a religious faith. Proponents of this view hold that Islam is a political ideology, not a religion, and therefore is not protected by the freedom-of-religion clause. Geert Wilders has claimed that Islam is not a religion but a totalitarian ideology, and therefore "the right to religious freedom should not apply to Islam".[17] Moorthy Muthuswamy takes a similar tack in his book *Defeating Political Islam*. Islam, he maintains, is basically a political ideology. Likewise, Gregory Davis, the author of *Religion of Peace? Islam's War against the World*, argues that we need to reorient our thinking about Islam: "The first task for the West must be to reclassify Islam as a political system with religious aspects rather than a religion with political aspects".[18] More recently, Rebecca Bynum has written a book that explains why Islam does not qualify as a religion.[19] "How do you solve a problem like Sharia?" asks Mark Steyn in a playful paraphrase of the Broadway song. The simple answer is that you reclassify Islam as a political organization.

But for hundreds of years Islam has been thought of as a religion—one of the world's "great" religions, according to most history books. While it's undoubtedly true that many Islamic leaders cynically use religion as a cover for political ambitions, it's also certainly true that many Muslims feel that in practicing Islam they are being obedient to God's commands. For this and a number of other reasons, it would be difficult to make a case that Islam is not in any sense a religion.

If Islam is treated as a religion and is therefore protected by the free-exercise clause, what then? The First Amendment has never been interpreted to give people the freedom to do whatever they want, just as long as they do it in the name of religion. In the late nineteenth-century, Congress outlawed the Mormon practice of polygamy in the territories, and when the Mormons appealed the law, the Supreme Court upheld the ban. Thus, the Congress prohibited the free exercise of a particular Mormon custom. Congress and the states would certainly also have the power to prohibit the free exercise of many Islamic customs, laws, and obligations that are in flagrant violation of federal or state laws.

In a very real sense, US laws already prohibit the free exercise of Islam. That's because the full practice of Islam requires compliance with Islamic laws—laws that are believed to be divine commandments. The trouble is that many of these divine commandments are violations of state and federal laws. For example, under sharia:

- a Muslim girl can be contracted for marriage at any age; the marriage can be consummated when she is nine;

- a man can marry up to four wives (simultaneously);

- a man can easily divorce his wife, but a woman cannot divorce her husband without his consent;

- Muslim women are forbidden from marrying non-Muslims;

- the testimony of a woman in court is worth half the value of a man's testimony;

- Muslim men have permission to beat their wives for disobedience;

- adultery is punishable by lashing or stoning to death; thieves may be punished with amputation;

- parents and grandparents are "not subject to retaliation" for the killing of a child or a grandchild—as, for example, in an honor killing.

In short, what is considered lawful under sharia is quite often considered criminal under current US laws. Moreover, Islamic laws are not like the old "blue laws" in the United States, which remained on the books long after people stopped enforcing them or paying attention to them. Not only is sharia strictly enforced in many Muslim countries, but it is also widely supported. For example, the Pew Global Attitudes Survey of Pakistani Public Opinion conducted in 2009 found that 83 percent of Pakistanis favor stoning adulterers, 80 percent favor whipping thieves or cutting off their hands, and 78 percent favor death for those who leave Islam.[20] A 2011 Pew survey of Egyptians showed almost identical results. The First Amendment to the US Constitution prevents Congress from passing laws that prohibit the free exercise of religion. Does this make the exercise of religion an absolute right to do anything in the name of religion? Should the free-exercise clause be extended to protect suicide cults or virgin sacrifice? The First Amendment also prohibits the establishment of a state religion, but one of the main purposes of Islam is to establish itself as the state religion. It can be argued that Islam's *raison d'être* is to be the established religion in every nation. Hence another question that must be asked: Does the First Amendment protect its own abolishment?

The difficulty of reconciling Islam with the First Amendment raises the larger question of whether Islam can be reconciled with our overall system of government. The founders of the American republic assumed a connection between religion and good government. As John Adams put it, "Our Constitution was made only for a moral and religious people. It is wholly inadequate for the government of any other." Ever since then, prominent Americans have echoed that sentiment. Even William O. Douglas, the most liberal member of the Supreme Court at the time, and not a particularly religious man, opined in a

1952 decision, "We are a religious people, whose institutions presuppose a Supreme Being." But which Supreme Being did he have in mind? Likewise, when John Adams said our Constitution was made "only for a moral and religious people", what religion and what morality did he have in mind?

For a long time, we have had the luxury of not having to think very deeply about the relationship between our form of government and our religious tradition. Now that mosques are popping up all over, it's time to ask whether our institutions presuppose merely a generic religion or whether they are linked to a specific religious tradition. The question is, are religions interchangeable? Will any religion provide a proper foundation for our form of government? Or were Adams and the other founders implicitly assuming a Judeo-Christian framework?

In a way, it's the same question that was raised earlier in connection with interfaith dialogue: "Do we all worship the same God?" According to the Declaration of Independence, "all men are created equal" and "are endowed by their Creator with certain unalienable rights". But to which Creator does the Declaration refer? It would make no sense to claim that Allah would qualify for the position, because in Islam all men are not created equal. Muslims, who are described in the Koran as "the best of people", are considered to be decidedly superior to non-Muslims. For example, under sharia, a Muslim who kills another Muslim may have to pay with his life, but a Muslim who kills a non-Muslim need only pay "blood money" to the murdered man's relatives. For the Shafii school of jurisprudence, the lives of Jews and Christians are worth one-third of those of Muslims, while the lives of Zoroastrians are worth only one-fifteenth. In other words, the Supreme Being assumed in the Declaration of Independence is an entirely different sort of being from the one assumed in Islamic law and tradition.

At the time the Ground Zero mosque was being debated, Steve Chapman, a columnist for the *Chicago Tribune*, wrote a piece criticizing opponents of the project. He maintained that even if Islam were "inherently violent and totalitarian" it would still deserve the full protection of the First Amendment.[21] Can that really be true? Are we to disagree with Muslims' head-chopping policy but defend to the death their right to exercise it? Even Voltaire would have balked at that. If the main goal of a religion is the subjugation of all other religions and governments, along with the establishment of a totalitarian legal system, it seems legitimate to put restrictions on its agenda. Whether Islam is a political ideology or a hybrid of religion and political ideology may not matter for practical purposes. If it is a religion that aims to impose a system of laws that will end freedom of religion and freedom of speech, it seems to disqualify itself from the full protection of the First Amendment.

Conservative blogger and essayist Lawrence Auster, who has written extensively about both Islam and constitutional issues, has made the argument that because Islam is fundamentally different from other religions, it shouldn't be covered by the First Amendment. He writes, "I believe that it is possible that Islam's First Amendment protections can be removed, through a law or constitutional amendment stating that Islam is both a religion AND a tyrannical political movement, and that as such Islam shall not be considered a religion under the First Amendment." [22]

Auster admits that this is a radical proposal but argues that Islam is *sui generis* and must not be treated as though it were a religion like all other religions. He also makes the case that such legislation, because it would be Islam-specific, would avoid the slippery-slope problem whereby increased regulation of Islam would lead to increased regulation of Christianity and Judaism. As long as the First Amendment is interpreted to mean that all religions must receive equal treatment, any attempt to ban the burqa will elicit demands that nuns be forbidden to wear habits. Likewise, it will be argued that if Muslims can't wear distinctive garb, Christians shouldn't be allowed to wear crosses and Jews to display the Star of David. And if you're going to monitor mosques and madrassas for un-American activities, why not monitor churches, homeschools, and Christian schools as well? Granting the government sweeping supervisory powers over Islam might provide it with just the leverage it needs to haul Pastor Jones off to jail the next time he says the wrong thing about gay "marriage". Come to think of it, a certain Pastor Jones was almost hauled into court for threatening to burn the Koran. Although a constitutional amendment seems extreme, Auster argues that any measure short of that would create an opportunity for government restrictions on all religions.

Auster concedes that, given the current political and social climate, the passage of such a law is highly unlikely. But it's worth talking about, if only to help people realize that in Islam we are faced with a unique threat that cannot be fully understood—let alone addressed—within our existing legal and mental frameworks. Do our laws require us to maintain strict neutrality between the religion on which our civilization is founded and the religion that aims to dismantle it? Freedom of religion is a more complex proposition than it at first appears.

Auster's proposal for a constitutional amendment will not only strike some as extreme; it will strike many as un-Christian; so too will the Team B proposal to halt the immigration of Muslims who adhere to sharia. Since adherence to sharia is an obligation of the Islamic faith, this means, in effect, that all devout Muslims would be denied immigrant status. Aside from offending Muslims, such a measure seems designed to offend a lot of Christians as well. Most Christian churches take a very welcoming stand toward immigration. American Catholic bishops, in particular, like to remind their flock that the Catholic Church is itself an immigrant Church and that welcoming the stranger is a corporal work of mercy. European Catholic bishops also favor liberal immigration policies. So do their Protestant counterparts. Geert Wilders' call for a ban on Muslim immigration was roundly condemned by prelates across Europe.

On the other hand, polls show that many Americans question current immigration law. Moreover, the fastest-growing political parties in Europe all advocate restricting Muslim immigration. Why? Perhaps because they are seeing the truth of something Irish columnist Kevin Myers recently observed:

> Not merely is there not a single stable, prosperous Muslim democracy in the world, free of terrorism and fundamentalism, there is no society that has received large numbers of Muslims that has not soon been confronted by an Islamic defiance of existing societal norms.[23]

Myers is not alone in his observation, and other Europeans like him are beginning to look upon Muslims settling in Europe not as a migration but as an invasion. Muslims, they fear, are coming not to assimilate but to dominate. In this connection it's worth noting that mass migration and Islamic conquest have been linked since the time of Muhammad. In fact, the Islamic calendar is dated not from the year of Muhammad's first revelation in 610 but from 622, the year he and his followers migrated from Mecca to Medina. During the twelve-year Meccan period, Muhammad never had more than one hundred followers. It was only after the move to Medina and the commencement of raiding and looting that Muhammad was able to attract enough followers to begin the conquest of Arabia. In *Modern Day Trojan Horse: The Islamic Doctrine of Immigration*, Sam Solomon and Elias Al Maqdisi point out that "Hijra or migration is binding on all Muslims for numerous reasons; the most important being that migration is preparatory to jihad with an aim and objective of securing victory for Islam."[24] Roland Shirk, writing in *FrontPage* magazine, asserts that European imams see "the movement of Muslims into Europe as akin to Muhammad's hijra into Medina. Within a few years, he ruled that city as a theocracy, and used it to launch wars of conquest."[25]

It seems likely that if Europeans come to view Muslim immigration as an invasion, they will increasingly turn away from immigration policies that favor Muslims. At the same time, many will likely turn away from the Church because of the pro-immigration stance of the bishops. Obviously, the bishops shouldn't change their stance to please the crowd, but they also shouldn't be deaf to valid concerns. In some quarters in Europe, multiculturalism is not looked upon as a well-intentioned but misguided experiment, but rather as a deliberate attempt to undercut Western freedoms. Here is an excerpt from a 2011 speech by Geert Wilders:

> All over Europe multicultural elites are waging total war against their populations. Their goal is to continue the strategy of mass-immigration, which will ultimately result in an Islamic Europe—a Europe without freedom: Eurabia.[26]

Wilders doesn't blame the Christian churches, but others do—such as John Derbyshire, an Englishman who writes for the *National Review*. Christianity, he writes, has "been the great enabler" of Islam. And the main way it has done that, he asserts, is by backing indiscriminate immigration. "It beggars belief", he writes, "that anyone should hold such a civilizationally-suicidal view, but many Christians do." He adds, "As the darkness, cruelty, and obscurantism of jihadist Islam . . . descend on our lands, our souls rise joyfully to greet them."[27]

Derbyshire has never been a friend of Christianity, so his comments should be read with that in mind. Still, if one peruses the European websites dedicated to the threat from Islam, one sees an increasing conviction that mass Muslim immigration is an elite agenda imposed on an unwilling populace. In many instances, the bishops have appeared to stand with the elites—not only on the question of immigration, but also in their opposition to banning the burqa and in their criticism of the Swiss vote to ban minarets. In response to the Swiss vote, Cardinal Jean-Louis Tauran, the president of the Pontifical Council for Interreligious Dialogue, gently scolded the voters: "I wonder", he said, "if these persons know Muslims, if they have ever opened the Qur'an." [28] But at least he didn't imply that they were bad Christians. In the Netherlands, Christian ministers went a bit further: in a 2010 poll, 75 percent of Protestant church leaders said that a Christian cannot vote for Geert Wilders' anti-immigration party, because, as one minister put it, "Wilders and the PVV's views contradict Christianity." [29] But if Wilders is right, Christians in the Netherlands will find themselves a subjugated people: the recipients of the kind of treatment that Christians now receive in Egypt, Pakistan, and Iraq. Can it be anti-Christian to want to prevent the subjugation and possible elimination of Christianity? Were all the popes and bishops who resisted the Islamization of Europe in past centuries anti-Christian?

Bishops in Europe and America shouldn't trim their sails just to fit the prevailing winds, but it may be time to develop a more nuanced stance on immigration. Should immigration be indiscriminate, or should the motives and agendas of immigrant groups be taken into account? Should host cultures be forced to accept immigrants who carry the seeds of a hostile ideology? Do attempts to do justice to one group create grave injustices for another? Catholic doctrine doesn't dictate any specific immigration policy, but it has always prohibited suicide, and in Europe, at least, current immigration policy seems set on a suicidal course.

It might be another story if Europeans had taken the effort to assimilate previous generations of immigrants. In the case of Christians, that would have meant attempts to evangelize Muslims. But this is something Christians have been reluctant to do. Is it time now to start thinking about the conversion of Muslims? The next chapter explores that possibility.

A Fast-Approaching Future

David P. Goldman, who writes under the name of Spengler for *Asia Times*, has a solution to Christian Europe's birth dearth:

> As I wrote in 2005, "Now that everyone is talking about Europe's demographic death, it is time to point out that there exists a way out: convert European Muslims to Christianity." Today's Europeans stem from the melting-pot of the barbarian invasions that replaced the vanishing population of the Roman Empire. The genius of the Catholic Church was to absorb them. If Benedict XVI can convert this new wave of invaders from North Africa and the Middle East, history will place him on par with his great namesake, the founder of the monastic order that bears his name.[1]

Converting Muslims is a long shot, but sometimes long shots pay off. After all, in its earliest days, Christianity itself was a decided long shot. Let's look at the present possibilities.

On Easter Sunday 2008, Pope Benedict XVI baptized Magdi Allam, a prominent Muslim journalist who had converted to Christianity. Was this wise? The pope's actions were widely viewed as provocative, not only by Muslims but also by many non-Muslims. To add fuel to the fire, Allam is well known in Italy as a vocal critic of Islam. As part of the Easter liturgy, Allam's baptism (along with that of six non-Muslim converts) became a high-profile event, broadcast to television sets all over the world.

Why couldn't Allam have been quietly baptized by a local priest in a local church so as not to offend Muslims, so as to keep the peace and to avoid repercussions? To ask this question is, of course, to acknowledge the extent to which we have already adopted the dhimmi attitude: the attitude of submission and deference that sharia requires of non-Muslims. Dhimmis are expected to know their place. They may be allowed to practice their religion, but they must do it as quietly and unobtrusively as possible. Above all, they must never challenge or criticize Islam.

The pope's purpose was probably to keep a foot in the door that others would like to close in the name of sensitivity. Although the pope has sometimes appeared to lean too far in the direction of finding common ground with Islam, he is clear about other issues. As he well understands, the right to religious freedom is far more important than a so-called right not to be offended. People have a right to choose their religion. Christian churches have a right to baptize converts. In other words, the pope was refusing to play the appeasement game, refusing to accept the dhimmi role that Muslim leaders as well as many European leaders now expect of non-Muslims.

In a way, Allam's baptism was a revolutionary act. Conversion away from Islam is a crime punishable by death under Islamic law. From an Islamic viewpoint, the pope's action makes him an accomplice to a crime. Allam himself looked upon his baptism by the pope as a historical and revolutionary moment:

> His Holiness has sent an explicit and revolutionary message to a Church that until now has been too prudent in the conversion of Muslims, abstaining from proselytizing in majority Muslim countries and keeping quiet about the reality of converts in Christian countries. Out of fear. The fear of not being able to protect converts in the face of their being condemned to death for apostasy and fear of reprisals against Christians living in Islamic countries. Well, today Benedict XVI, with his witness, tells us that we must overcome fear and not to be afraid to affirm the truth of Jesus even with Muslims.[2]

Where will the Church find the missionaries to evangelize Muslims? Allam suggests that many of them will come from the ranks of Muslims themselves. He says there are many Muslim converts to Christianity in Europe who lead a "catacomb" existence because of "the silence of the Church itself". He hopes that his public baptism may change that:

> I hope that the Pope's historical gesture and my testimony will lead to the conviction that the moment has come to leave the darkness of the catacombs and to publicly declare their desire to be fully themselves.[3]

Despite Allam's hope, it must be conceded that the conversion of Muslims in Europe would be a formidable task. How about converting

Muslims in Muslim countries? That seems even more unlikely. Yet one of the untold stories of our time is that many such conversions are being effected by a few brave missionaries (many of them ex-Muslims) living in Muslim lands and also by evangelists who make use of the Internet and satellite television.

One of the best television evangelizers is the Coptic priest mentioned previously, Fr. Zakaria Botros, who, along with other missionaries—mostly Muslim converts—appears on Life TV. Father Botros, who is well versed in Islamic teachings, uses a combination of techniques: sometimes raising controversial aspects of Islamic law that average Muslims find troubling, sometimes engaging in forceful but reasoned debate with callers or with Islamic experts, sometimes presenting readings from the Bible. The result, according to an article by Raymond Ibrahim, has been impressive:

> Mass conversions to Christianity—if clandestine ones. The very public conversion of high-profile Italian journalist Magdi Allam . . . is only the tip of the iceberg. Indeed, Islamic cleric Ahmad al-Qatani stated on *al-Jazeera* TV a while back that some six million Muslims convert to Christianity annually, many of them persuaded by Botros's public ministry.[4]

Can the elderly Father Botros—who has been labeled Islam's public enemy number one—really be that effective? The answer came in August 2008, when al-Qaeda put a $60 million bounty on his head—considerably more than the $25 million US bounty on Osama bin Laden. Since Saint Francis of Assisi gave up on converting the Muslims, they have been considered immune to conversion, but recent events suggest otherwise.

Make no mistake: the conversion of Muslims is no easy thing. On the other hand, the hope for religious conversions is probably more realistic than the expectation that the West can convert Islamic nations to Western-style democracies. After all, Muslims have had a lot more experience with religion than they have had with democracy. The importance of the spiritual life has always been recognized in Islam; the importance of the vote has not. Raymond Ibrahim puts it this way:

> Many Western critics fail to appreciate that, to disempower radical Islam, something theocentric and spiritually satisfying—not secularism, democracy, capitalism, materialism, feminism, etc.—*must* be offered in its place. The truths of one religion can only be challenged and supplanted by the truths of another.[5]

In addition, evangelization happens to be an obligation for Christians. There is no duty to wage holy war to spread the gospel, but Christians *are* supposed to share the good news with others. As Pope Benedict XVI said, "Those who have recognized a great truth, those who have discovered a great joy, must pass it on; they cannot keep it to themselves." [6]

Satellite television and the Internet have created a new field for missionaries. They now can convey a plentitude of information about Christianity to millions of Muslims who previously would have had little or no access to such knowledge. It's possible, for example, to show all the humanitarian work done by Christians around the world (some of it for the benefit of Muslims). It's also possible to convey the Gospel story of Christ in its power and fullness, so that Muslims can see for themselves that in comparison, the Koran story of Isa is thin and unconvincing.

For that matter, the whole Christian account of salvation, from Adam's fall through the prophecies of a messiah, to the birth of Christ and his passion, death, and resurrection, forms a much richer and more meaningful and cohesive story than anything to be found in the Koran (which is sadly lacking in any overall story). Through the medium of film, the Christian story can be presented in a condensed but powerful way. Many Christian filmmakers have become considerably more sophisticated at their trade. For example, the one-minute introductory to EWTN's daily Mass program is an amazingly powerful montage of images and symbols that wordlessly and convincingly conveys the Catholic belief in the interconnectedness of the Last Supper, the Crucifixion, and the Eucharist. There's a high rate of illiteracy in the Muslim world, but pictures speak to everyone. Moreover, images of Christians at worship can show Muslims that Christians have developed beautiful and reverent forms of worship that are a fitting response to the mystery and transcendence of God. Such images would also help dispel the widespread Muslim stereotype that Christians are irreverent, materialistic, and lacking in true spirituality.

Evangelizing does not necessitate heavy-handed, Bible-thumping proselytizing. For example, the simple testimony of a Muslim who has found Christ is more effective than half an hour of sermonizing (which may serve only to remind the audience of their local imam). Programs that compare and contrast Islam and Christianity in an objective, fact-based format could also be aired. Such programs should demonstrate that the Islamic viewpoint on various issues is thoroughly understood, while presenting the reasons Christians take different positions. Short documentaries laying out the historical and archaeological evidence for the authenticity of the Gospels could also be provided. These are only a few of the possibilities. There are dozens of ways to build bridges to the Muslim world.

On the one hand, evangelizing Muslims is a daunting prospect; on the other hand, the Christian message of love and redemption is immensely liberating. To many in the West, it seems like an old story— one that has been sanitized, diluted, and explained away. But for many in other cultures who are encountering it for the first time, it's a different story—one of great joy. The power of that story should not be underestimated. It's the perennial story that people keep coming back to—or find anew—when all the other story lines have failed or faded.

There are good reasons to believe that, given enough time, Muslims can be converted. Unfortunately, time is precisely the thing we seem to be running out of. In an article titled "Christianity Face to Face with Islam", Robert Louis Wilken concludes that "in the decades to come the greatest challenge for Christians will be to fashion, within the cultural and political conditions of the twenty-first century, a new kind of Christendom." [7] Well, yes, that's similar to my own contention: the Islamic threat is upon us—it's time to shape up. But "in the decades to come"? How many decades does the professor think we have?

In his opening paragraph, Wilken concedes that "within a decade three major cities in the Byzantine Christian Empire—Damascus in 635, Jerusalem in 638, and Alexandria in 641—fell to the [Muslim] invaders." [8] Let's see, Alexandria is about six hundred camel miles from Jerusalem, and A.D. 641 minus 638 is three years. So the people of Alexandria had only a few years to get ready for a threat that was still six hundred miles away, yet we are supposed to believe that we have decades to prepare ourselves for a threat that is already comfortably ensconced within our own borders. Meanwhile, outside our borders, events are moving at a breathtaking speed. Considering how quickly Islamic revolutions have spread through the Middle East and North Africa in recent months, it does not seem wise to conclude that time is on our side.

Still, the belief that we have plenty of time to sort things out seems to be widely shared. Hence, there are a lot of fence-sitters in our society who don't know what to believe about this Christianity-Islam-atheism business but plan to give it some thought in the next decade or so. Let's hope they're right about the timing. Otherwise, someday soon there might not be any fences for the fence-sitters to sit on: no neutral ground from which to observe events. Their observation posts may turn out to be about as secure as that of a UN observer on the southern border of Lebanon. The undecideds can no longer afford to get by with only a surface knowledge of Christianity and its adversaries. If we are in the middle of a cultural world war, there is a certain obligation to get the facts straight about the religious and ideological forces in play. To paraphrase the old song, "Apply yourself, it's later than you think."

Fellow Travelers

"Religion is but myth and superstition that hardens hearts and enslaves minds." So said a large placard placed in the Washington state capitol rotunda during the 2008 Christmas season by the Freedom from Religion Foundation.[1] The foundation places a similar sign each Christmas at the Wisconsin state capitol. The aggressive atheist campaign of the last two decades is beginning to have the intended effect. Perhaps the country is not facing "The End of Christian America" described in *Newsweek*'s 2010 Holy Week cover story, but statistically speaking, America is less Christian than it used to be. For example, among Americans ages 18 to 29, a fourth now classify themselves as agnostic, atheist, or of no religious faith.[2]

Atheists alone aren't sufficient in numbers to undo a society, but that doesn't mean that there is no cause for alarm. Many secularists are, in effect, functional atheists. They may have a nominal belief in God; but for the most part, they act as though he does not exist. Without theism, men tend to gravitate toward "meism"; and judging from the destructive fallout of the sixties and seventies, meism is inimical to the social order: people who live only to gratify themselves in the moment are generally disinclined to have children or to care for them if they do have them. In the long run, the lack of stable families spells disaster for a society, but the activist secularists don't seem to want to wait for the long run. Instead they're busy doing what they can to speed up the disaster process.

A still greater cause for alarm is that atheists and secularists have found a new confederate in their struggle against Christians. One of the more ominous developments accompanying the rebirth of Islam as a force to be reckoned with is the formation of a tacit alliance between Islamists and secular leftists. For example, most of the demonstrators who showed up on September 11, 2010, to support the Ground Zero

mosque were members of various leftist, socialist, and communist organizations. Unlike their counterparts in the anti-mosque rally, who carried hand-painted signs, the leftists wielded pre-printed posters—a telltale
sign that the demonstrators were members of well-organized groups
with extensive experience in staging rallies and protests. That many of
the signs carried standard socialist slogans was another giveaway.

In his book *United in Hate*, historian Jamie Glazov provides detailed
evidence of the left's affinity for Islam. As he demonstrates, leftists
tend to ally themselves with anti-American, anti-Western forces. Right
now, one of the most powerful of these is Islam. Islam's opposition to
left/liberal values such as sexual permissiveness might seem to present
an obstacle to the alliance, but because of its overriding hatred of the
West, the left is willing to overlook its differences with Islam.[3] In *The
Closing of the Muslim Mind*, Robert Reilly makes a similar point. During the twentieth century, Islamic theorists and revolutionaries were
attracted at different times to both Nazism and communism. The attraction, says Reilly, results from the affinity of one totalitarian group for
another and from a philosophical similarity. Like Nazism and communism, Islamism (the term Reilly prefers) is an ideology based on
the primacy of will and power.[4]

Whether or not we wish to look deeper into the philosophical reasons for the existence of leftist/Islamic alliances, we need to realize
that they exist. Moreover, these alliances exist on the local as well as
the global level. Islam is supported not only by leftist dictators in Ven-
ezuela and North Korea, but also by left-leaning legislators, judges,
media personalities, educators, and labor organizers in your own city
or state.

This connection considerably amplifies the power of stealth jihadists. It is often argued that because Muslims make up only about 1 to
2 percent of the American population, there is simply no reason to
think that Islam can have any real power in our society. Yet, as mentioned earlier, homosexuals make up only 2 to 3 percent of the population, and they are close to controlling the national agenda in certain
key areas. Almost all public schools have become gay-affirmative. And
things that were unthinkable fifteen years ago—gay "marriage", gays
serving openly in the military—now seem uncontroversial. Moreover,
the gay lifestyle now seems beyond criticism—as a New York guber-
natorial candidate discovered two years ago when he stated that he
didn't think children should be taken to gay-pride parades. He was

roundly condemned by the media, by the opposition party, and by fellow party members. Almost no one came to his defense. How did gays come to wield so much power despite their numbers? The answer is that they have the backing of the same left-leaning educators, bureaucrats, and opinion makers who support Islam.

The irony is that Islam is advancing in the West by employing the same tactics pioneered by leftist and liberal activist groups. Muslim activists may have no love for homosexuals or secularists, but they appreciate their strategies. When gay activists learned to silence their opponents by crying "homophobia" at every opportunity and by branding every criticism of gays as a hate crime, Muslim activists took note. They quickly became adept at marshaling the epithets of the multicultural left—*racism, bigotry, intolerance,* and, of course, *Islamophobia*—for their own purposes. The term *Islamophobia* did not emerge spontaneously but was invented at a meeting of the International Institute for Islamic Thought (a Muslim Brotherhood organization) in northern Virginia. The coinage was deliberately modeled on the term *homophobia* in the hopes that Muslims too could portray themselves as victims.[5] Likewise, just as gay activists and their enablers in the media and the courts have managed to criminalize criticism of homosexuality in many places in the West, Muslim activists have succeeded in criminalizing criticism of Islam in the same places. In short, Islamic activists were quick to make use of the opportunities opened up by gays and other militant secularists.

The question is, what happens when Islamic sensitivities conflict with the sensitivities of gays and other secular activists? According to Bruce Bawer, the secular establishment in Europe won't stand up against the Muslims. Instead it quickly abandons liberal principles whenever they come into conflict with Islamic principles—whether it's a case of bending the school curriculum to suit Muslim demands or of looking the other way when gays or Jews are harassed or beaten.

Militant secularists have become the unwitting enablers of Islam. Once they have served their purpose, however, they will be pushed aside. Far from realizing this, the secularists are still focusing their ire on the one force that is capable of cutting through the relativist haze and confronting Islam's twisted beliefs: Christianity. The secularist campaign to silence and discredit Christians hasn't been entirely successful, but it has taken its toll. If it succeeds in silencing the churches, the hand of Islam will be considerably strengthened.

Secularists aren't the only ones who have difficulty in determining where the main threat lies. For many decades, Christian leaders have been focused almost exclusively on the threat from the secular left. It was and still is, of course, a dire threat. Unfortunately, the struggle against secularism may have caused church leaders to underestimate the equally serious threat from Islam. Indeed, many Christians have seen Islam as an ally in the war against secularism. And on some occasions it has been an ally. During the nineties, Catholics and Muslims stood together against various attempts to introduce contraception, abortion, and other forms of population control into Third World countries. Like many Christians, Muslims were and are concerned about the socially destructive effects of sexual liberation.

It is questionable, however, if Muslims oppose population control for the same reasons that Catholics do, or whether they can be counted on as reliable allies. While Muslims may be interested in growing the Muslim population, recent events in Africa and the Middle East suggest that they have much less concern for the fate of Christian populations. Moreover, just as Muslims were willing to ally themselves with Christians for strategic reasons, they now seem willing to ally themselves with the secular left for other strategic purposes.

Many church leaders seem to be relying on the hope that Muslims, because they believe in God, are on the same side as Christians. For example, Pope John Paul II tended to view the world in terms of a struggle between atheism and religion. And for much of his life, the atheist ideologies of Nazism and communism were indeed the main threat to believers. To a man who had battled the forces of atheism all his life, the Islamic issue must have seemed of secondary importance. Pope Benedict seems more concerned than his predecessor about the dangers posed by Islam, but he also sometimes frames the world situation as a conflict between religion and irreligion. When asked in an interview if the Vatican was following a different policy from earlier popes who "thought it their duty to save Europe from Islamization", the pope replied: "Today we are living in a completely different world, in which the battle lines are drawn differently. In this world, radical secularism stands on one side, and the question of God, in its various forms, stands on the other".[6]

It may be, however, that Rome's situation is not so different from that faced by earlier popes. It may be even more hazardous. Christianity's ancient enemy, Islam, has not gone away, and now there is a new enemy—radical secularism. Rather than speak in terms of religion versus irreligion, it may be more accurate to speak in terms of religion versus irreligion on the one hand and religion versus religion on the other. Another way to frame the current situation is to think in terms of one religion (Christianity) versus two totalitarian ideologies— two ideologies that, despite their differences, are united in their hatred of Christianity and the West. Consider this observation by Soeren Kern, a senior fellow at the Madrid-based Strategic Studies Group:

> Many of the mosque projects in Italy have been promoted by left wing politicians, who are waging an ideological war with the Roman Catholic Church. As in many other European countries, multiculturalists in Italy hope that by promoting Islam, they will eventually succeed in destroying the country's Judeo-Christian heritage.[7]

After the collapse of the Soviet empire, many leftists fell into a state of despondency. The events of 9/11, however, gave them new hope and a new cause. As Glazov points out, leftists saw in radical Islam many of the qualities they cherished in their own secular religion: an apocalyptic mindset, a desire to purify the world, and a willingness to shed blood in order to do it. Thus, like many Muslims around the world, leftists saw 9/11 as a cause for celebration. Norman Mailer responded to the destruction of the World Trade Center in these words: "Everything wrong with America led to the point where the country built that tower of Babel which consequently had to be destroyed."[8] Dario Fo, the Italian Marxist and Nobel Prize winner, exclaimed that the American economy "kills tens of millions of people with poverty, so what is twenty thousand dead in New York?"[9] German composer Karlheinz Stockhausen said that 9/11 was "the greatest work of art for the whole cosmos".[10] In Islam, the leftists had found a new champion to fight the capitalist foe.

In the years after 9/11, prominent leftists such as Noam Chomsky, Michael Moore, and Tom Hayden undertook pilgrimages to the Middle East to endorse and embrace the leaders of terrorist groups such as Hamas and Hezbollah, just as in previous generations leftists had embraced Castro, Ho Chi Minh, and Stalin. In the early years of the Stalin era, liberal newspapers carried glowing reports of the Soviet paradise while covering up Stalin's deliberate starvation of millions of Ukrainians. Today a compliant media does its best to present a Potemkin village picture of Muslim life in television series such as *All-American*

Muslim and *Little Mosque on the Prairie*, while going to extraordinary lengths to cover up the links between Islam and violence.

Meanwhile on university campuses, leftist professors and students work with Muslim students to further the anti-Semitic agenda of the Muslim Student Association. At the same time, leftist legal groups such as the ACLU, the National Lawyers Guild, and others have worked to block efforts to prosecute terrorists and to strengthen homeland security. Other groups have endeavored to silence criticism of Islam. Although the term *Islamophobia* was invented by Muslims, the campaign to eliminate Islamophobia has been mostly engineered by the left. Leftwing groups such as Fairness and Accuracy in Reporting, the Southern Poverty Law Center, and the *Huffington Post* have issued reports with lists of "anti-Muslim bigots" and "Islamophobes".[11] In 2011, working hand in hand with CAIR, the considerably left-of-center Center for American Progress produced a report titled *Fear Inc: The Roots of the Islamophobia Network in America.*[12]

David Horowitz, a former leftist whose name appears on almost all the Islamophobe lists, has termed the union of the secular left and radical Islam an "unholy alliance". Unfortunately, the efforts of the unholy alliance have succeeded in making America and the West more vulnerable—to both stealth jihad and violent jihad. With the help of the media, the alliance has managed to brand legitimate criticism of Islam as Islamophobia. With the help of the Department of Justice, it has undercut the ability of law-enforcement groups to uncover terrorist activity and terror plots.

Jamie Glazov writes, "The lust for destruction is at the heart of Marxism. In Marx's apocalyptic mindset, catastrophe gives rise, ultimately, to a new, perfect world."[13] The vision of many Muslim leaders is not that different. In Iran, President Ahmadinejad, Ayatollah Khamenei, and others talk openly of the catastrophic events that will be needed to ensure that the Mahdi returns to establish a new world order. As we saw in an earlier chapter, Islamic theorist Sayyid Maududi described Islam as "a revolutionary ideology and programme" that seeks to alter and rebuild the entire social order.

The many parallels between the messianic faith of secular leftists and the apocalyptic faith of Islam should give pause to Christians who hope to make a common cause with Muslims against radical secularism. Islam is inherently opposed to secular rule, but Islamists recognize that they can make good use of the secular left. Lenin spoke disparagingly of the "useful idiots" who naïvely served the Communist cause. It's beginning to look as though the leftists themselves have become useful idiots in the service of Islam. Leftists and Islamists have become fellow travelers, but if the leftists are helping pay for the tickets, it's the Islamists who are choosing the destination.

It is possible to imagine scenarios in which the secular left, or a large part of it, is absorbed by Islam. Many leftists will convert to Islam just as many seventh-century Arab warriors converted—not because they had no doubts about Muhammad's revelations but because they had no doubts about his power. In this regard, it's noteworthy that the PLO, which began as a leftist secular movement, has been largely superseded by terrorist groups of a more religious bent. For that matter, the majority of secular governments in the Muslim world have given way to rule by true believers.

As Islam grows stronger, it will attract more converts. Will Christians also be tempted to convert? The Bible warns of a great apostasy—a time when many will turn away from the faith. When speaking of the last days, Christ cautioned his followers about just such a betrayal: "And then many will fall away, and betray one another, and hate one another. And many false prophets will arise and lead many astray" (Mt 24:10–11). Saint Paul also warned that the return of Jesus would be preceded by apostasy: "Let no one deceive you in any way; for that day will not come, unless the rebellion comes first" (2 Thess 2:3).

Joel Richardson's *The Islamic Antichrist* is a trenchant analysis of end-times prophecies in the Bible and in Islam. Toward the end of the book, he discusses the possibility of mass conversions to Islam as it grows larger:

> I expect that we will see a "tipping point" just before Islam actually bypasses Christianity when there will be a sudden burst forward of bandwagon conversions and growth. At this time, the power of testimony will be a powerful tool for Muslims. As more and more Westerners convert, the claims and challenges of Islam will become far more difficult for many Western Christians to brush aside.[14]

A question that secular leftists and lukewarm Christians may both begin to ask will be like the question we find in the book of Revelation: "Who is like the beast, and who can fight against it?" (Rev 13:4).

Does this mean the situation is hopeless? No, not at all. My purpose in writing this book is not to dash hopes but to provide Christians with an accurate picture of what they're up against. Those who are acquainted with the grim possibilities are in a better position to prevent them from happening. The first rule of war is to know your enemies. The best weapon in the battle against the two forces arrayed against us is knowledge. If Christians have been losing the war of ideas, it's because they have been deluding themselves that there is no war. Too often they have confined their thinking to the narrative established by secularists and multiculturalists—a narrative that says the world's troubles are of our own making and can be solved only if we show more tolerance and give less offense. Christians have become trapped in a fog of propaganda and disinformation. It's time to cut through the haze.

The combined forces of Islam and the secular left seem to be increasing in size and power. But let's not be intimidated by sheer size. As Roy Schoeman observes in *Salvation Is from the Jews*, "The relationship between God and mankind is not established and maintained on the basis of 'averages', or on the behavior of the majority", but rather on the fervor and faith of a relatively small number of people.[15] Christians were decidedly outnumbered in the early centuries of the Church's existence, yet their faith proved stronger than that of all their enemies.

As we can see from history, the battle is not always to the strong. Christians defeated numerically superior Muslim forces at the Battle of Tours in 732 and at the gates of Vienna in 1683. A small band of RAF fighter pilots withstood the might of Nazi Germany during the Battle of Britain. The expansion of the Soviet empire was halted and then reversed due largely to the efforts and determination of three people—Ronald Reagan, Margaret Thatcher, and Pope John Paul II.

The Cold War was, for the most part, an ideological struggle, and its resolution should provide us with confidence that we can win the current war of ideas. Another reason for hope is that both Islam and the left stand on very shaky ideological ground. Both can survive only in a climate of ignorance and repression; both engage in incessant propaganda; and both devote much energy to silencing opposing voices. Islam is particularly weak. Its central document is a crudely constructed fabrication; and it is only by constant agitation and warfare that Islamic ideologues manage to divert attention away from the hollowness of its doctrines. Ali Sina, the author of *Understanding Muhammad*, asserts that Islam is built on sand: "To defeat Islam ideologically we must talk about it openly and allow it to be questioned. Islam cannot stand criticism. It is held together like a house of cards and will fall just as easily." [16]

Christians should take courage from knowing that in this war of ideas, all the best ideas are on their side. Although the secular left talks the language of human dignity and although Islam's representatives have learned to do the same, neither provides any basis for human dignity or human rights. In Islam, human beings are nothing more than slaves of a capricious Allah. Likewise, secular systems don't provide any reasons for believing in human rights and human dignity; they only assume them as a given. We tend to forget that these concepts are now a given because they were given to the world by Christians. Before Christianity, the idea that all human beings are endowed with intrinsic value was not considered "self-evident"; it was considered ludicrous. As theologian David Bentley Hart puts it, "All of us today in the West, to some degree or another, have inherited a conscience formed by Christian moral ideals". [17]

Professor Hart presents a convincing historical case that our present concern with humanity would simply not have come into being without Christianity; and without a strong Christian presence, he asserts, it is reasonable to expect that our concern for humanity will evaporate. The strongest argument for the infinite value of every human life is that the infinite God became a man both to share our humanity and to redeem it, thus making it possible for humans to share in his divinity. Pope John Paul II observed that Christ does not just reveal God to man, but "reveals man to man". Gladiatorial combats and slavery didn't go out of fashion because societies evolved, but because people began to see one another in the light of that revelation. Christianity does not promise a perfect earthly society of the type that Marxists and Islamists believe will arrive with the next revolution. It does, however, offer the best chance of creating a good society.

I have suggested that we may be approaching a tipping point—a point at which the balance tips in favor of Islam. But it is possible to envision another kind of tipping point—the point at which enough people wake up and realize that they have been duped both by multiculturalists and Islamic propagandists, as well as by media censors determined to control what people know and think. At that point, they will see clearly why Christianity is under attack and why, despite centuries of such attacks, it has endured. That is the point at which Christians and others of good faith can successfully push back against the ideological tides. Christians have the weight of truth and reason on their side, but it won't be of help to them unless they rediscover that fact. A combination of events and forces is pushing us toward a pivotal juncture. Which way the balance tips will depend—as it always has—on a faithful, determined, and clear-headed few.

ACKNOWLEDGMENTS

Sections of chapters 5 and 14 first appeared in the *Catholic World Report*. Portions of chapters 3, 8, and 9 first appeared in *FrontPage* magazine.

I am especially grateful to Ignatius Press for its generous support of my work. I also owe special thanks to the Earhart Foundation for supporting the research into multiculturalism that initially led me to embark on this book.

NOTES

INTRODUCTION

1. "Rifqa Bary: 'I Want to Be Free'", *Atlas Shrugs* (blog), August 12, 2009, http://atlasshrugs2000.typepad.com/.

2. Ibid.

3. Quoted in Raymond Ibrahim, "Lessons on the Long Road to Hijab", *Jihad Watch* (blog), December 28, 2011, http://www.jihadwatch.org/2011/12/raymond-ibrahim-lessons-on-the-long-road-to-hijab.html.

4. Catherine Herridge, "Extremist Teachings Remain in Saudi Text-books Despite Kingdom's Claims of Reform", Fox News, December 21, 2011, http://www.foxnews.com/world/2011/12/21/extremist-teachings-remain-in-saudi-textbooks-despite-kingdoms-claims-reform/#ixzz1hFKF1iC.

CHAPTER ONE: The Crisis of Faith

1. Robert Spencer, *Religion of Peace?: Why Christianity Is and Islam Isn't* (Washington, DC: Regnery Publishing, 2007), p. 3.

2. Bruce Bawer, *While Europe Slept* (New York: Broadway Books, 2006), p. 215.

3. "UK Cops Stop Christian Preachers in Muslim Areas, Call Preaching a 'Hate Crime'", *Jihad Watch* (blog), June 1, 2008, http://www.jihadwatch.org/.

4. Soeren Kern, "Britain: Islam In, Christianity Out", Gatestone Institute, December 1, 2011, http://www.gatestoneinstitute.org/2634/britain-islam-christianity.

5. Soeren Kern, "France Goes Halal", Gatestone Institute, February 28, 2012, http://www.gatestoneinstitute.org/2886/france-halal.

6. Bruce Thornton, *Decline and Fall: Europe's Slow Motion Suicide* (New York: Encounter Books, 2007), p. 32.

7. Stanley Kurtz, "Saudi in the Classroom", *National Review Online*, July 25, 2007, http://www.nationalreview.com/.

8.   Michelle Malkin, "Whitewashing Jihad in the Schools", *National Review Online*, April 4, 2007, http://www.nationalreview.com/.

9.   Daniel Greenfield, *Muslim Hate Groups on Campus* (Sherman Oaks, CA: David Horowitz Freedom Center, 2011), p. 10.

10.   Rabbi Aryeh Spero, "Academic Prohibition", *FrontPage*, August 10, 2007, http://archive.frontpagemag.com/.

11.   Spencer, *Religion of Peace?*, p. 102.

12.   Author's recollection of a Dennis Prager radio broadcast.

13.   Audrey Barrick, "Study: Christianity No Longer Looks like Jesus", *Christian Post*, September 25, 2007, http://www.christianpost.com/.

14.   Thornton, *Decline and Fall*, p. 75.

15.   Spencer, *Religion of Peace?*, p. 5.

CHAPTER TWO: The Islamization of the World

1.   See, for example, Jed Babbin, *In the Words of Our Enemies* (Washington, DC: Regnery Publishing, 2007).

2.   "The Strategy of Consensual Dissimulation", *Melanie Phillips* (blog), July 3, 2007, http://melaniephillips.com.

3.   "Gullible Gordon's Pentagon PC", *Investors Business Daily*, January 22, 2008, http://news.investors.com.

4.   "Predicting a Majority-Muslim Russia", *Daniel Pipes* (blog), August 6, 2005, http://www.danielpipes.org.

5.   Quoted in Mark Steyn, *America Alone*, first paperback ed. (Washington, DC: Regnery Publishing, 2008), p. 146.

6.   Population Reference Bureau, "2006 World Population Data Sheet", http://www.prb.org.

7.   Steyn, *America Alone*, pp. xxiii, 10.

8.   Ibid., p. 6.

9.   Ibid., p. 34.

10.   Quoted in Fjordman, "Jihad and the Collapse of the Swedish Model", *Islam Watch* (blog), April 20, 2007, http://islam-watch.org/Fjordman/Jihad-Collapse-Sweden.html.

11.   Anthony Watts, "Tipping Points and Beliefs—the 10% Solution", *Watts Up with That?* (blog), July 27, 2011, http://wattsupwiththat.com/2011/07/27/tipping-points-and-beliefs.

12.   Christopher Caldwell, *Reflections on the Revolution in Europe: Immigration, Islam, and the West* (New York: Doubleday, 2009), p. 12.

13.   Ibid., p. 7.

14.   Ibid., pp. 12, 17.

15.   Ibid., p. 118.

16.   Soeren Kern, "Europe's Ticking Demographic Time Bomb", PJ Media, March 8, 2011, http://pjmedia.com/.

17.   Caldwell, *Reflections on the Revolution in Europe*, p. 9.

18.   Soeren Kern, "Britain vs. Muslim Immigration", *Pundicity* (blog), April 21, 2011, http://kern.pundicity.com/.

19.   Walter Laqueur, *The Last Days of Europe* (New York: Thomas Dunne Books, 2007), p. 41.

20.   Soeren Kern, "Britain vs. Muslim Immigration".

21.   Caldwell, *Reflections on the Revolution in Europe*, p. 150.

22.   Soeren Kern, "European Concerns over Muslim Immigration Go Mainstream", *Pundicity* (blog), August 15, 2011, http://kern.pundicity. com/10122/european-concerns-muslim-immigration.

23.   Ibid.

24.   Ibid.

25.   Soeren Kern, "Turks in Germany: The Guests Take Over the House", *Pundicity* (blog), November 7, 2011, http://kern.pundicity.com/ 10662/turks-germany.

26.   Quoted in Dinesh D'Souza, *The Enemy at Home: The Cultural Left and Its Responsibility for 9/11* (New York: Doubleday, 2007), p. 117.

27.   Soeren Kern, "European Concerns over Muslim Immigration Go Mainstream".

28.   Serge Trifkovic, *Defeating Jihad* (Boston: Regina Orthodox Press, 2006), p. 69.

29.   Cal Thomas, "Segregation: Muslim Style", *Human Events*, January 7, 2008, http://www.humanevents.com/.

30.   Philip Johnston, "Emigration Soars as Britons Desert the UK", *Telegraph*, November 15, 2007, http://www.telegraph.co.uk.

31.   Cited in "Emigration Rate at 50-Year High", *American Renaissance*, March 7, 2005, http://amren.com/.

32.   Craig S. Smith, "Europe Fears Threat from Its Converts to Islam", *Religion News Blog*, July 19, 2004, http://www.religionnewsblog. com/; Jumana Farouky, "Allah's Recruits", *Time*, August 20, 2006; Peter Ford, "Why European Women Are Turning to Islam", *Christian Science Monitor*, December 27, 2005, http://www.csmonitor.com/.

33.   Farouky, "Allah's Recruits."

34.   Smith, "Europe Fears Threat from Its Converts to Islam".

35. Ford, "Why European Women Are Turning to Islam".

36. Soeren Kern, "Europeans Increasingly Converting to Islam", Gatestone Institute, January 27, 2012, http://www.gatestoneinstitute. org/.

37. Matthew Arnold, "Dover Beach", in G. K. Anderson and K. J. Holzknecht, *The Literature of England* (Chicago: Scott, Foresman and Company, 1953), p. 894.

38. Robert Ferrigno, *Prayers for the Assassin* (New York: Scribner, 2007).

39. Melanie Phillips, *Londonistan* (New York: Encounter Books, 2006), p. 15.

40. Ibid., pp. 67, 68.

41. Ronni L. Gordon and David M. Stillman, "Prince Charles of Arabia", *Middle East Quarterly* 4, no. 3 (September 1997): pp. 3–7.

42. Phillips, *Londonistan*, p. 66.

43. Peter Hitchens, "Will Britain Convert to Islam?", *Mail Online*, November 2, 2003, http://www.dailymail.co.uk/.

44. Phillips, *Londonistan*, p. 68.

45. "Muslims on the Inside: Results from a Survey of Incarcerated Muslims", *Citizens against Recidivism Blog*, June 21, 2010, http:// citizensinc.wordpress.com/.

46. Erick Stakelbeck, *The Terrorist Next Door: How the Government Is Deceiving You about the Islamist Threat* (Washington, DC: Regnery Publishing, 2011), pp. 96–97.

47. Ibid., pp. 97, 204.

48. Daniel Greenfield, "The Islamic Political Takeover of America", *FrontPage*, August 19, 2011, http://frontpagemag.com/2011/08/ 19/the-islamic-political-takeover-of-america.

49. Stakelbeck, *The Terrorist Next Door*, p. 198.

50. Ibid., p. 199.

51. "Obama Appointment: Arif Alikhan, Asst Secretary DHS", *Atlas Shrugs* (blog), June 7, 2009, http://atlasshrugs2000.typepad. com/.

52. Andrew C. McCarthy, *The Grand Jihad: How Islam and the Left Sabotage America* (New York: Encounter Books, 2010), p. 292.

53. Greg Miller, "At CIA, a Convert to Islam Leads the Terrorism Hunt", the *Washington Post*, March 24, 2012, http://www. washingtonpost.com/world/national-security/at-cia-a-convert-to-islam-leads-the-terrorism-hunt/2012/03/23/gIQA2mSqYS_story.html.

54. Walid Shoebat and Ben Barrack, "U.S. Ignores Hillary Clinton's Powerful Aide Huma Abedin at Its Own Risk", *Human Events*, June 30, 2011, http://www.humanevents.com/article.php?print=yes&id=44549us-ignores-hillary-clintons-powerful-aide.

55. McCarthy, *The Grand Jihad*, p. 292.

56. Quoted in McCarthy, *The Grand Jihad*, p. 58.

57. Quoted in Pamela Geller, *Stop the Islamization of America: A Practical Guide to the Resistance* (Washington, DC: WND Books, 2011), p. iv.

58. Byron Tau, "Muslim Brotherhood Delegation Meets with White House Officials", *Politico*, April 4, 2012, http://www.politico.com/politico44/2012/04/muslim-brotherhood-delegation-meets-with-white-house-119647.html.

59. Jon Meacham, "The End of Christian America", *Newsweek*, April 13, 2009; Daniel Stone, "One Nation under God?" (results of *Newsweek* poll), *Newsweek*, April 13, 2009.

60. Charles J. Sykes, *A Nation of Victims* (New York: St. Martin's Press, 1992), pp. 135–36.

61. Nonie Darwish, *Now They Call Me Infidel: Why I Renounced Jihad for America, Israel, and the War on Terror* (New York: Sentinel, 2006), p. 201.

62. "Is an Islamic Orphanage Better for Children Than a Christian Mother?", *Jihad Watch* (blog), January 13, 2008, http://www.jihadwatch.org/.

63. Qaiser Felix, "Pakistani Judge Rules 'Marriage' and Forced Conversion Legal", *Catholic Online*, August 23, 2008, http://www.catholic.org/.

64. Raymond Ibrahim, "Christmas under Islam: Hardly a Season to Be Jolly", PJ Media, January 17, 2012, http://pjmedia.com/blog/christmas-under-islam-hardly-a-season-to-be-jolly/.

65. Spencer, *Religion of Peace?*, p. 49.

66. Ayaan Hirsi Ali, "The Rise of Christophobia", *Newsweek*, February 13, 2012, p. 34.

67. Spencer, *Religion of Peace?*, p. 49.

68. "Crackdown on Christians Could Go Nationwide", *WorldNetDaily*, May 5, 2007, http://www.wnd.com/.

69. Serge Trifkovic, "Islamism's Other Victims: The Tragedy of East Timor", *FrontPage*, November 25, 2002, http://archive.frontpagemag.com/.

70. Paul H. Liben, "Murder in the Sudan", *First Things*, August/September 1995, pp. 42–44.

CHAPTER THREE: The Cover-Up

1.   TheReligionofPeace.com. This site keeps track of Islamic terrorist attacks since 9/11. As of May 11, 2012, there were 18,889.

2.   "Shooter Advised Obama Transition", *WorldNetDaily*, November 6, 2009, http://www.wnd.com/.

3.   John Brennan, speech to CSIS, May 10, 2010, quoted in *Sharia: The Threat to America* (Washington, DC: Center for Security Policy Press, 2010), p. 253.

4.   "Gullible Gordon's Pentagon PC".

5.   John Nichols, "Horror at Fort Hood Inspires Horribly Predictable Islamophobia", *Nation* (blog), November 5, 2009, http://www.thenation.com/.

6.   Robert Spencer, "Latest Jihad Plot Shows Need to Know Koran", *Human Events*, September 24, 2009, http://www.humanevents.com/.

7.   "Unrepentant Times Square Bomber Pleads Guilty '100 Times'", *Express Tribune*, June 22, 2010, http://tribune.com.pk/.

8.   Cited in John R. Guardiano, "Understanding the Norway Massacre", *American Spectator*, July 25, 2011, http://spectator.org/archives/2011/07/25/understanding-the-norway-massa.

9.   Susan Brooks Thislethwaite, "When Christianity Becomes Lethal", *Washington Post*, July 25, 2011, http://www.washingtonpost.com/blogs/on-faith/post/norway-attacks-when-christianity-becomes-lethal/2011/07/25/gIQAPRw5YI_blog.html.

10.   "Ground Zero Mosque Protest: Where Was the American Press?", *PPJ Gazette*, July 12, 2010, http://ppjg.me/.

11.   Pamela Geller, "Countering the Lies of the MSM: The Ground Zero Mosque War in the Information Battlespace", *Breitbart, Big Journalism*, September 13, 2010, http://www.breitbart.com/Big-Journalism.

12.   From Channel 12 WBNG. Cited in Mark Steyn, "Another Case of PTSD?", *National Review Online*, December 6, 2009, http://www.nationalreview.com/.

13.   "Story of Buffalo Beheading Has No Legs", *I Hate the Media!* (blog), February 15, 2009, http://www.ihatethemedia.com/.

14.   Mary Papenfuss, "Daughter's 'Honor Killing' Hitting Arizona Court", *Newser*, January 3, 2011, http://www.newser.com/.

15.   "Five Muslim Soldiers Arrested at Fort Jackson for Trying to Poison the Food Supply", *CBN News*, February 18, 2010, http://blogs.cbn.com/.

16. "Time for Restraint, as after September 11", *Globe and Mail*, November 7, 2009, http://www.theglobeandmail.com/.

17. See, for example: Maureen Dowd, "A Nope for Pope", *New York Times*, March 27, 2010; http://www.nytimes.com/; John Hooper, "Pope Accused of Sparing Priest Suspected of Sex Abuse Attacks", *Guardian*, March 25, 2010, http://www.guardian.co.uk; John Rondy, "Pope Accountable for Hiding Priest Abuses: U.S. Victim", Reuters, March 25, 2010, http://reuters.com/; Christopher Hitchens, "The Great Catholic Cover-up", *National Post*, March 18, 2010, http://fullcomment.nationalpost.com/.

18. S. E. Cupp, *Losing Our Religion: The Liberal Media's Attack on Christianity* (New York: Simon & Schuster, 2010).

19. Phyllis Chesler, "Islamic Homosexual Pederasty and Afghanistan's 'Dancing Boys'", PJ Media, April 21, 2010, http://www.phyllis-chesler.com/758/islamic-homosexual-pederasty-and-afghanistans.

20. Cited in ibid.

21. Stephen O. Murray, *Homosexualities*, Worlds of Desire: The Chicago Series of Sexuality, Gender and Culture (Chicago: University of Chicago Press, 2011), pp. 128, 161, 188; Raphael Patai, *The Arab Mind* (New York: Hatherleigh Press, 2002), pp. 143–44; Ibn Warraq, *Why the West Is Best: A Muslim Apostate's Defense of Liberal Democracy* (New York: Encounter Books, 2011), pp. 86–87; *Encyclopedia of Islam and the Muslim World* (New York: Macmillan Reference USA, 2004), p. 316; See also, Arno Schmitt and Jehoeda Sofer, eds., *Sexuality and Eroticism among Males in Muslim Societies* (Binghamton, NY: The Haworth Press, 1992); Ibn Warraq, *Why I Am Not a Muslim* (Amherst, NY: Prometheus Press, 2003), pp. 340–43.

22. "A Question of Honour: Police Say 17,000 Women Are Victims Every Year", *Independent*, February 10, 2008, http://www.independent.co.uk.

23. U.S. Department of Health and Human Services, Office on Women's Health, "Female Genital Cutting Fact Sheet", http://www.womenshealth.gov/.

24. "Four Christians Arrested outside Arab Festival", *Christian Examiner*, June 2010, http://www.christianexaminer.com/.

25. "Christian Preacher on Hooligan Charge after Saying He Believes That Homosexuality Is a Sin", *Mail Online*, May 1, 2010, http://www.dailymail.co.uk/.

26.   Matt Cover, "UN Jurist Calls for Pope to Be Tried in International Court", CNSNews.com, April 13, 2010, http://cnsnews.com/.

CHAPTER FOUR: Secularists: Lights Out for the Enlightenment

1.   "'Imagine No Religion,' Says Atheists' Display", *WorldNet-Daily*, Dec. 9, 2007, http://www.wnd.com/.

2.   Ayaan Hirsi Ali, *Infidel* (New York: Free Press, 2007).

3.   Ibid., p. 282.

4.   Ibid., p. 272.

5.   Ibid., p. 281.

6.   Ibid., p. 272.

7.   Ibid., p. 293, p. xii.

8.   Mark Steyn, "She Said What She Thought," *Atlantic*, December, 2006, http://www.theatlantic.com/.

9.   Tunku Varadarajan, "An Interview with Oriana Fallaci", *Wall Street* Journal, June 23, 2005, http://www.mdtaxes.org/NEWS-STORIES-2005/WSJ.Tunku.Varadarajan.Oriana.Fallaci.6.23.05.htm.

10.   Joseph Cardinal Ratzinger, "If Europe Hates Itself", *Avvenire*, May 14, 2004, quoted in Varadarajan, "An Interview with Oriana Fallaci".

11.   Joseph Cardinal Ratzinger, *Christianity and the Crisis of Culture* (San Francisco: Ignatius Press, 2006), p. 48.

12.   Ibid.

13.   Quoted in George Weigel, *The Cube and the Cathedral: Europe, America, and Politics without God* (New York: Basic Books, 2005), pp. 108–9.

14.   Ibid., p. 112.

15.   Ratzinger, *Christianity and the Crisis of Culture*, p. 21.

16.   Quoted in Weigel, *The Cube and the Cathedral*, p. 112.

17.   Hirsi Ali, *Infidel*, p. 240.

18.   Ratzinger, *Christianity and the Crisis of Culture*, p. 42.

19.   Dinesh D'Souza, *What's So Great about Christianity* (Washington, DC: Regnery Publishing, 2007), p. 213.

20.   Father Alfonso Aguilar, "Learning from the Example of the Spanish Martyrs", *National Catholic Register*, November 18, 2007.

21.   "Together Facing the New Totalitarianism", quoted in BBC News, March 1, 2006, http://news.bbc.co.uk/.

22. Ibid.

23. Quoted in Rabbi David G. Dalin, *The Myth of Hitler's Pope: Pope Pius XII and His Secret War against Nazi Germany* (Washington, DC: Regnery Publishing, 2005), p. 38.

24. Ibid, p. 73.

25. Weigel, *The Cube and the Cathedral*, p. 172.

26. "Bardot Fined for 'Race Hate' Book", *BBC News*, June 10, 2004, http://news.bbc.co.uk.

27. Roger Kimball, "Libel Tourism, Coming Soon to a Town near You," PJ Media, December 8, 2007, http://pjmedia.com/.

28. Ibid.

29. Mark Steyn, "Best Not to Mention It," *National Review Online*, December 8, 2007, http://www.nationalreview.com/.

30. Art Moore, "Bible Verses Regarded as Hate Literature," *WorldNetDaily*, February 18, 2003, http://www.wnd.com/.

31. Michael D. O'Brien, "Same-Sex 'Marriage,' 'Hate Crimes,' and the New Totalitarianism", *LifeSiteNews.com*, February 28, 2005, http://www.lifesitenews.com/.

32. "Catholic League Notes Result of Homosexual Hate Crime Law in Other Countries as Warning to Canada", *LifeSiteNews.com*, April 30, 2004, http://www.lifesitenews.com/.

33. Mark Steyn, "The Case of the Part-Time Pedophile", *SteynOnline* (blog), Feb. 19, 2011, http://www.steynonline.com/.

34. Arthur Legger, "Shrugging off Spinoza", *Tidsskriftet Sappho* (blog), January 17, 2010, http://www.sappho.dk/.

35. "Lars Hedegaard Found Guilty of Hate Speech", International Free Press Society, May 3, 2011, http://www.internationalfreepresssociety.org/. In 2012 Denmark's Supreme Court dismissed the conviction.

36. Speech by Geert Wilders, Cornerstone Church, Nashville, May 12, 2011. Reprinted in *American Thinker*, May 12, 2011, http://www.americanthinker.com/.

37. Daniel Pipes, "How Dare You Defame Islam," *Commentary*, November 1999, http://www.commentarymagazine.com/.

38. "Israeli Apartheid Week on U.S. Campuses", *FrontPage*, February 22, 2007, http://archive.frontpagemag.com/; Joy Resmovits, "Horowitz Lambasts Columbia, Liberals", *Columbia Spectator*, October 29, 2007, http://www.columbiaspectator.com/; Patrick Poole, "Jihad U", *FrontPage*, February 14, 2007, http://archive.frontpagemag.com/.

39.   E-mail message from David Horowitz Freedom Center, February 9, 2012.

40.   Cited in Brigitte Gabriel, *Because They Hate: A Survivor of Islamic Terror Warns America* (New York: St. Martin's Press, 2006), pp. 161–62.

41.   Darwish, *Now They Call Me Infidel*, p. 223.

42.   Phillips, *Londonistan*, pp. 90–91.

43.   Sara Dogan, "Women's Studies Departments Ignore the Plight of Women in Islam", *FrontPage*, October 9, 2007, http://archive.frontpagemag.com/.

44.   Christina Hoff Sommers, "The Subjection of Islamic Women and the Fecklessness of American Feminism", *Weekly Standard*, May 21, 2007, http://staging.weeklystandard.com/Content/Public/Articles/000/000/013/641szkys.asp.

45.   Quoted in Sommers, "The Subjection of Islamic Women".

46.   Ibid.

47.   Christina Hoff Sommers, "Persistent Myths in Feminist Scholarship", *Chronicle of Higher Education*, June 29, 2009, http://chronicle.com/.

48.   Quoted in Robert Spencer, "Feminists Betray Muslim Women", *FrontPage*, May 21, 2009, http://archive.frontpagemag.com/.

49.   Mark Steyn, "The Silence of the Artistic Lambs", *Maclean's*, November 22, 2007, http://www.macleans.ca/.

CHAPTER FIVE: Atheists: The Descent of Man

1.   Warraq, *Why I Am Not a Muslim*, p. 40.

2.   Christopher Hitchens, *God Is Not Great: How Religion Poisons Everything* (New York: Twelve Books, 2007), pp. 38–39.

3.   Ibid., p. 38.

4.   Ibid., pp. 135, 102, 176.

5.   Kevin Miller and Ben Stein, *Expelled: No Intelligence Allowed* (film), directed by Nathan Frankowski (Premise Media Corp., 2008).

6.   G. K. Chesterton, *Orthodoxy* (Garden City: Image Books, 1959), p. 144.

7.   Pope John Paul II, *Evangelium Vitae* (March 1995), http://www.vatican.va/holy_father/john_paul_ii/encyclicals/documents/hf_jp-ii_enc_25031995_evangelium-vitae_en.html.

8.   Hitchens, *God Is Not Great*, pp. 281–82.

9.   Ibid., p. 283.

10. Miller and Stein, *Expelled* .

11. Lee Harris, *The Suicide of Reason: Radical Islam's Threat to the West* (New York: Basic Books, 2007), p. 35.

12. Ibid., p. xxi.

13. Ibid., p. xvi.

14. Ibid., p. xvii.

CHAPTER SIX: Multiculturalists: Why Johnny Can't Read the
Writing on the Wall

1. "Nicholas Sarkozy Joins David Cameron and Angela Merkel View That Multiculturalism Has Failed", *Mail Online*, February 11, 2011, http://www.dailymail.co.uk/.

2. James Kirkup, "Muslims Must Embrace Our British Values, David Cameron Says", *Telegraph*, February 5, 2011, http://www.telegraph.co.uk/.

3. "Nicholas Sarkozy Joins David Cameron and Angela Merkel View That Multiculturalism Has Failed".

4. Dorothy Rabinowitz, "Major Hasan, 'Star Officer'", *Wall Street Journal*, February 16, 2011, http://online.wsj.com/.

5. Ibid.

6. Ken Russell, "General Casey's Diverse Army", *American Thinker*, November 11, 2009, http://www.americanthinker.com/.

7. Dave Bohon, "Alberta Law Would Ban Homeschool Parents from Teaching against Homosexuality", *The New American*, March 1, 2012, http://www.thenewamerican.com/world-news/north-america/item/10674-alberta-law-would-ban-homeschool-parents-from-teaching-against-homosexuality.

8. Kevin Whiteman, "European Union Calendar Omits Christmas", *Examiner.com*, January 13, 2011, http://www.examiner.com/.

9. "Number of Gay-Straight Alliance Registrations Passes 3,500", Gay, Lesbian and Straight Education Network, July 2, 2007, http://www.glsen.org/.

10. Brian Lippincott, Ph.D., "Tips for Parents and Schools Regarding the Anniversary of September 11". This document is no longer available from the NEA but can be found at other online sources.

11. Quoted in Spencer, *Religion of Peace?*, p. 2.

12. Ibid., p. 3.

13. Quoted in Sandra Stotsky, *Losing Our Language: How Multiculturism Undermines Our Children's Ability to Read, Write and Reason* (New York: The Free Press, 1999), p. 143.

14. Mark Steyn, *The Face of the Tiger* (Montreal: Stockade Books, 2002), p. 336.

15. Don Feder, "The Jihad: We're All in This Together", *Human Events*, December 11, 2006, http://www.humanevents.com/.

16. Kurtz, "Saudi in the Classroom".

17. Elizabeth Gaynor Ellis and Anthony Esler, *World History: Connections to Today* (Upper Saddle River, NJ: Pearson Prentice Hall, 2007), p. 306.

18. Iftikhar Ahmad, Herbert Brodsky, Marylee Susan Crofts, and Elizabeth Gaynor Ellis, *World Cultures: A Global Mosaic*, teacher's ed. (Upper Saddle River, NJ: Pearson Prentice Hall, 2004), p. 571.

19. Roger B. Beck, *Modern World History: Patterns of Interaction* (Evanston, IL: McDougal Littell, 2007), p. 270.

20. Roger B. Beck, Linda Black, Larry S. Krieger, et al., *Modern World History: Patterns of Interaction*, teacher's ed. (Evanston, IL: McDougal Littell, 2005), p. 15.

21. Ibid., pp. 14–15.

22. Sarah Bednarz, Miyares, Shug, et al., *World Cultures and Geography: Eastern Hemisphere and Europe*, teacher's ed. (Evanston, IL: McDougal Littell, 2005), p. 209a.

23. Gilbert T. Sewall, *Islam in the Classroom: What the Textbooks Tell Us* (New York: American Textbook Council, 2008), p. 23. For a comparison of the Atlantic slave trade and the Arab slave trade, see Warraq, *Why the West Is Best*, pp. 104–15.

24. Julia Corbett Hemeyer, *Religion in America*, 5th ed. (Upper Saddle River, NJ: Pearson, 2006), p. 44.

25. Ibid.

26. Ibid., p. 46.

27. Ibid., p. 52.

28. Quoted in Amir Taheri, *Holy Terror: Inside the World of Islamic Terrorism* (Bethesda: Adler & Adler, 1987), pp. 241–3.

29. Quoted in news reports at the time. The word *tragedy* is commonly found in articles and books about the massacre.

30. Phillips, *Londonistan*, pp. 62–63.

31. Ibid., p.xxi.

32. Ibid., p. 51.

33.   Ibid., p. xxiii.

34.   Paul Weston, "Multiculturalism Has Destroyed the British Police", *Gates of Vienna* (blog), October 15, 2009, http://gatesofvienna.blogspot.com/.

35.   Harry Phibbs, "The Police in London Should Learn from Those in Manchester and Elsewhere", *Mail Online*, August 11, 2011, http://www.dailymail.co.uk/debate/article-2024308/UK-riots-2011-London-police-learn-Manchester.html.

36.   Phillips, *Londonistan*, p. 64.

37.   "Sharia Law in UK Is 'Unavoidable'", BBC News, February 7, 2008, http://news.bbc.co.uk/.

38.   Phillips, *Londonistan*, p. 139.

39.   Robert Spencer, "Is Multiculturalism Evil?", *Crisis*, November 8, 2011, http://www.crisismagazine.com/2011/is-multiculturalism-evil.

40.   Donna Jean Kemmetmueller, FSP, *My Muslim Friend: A Young Catholic Learns about Islam* (Boston: Pauline Books & Media, 2006), back cover.

41.   Ibid., p. 26.

42.   Ibid., p. 45.

43.   "L.A. Police Shelves Controversial Plan to Map Muslim Neighborhoods", Fox News, November 14, 2007, http://www.foxnews.com/.

CHAPTER SEVEN: Christian Enablers

1.   Faith J. H. McDonnell, "Guess Who's Coming to the Cathedral?", *FrontPage*, March 2, 2010, http://frontpagemag.com/.

2.   Dayna Harpster, "Islamic center, Fort Myers church team up," *Fort Myers News-Press*, July 23, 2010, p. B-1.

3.   Ahmad ibn Naqib al-Misri, *Reliance of the Traveller: A Classic Manual of Islamic Sacred Law*, trans. Nuh Ha Mim Keller (Beltsville, MD: Amana Publications, 2011).

4.   Peter Kreeft, *Between Allah and Jesus: What Christians Can Learn from Muslims* (Downers Grove, IL: IVP Books, 2010), pp. 18–20.

5.   Ibid., p. 110.

6.   Ibid., p. 9.

7.   Ibid., p. 12.

8.   Darwish, *Now They Call Me Infidel*, p. 80.

9. Wafa Sultan, *A God Who Hates* (New York: St. Martin's Press, 2009), p. 13.

10. Ibid., p. 14.

11. Kreeft, *Between Allah and Jesus*, pp. 170, 60, 43.

12. Ibid., pp. 141, 160.

13. Samir Khalil Samir, S.J., with Giorgio Paolucci and Camille Eid, *111 Questions on Islam* (San Francisco: Ignatius Press, 2008), p. 62.

14. Darwish, *Now They Call Me Infidel*, p. 201.

15. Raphael Patai, *The Arab Mind* (New York: Hatherleigh Press, 2002), p. 113.

16. Yale Center for Faith and Culture, "Loving God and Neighbor Together", November 18, 2007, http://www.yale.edu/faith.

17. "Pope Benedict's Remarks during Visit to the Dome of the Rock", Catholic News Service, May 12, 2009, http://cnsblog.wordpress.com/.

18. *Lumen Gentium*, no. 16 in *Catechism of the Catholic Church*, no. 841.

19. *Nostra Aetate*, no. 3.

20. Raymond Ibrahim, "Muslim Prayers of Hate", PJ Media, November 7, 2011, http://pjmedia.com/blog/muslim-prayers-of-hate/.

21. Ibid.

CHAPTER EIGHT: Questioning the Koran

1. *L'Osservatore Romano*, March 5, 1989. For a more thorough discussion of the response to the Rushdie affair, see Daniel Pipes, *The Rushdie Affair: The Novel, the Ayatollah, and the West* (New York: Birch Lane, 1990).

2. The argument that the Koran should be understood as typical of the prophetic-utterance genre is also an argument against the unique and matchless quality that orthodox Muslims claim for it. It suggests that Allah is unable to transcend a widely used literary form.

3. Hitchens, *God Is Not Great*, p. 129.

4. Serge Trifkovic, *The Sword of the Prophet: Islam, History, Theology, Impact on the World* (Boston: Regina Orthodox Press, 2002), p. 82.

5. Ibid., pp. 76–77.

6. Erich Auerbach, *Mimesis* (Princeton: Princeton University Press, 1953), pp. 42, 43, 44, 46.

7. Ibid., p. 45.

8. C. S. Lewis, *God in the Dock* (Grand Rapids: Eerdmans Publishing, 1970), p. 101.

9. The Muslim reply to the argument that the Koran is an anticlimax is that Jews and Christians had altered and distorted the original books given to Moses and to Jesus. Therefore, much of the Old and New Testaments are unreliable or false accounts that had to be corrected by the revelation to Muhammad. By this account the Trinity and the Incarnation are fabrications that contradict the pure monotheistic message actually given to Jesus—a revelation completely consonant with the Koran. Because these original, true scriptures no longer exist, the only way to discern their original content is to refer to the Koran. Of course, the chances are exceedingly slim that at some point, the original texts and the copies of them were rounded up and destroyed without leaving a trace (as many Muslims claim). This thesis flies in the face of the enormous array of documentary evidence which demonstrates that the New Testament versions that exist today—and which existed in Muhammad's time—are virtually the same as those that existed in the first century. For more on the historical reliability of the New Testament, see chap. 5.

10. N. J. Dawood, introduction to *The Koran* (London: Penguin Books, 2000), p. x.

11. *Encyclopedia Britannica*, 11th ed., s.v. "Koran", quoted in Warraq, *Why I Am Not a Muslim*, p. 111.

12. Mark Twain, "Fenimore Cooper's Literacy Offences", in *The Complete Humorous Sketches and Tales of Mark Twain*, ed. Charles Neider (Garden City: Doubleday, 1961), p. 632.

The criticism I offer here applies mainly to the stories narrated in the Koran, but problems with coherence and transitions can be found throughout. While one would not necessarily expect each new prophetic utterance to be linked to the one before it, one would expect some internal consistency or unity within each individual sura. This is quite often not the case in the Koran.

13. Malcolm Clark, *Islam for Dummies* (Indianapolis: Wiley Publishing, Inc., 2003), p. 109.

14. Thomas Carlyle, "The Hero as Prophet", chap. 2 in *On Heroes and Hero Worship*, http://www.online-literature.com.

15. Hitchens, *God Is Not Great*, p. 117.

16. For a thorough, well-documented refutation of *The Da Vinci Code*, see Carl E. Olson and Sandra Miesel, *The Da Vinci Hoax:*

Exposing the Errors in The Da Vinci Code (San Francisco: Ignatius Press, 2004).

17.   The largest community of Christians in Arabia at the time were Nestorians, a heretical sect that emphasized a separation between the divine and human natures of Jesus. Muhammad's denial of the divinity of Christ could be explained as a misinterpretation of Nestorian beliefs. On the other hand, the Gnostic heresy, which denied the humanity of Christ, was also widespread in that part of the world. The Koran's portrayal of Jesus as an otherworldly revealer who seems to exist in neither time nor space is similar to the depiction of Jesus in the Gnostic texts. Likewise, the Koran's insistence that Jesus was not really crucified echoes the belief, common among Gnostics, that another person was put on the Cross in place of Jesus.

18.   As indicated in footnote 9, Muslims contend that the Gospels that exist today cannot be a final revelation because they are not the true revelation given to Jesus, but a corruption of it. Therefore, the Koran would not be an anticlimax but rather Allah's way of setting the record straight. From this point of view, what is new and distinctive about Christianity is in reality a distortion of Allah's will.

CHAPTER NINE: Jesus of Nazareth versus Jesus of Neverland

1.   John Zmirak and Denise Matychowiak, *The Bad Catholic's Guide to Wine, Whiskey and Song* (New York: A Crossroad Book, 2007), p. 252.

2.   For a discussion of the possibility of miracles, see C. S. Lewis, *Miracles: A Preliminary Study* (New York: Macmillan, 1978). See also Craig L. Blomberg, *The Historical Reliability of the Gospels*, 2nd ed. (Downer's Grove, IL: InterVarsity Press, 2007), chap. 3.

3.   Ronald A. Knox, *The Hidden Stream* (New York: Sheed and Ward, 1953), p. 107.

4.   D'Souza, *What's So Great about Christianity*, pp. 295–96.

5.   Quoted in Josh McDowell, *The New Evidence That Demands A Verdict* (Nashville: Thomas Nelson Publishers, 1999), p. 34.

6.   Ibid.

7.   Ibid., pp. 34–38.

8.   Ibid., pp. 36–38.

9.   The game of "Telephone" is often used as an example of the inaccuracy of oral transmission. But it's not a good analogy. Why? First, people today don't have the kind of well-trained memories possessed

by people in oral cultures. Second, the whispering itself distorts the message. Whispered words are difficult to understand. By contrast, in oral cultures, histories and traditions were spoken aloud in front of many others who were familiar with the tradition and would have been able to correct distortions or variations in the message. Third, the message in the telephone game is a random one without any particular form, but this is not the case with oral traditions. For example, the sayings of Jesus, the "first player" in the Gospel "telephone game" were memorable and also phrased in a way that facilitated memorization. The parables were arresting short stories that were easily committed to memory, while the teachings were often expressed in striking images or in parallel phrases ("Blessed are the poor in spirit . . . ; blessed are those who mourn . . ."). Even today we have little trouble in passing on an interesting story or a joke we have just heard, and most of us can remember song lyrics and advertising jingles we heard as children. For those who think the telephone game proves anything about oral cultures, the best reply is found in the title of the 1948 Hollywood classic *Sorry, Wrong Number*.

For an extended discussion of oral transmission, see Gregory A. Boyd and Paul Rhodes Eddy, *Lord or Legend?: Wrestling with the Jesus Dilemma* (Grand Rapids, MI: Baker Books, 2007), chap. 5; also see Mark D. Roberts, *Can We Trust the Gospels?: Investigating the Reliability of Matthew, Mark, Luke, and John* (Wheaton, IL: Crossway Books, 2007), chap. 6.

10.   Dan Brown, *The Da Vinci Code* (New York: Doubleday, 2003), p. 234.

11.   The Gnostic gospels—the gospels that some believe predate those included in the Bible and were suppressed—seem to have been composed much later than the four Gospels and have far less claim to historical reliability. In addition, rather than portraying a more human Jesus, as *The Da Vinci Code* asserts, the Gnostic gospels present a picture of an abstract and spiritualized Christ who seems only vaguely human. For more on this see, Roberts, *Can We Trust the Gospels?*, chap. 13.

The Muslim claim that the original, uncorrupted gospel was supplanted by distorted accounts parallels *The Da Vinci Code* theory and, like it, has little basis in historical evidence.

12.   Boyd and Eddy, *Lord or Legend?*, p. 54.

13.   Ibid., p. 36.

14.   The Church Fathers had to wrestle with the question of authenticity as early as the second century because there were different accounts

of the life and teachings of Jesus circulating in the Mediterranean world
and it was necessary to determine which of them were reliable. The
four Gospels were subjected to a careful scrutiny very early on, and,
in fact, the Church Fathers applied many of the tests that modern
scholars now employ. They also avoided the temptation to "clean up"
the minor variations and apparent discrepancies in the four Gospels.
For example, a harmonized gospel was produced around the year 175
by Tatian, a Syrian Christian, but it never received official sanction.
Tatian melded the four Gospels into a single narrative that smoothed
away the differences; but the Church preferred to stick with the four
distinctive accounts of Matthew, Mark, Luke, and John, warts and all.
Moreover, no attempt was made to remove or alter material that cast
the apostles in a negative light. Simply put, there was no conspiracy in
the early Church to produce a more convenient Scripture. For a fuller
discussion of this, see Roberts, *Can We Trust the Gospels?*

15.   Boyd and Eddy, *Lord or Legend?*, p. 83. On page 16, Boyd and
Eddy list the criteria historians use to evaluate the reliability of ancient
documents. Here is a sample:

Do we possess copies of the ancient work that are reasonably close
   to the original?

Did the work intend to communicate reliable history, or was it
   intended to be read as fiction?

Was the author of the work in a position to record the history he
   or her claims to report?

How much did the biases of the author affect his or her historical
   reporting?

Do the works include the kind of detail that tends to accompany
   reports that are rooted in eyewitness testimony?

Does the work incorporate material that is "self-damaging"—that
   is, material that works counter to any bias the author seems to
   have, and thus material one might have expected the writer to
   leave out?

Is the work self-consistent or consistent with the other works that
   report on the same events?

16. Richard Dawkins, *The God Delusion* (Boston: Houghton Mifflin, 2006), p. 92.

17. C. S. Lewis, *Mere Christianity* (New York: Macmillan, 1952), pp. 40, 41.

18. Even if it could be established that the Koran we have today is the same as that which existed in Muhammad's time, the question of historical reliability is considerably muddied by the fact that there was only one witness to the Koranic revelation—namely, Muhammad himself. Moreover, what little the Koran has to say about Jesus seems to be based on historically unreliable sources, such as the apocryphal "infancy narratives" and the Gnostic accounts that were circulating in Arabia at the time. For those who are seeking solid knowledge of Jesus based on historical evidence, the Koran is not the place to look.

CHAPTER TEN: What Would Muhammad Do?

1. *Nostra Aetate*, no. 3.

2. *Sunan-Abu Dawud*, bk.37, no. 4310, trans. Ahmad Hasan, University of Southern California Center for Muslim-Jewish Engagement, http://cmje.org/.

3. For a fuller discussion see Joel Richardson, *The Islamic Anti-Christ* (Los Angeles, WND Books, 2009), pp. 55–57.

4. Quoted in Robert Spencer, *The Truth about Muhammad: Founder of the World's Most Intolerant Religion* (Washington, DC: Regnery Publishing, 2006), p. 185.

5. Malcolm Clark, *Islam for Dummies* (Indianapolis: Wiley Publishing, 2003), pp. 93–94.

6. Alfred Guillaume, trans., *The Life of Muhammad: A Translation of Ibn Ishaq's Sirat Rasul Allah*, (Oxford: Oxford University Press, 2004), pp. 463–64.

7. *Sahih al-Bukhari*, vol. 8, bk. 82, no. 797, trans. Muhammad Mushin Khan, USC Center for Muslim-Jewish Engagement, http://cmje.org/.

8. Gregory M. Davis, *Religion of Peace? Islam's War against the World* (Los Angeles: World Ahead Publishing, 2006), p. 43.

9. Ahmad ibn Naqib al-Misri, *Reliance of the Traveller*, p. 822.

10. Robert R. Reilly, *The Closing of the Muslim Mind* (Wilmington, DE: ISI Books, 2010), p. 69.

11. Ibid., p. 70.

12. Ibid., p. 74.

13. Ibid., p. 77.

14. Mark Durie, *Revelation?* (Upper Mt. Gravatt, Australia: City Harvest Publications, 2007), p. 113.

15. Lewis, *Mere Christianity*, p. 121.

CHAPTER ELEVEN: Don't Throw Out the Britney with the Bath Water

1. D'Souza, *The Enemy at Home*.

2. Quoted in ibid., p. 103.

3. Quoted in ibid., p. 115.

4. Quoted in ibid., p. 113.

5. Quoted in ibid., p. 117.

6. Cited in ibid., p. 188.

7. Robert Spencer, "The D'Souza Follies", *FrontPage*, January 30, 2007, http://frontpagemag.com/.

8. Robert Spencer, "How Britney Spears and I Cause Jihad", *Jihad Watch* (blog), February 1, 2007, http://www.jihadwatch.org/.

9. Spencer, *Religion of Peace?*, pp. 201, 203.

10. Katharine Boswell, "Bad Girls", *American Spectator*, December 7, 2007, http://spectator.org/.

11. Spencer, *Religion of Peace?*, p. 203.

12. Quoted in Spencer, *Religion of Peace?*, p. 173.

13. Cited in Lawrence Wright, *The Looming Tower: Al-Qaeda and the Road to 9/11* (New York: Alfred A. Knopf, 2006), p. 22.

14. C.S. Lewis, "Tolkien's *The Lord of the Rings*" in *On Stories*, ed. Walter Hooper (New York: Harcourt Brace Jovanovich, 1982), p. 85.

15. Ibid., p. 89.

16. G.K. Chesterton, *The Everlasting Man* (Garden City: Image Books, 1955), p. 253.

CHAPTER TWELVE: The Warrior Code versus the Da Vinci Code

1. Leon J. Podles, *The Church Impotent: The Feminization of Christianity* (Dallas: Spence Publishing Company, 1999), p. 12.

2. Ibid., p. xii.

3. Ibid.

4. Ibid., p. 23.

5. Ibid., p. 168.

6. Ibid., p. 193.

7. Kenneth Guentert quoted in Podles, *The Church Impotent*, p. 10.

8. Charlotte Allen, "Liberal Christianity Is Paying for Its Sins", *Los Angeles Times*, July 9, 2006, http://www.latimes.com/.

9. Podles, *The Church Impotent*, pp. 8–9.

10. Ibid., p. 67.

11. Federal Bureau of Investigation, "2011 National Gang Threat Assessment", http://www.fbi.gov/stats-services/publications/2011-national-gang-threat-assessment.

12. US House Ways and Means Committee, *Green Book 2003*, appendix M, "Data on Nonmarital Births to Adults and Teenagers and Federal Strategies to Reduce Nonmarital Pregnancies", http://waysandmeans.house.gov/media/pdf/greenbook2003/AppendixM.pdf.

13. Podles, *The Church Impotent*, p. 207.

14. Alain Besancon, "What Kind of Religion Is Islam?", *Commentary*, May 2004, p. 45.

15. Judith Miller, *God Has Ninety-Nine Names* (New York: Touchstone, 1997), pp. 26–27.

16. Roy H. Schoeman, *Salvation Is from the Jews: The Role of Judaism in Salvation History from Abraham to the Second Coming* (San Francisco: Ignatius Press, 2003), p. 297.

17. Ibid., p. 298.

18. Darwish, *Now They Call Me Infidel*, p. 81.

19. Harris, *The Suicide of Reason*, p. 272.

20. Mark Steyn, "Excusing the Men Who Ran Away", *Maclean's*, March, 5, 2009, http://www.macleans.ca.

21. Quoted in Bawer, *While Europe Slept*, p. 55.

22. Hirsi Ali, *Infidel*, p. 348.

23. "Onward, Christian Soldiers", lyrics by Sabine Baring-Gould (1865), music by Arthur S. Sullivan (1871).

CHAPTER THIRTEEN: The Moderate-Muslim Strategy

1. John McCain, speech on foreign policy, at meeting of World Affairs Council in Los Angeles, March 26, 2008, published on Council on Foreign Relations website, http://www.cfr.org/.

2. "Chertoff: 'Islam Has Been Hijacked by Ideologues'", *Jihad Watch* (blog), May 30, 2008, http://www.jihadwatch.org/.

3. Oliver North, "Politically Correct Terror Terminology", *Human Events*, May 16, 2008, http://www.humanevents.com/.

4. D'Souza, *The Enemy at Home*, p. 92.

5. Ibid., p. 93.

6. Ibid., p. 94.

7. Ibid.

8. Ibid., p. 93.

9. Quoted in ibid., p. 75.

10. "Indonesian Muslims Rally to Ban Ahmadiyya Sect", Reuters UK, July 18, 2008, http://uk.reuters.com/.

11. Mona Charen, "A Child Killer's Homecoming", *National Review Online*, July 18, 2008, http://www.nationalreview.com/.

12. John L. Esposito and Dalia Mogahed, *Who Speaks for Islam?: What a Billion Muslims Really Think* (New York: Gallup Press, 2007), pp. 69–70. See also Esposito and Mogahed, "What Makes a Muslim Radical?", *Foreign Policy*, November 16, 2006, http://www. foreignpolicy.com/. See also, Robert Satloff, "Just Like Us! Really?", *Weekly Standard*, May 12, 2008, http://www.weeklystandard.com/.

13. Quoted in Ajit Jain, "The Muslim Misconception", *Toronto Sun*, May 14, 2008, http://www.torontosun.com/.

14. Ibid.

15. Ibid.

16. Mark Steyn, "The Mod Squad", *SteynOnline* (blog), May 6, 2008, http://www.steynonline.com/.

17. Ibid.

18. Ibid.

19. Quoted in Spencer, *Religion of Peace?*, p. 18.

20. Quoted in ibid., p. 189. See also Phillips, *Londonistan*, pp. 122–23.

21. "Qaradawi's Ominous Return to Egypt", Investigative Project on Terrorism, February 17, 2011, http://www.investigativeproject.org/.

22. Quoted in Bawer, *While Europe Slept*, p. 67.

23. Ali Al-Faqir, interview on Al-Aqsa TV, May 2, 2008, cited in *Jihad Watch* (blog), May 10, 2008, http://www.jihadwatch.org/.

24. Quoted in Andrew Bostom, "A Study in Contrasts: Benedict, Tantawi, and the Jews", *National Review Online*, April 23, 2008, http://www.nationalreview.com/.

25. Ibid.

26.   Bill Warner, "The Two Kinds of Dhimmis", interview with Jamie Glazov, *FrontPage*, April 23, 2008, http://frontpagemag.com/.

27.   Spencer, *Religion of Peace?*, p. 85.

28.   Ibid., p. 87.

29.   Andrew C. McCarthy, "The Government's Jihad on *Jihad*", *National Review Online*, May 13, 2008, http://www.nationalreview.com/.

30.   "Council on American-Islamic Relations", Discover the Networks, http://discoverthenetworks.org/groupProfile.asp?grpid=6176.

31.   Pew Research Center, "Muslim Americans: No Signs of Growth in Alienation or Support for Extremism", Pew Research Center website, August 30, 2011, http://pewresearch.org.

32.   CNN News, May 18, 2008, http://edition.cnn.com/2008/WORLD/meast/05/17/iraq.quran/.

33.   "U.S. Soldier uses Qur'an for Target Practice" *Jihad Watch* (blog), May 18, 2008, http://www.jihadwatch.org/.

34.   Sarah Huisenga, "Gingrich Says Obama 'Surrendered' by Apologizing to Afghans", CBS News, February 23, 2012, http://www.cbsnews.com/8301-503544_162-57384194-503544/gingrich-says-obama-surrendered-by-apologizing-to-afghans/. See also "Senior Pentagon Official Apologizes to Muslims in Washington Area for Qur'an-Burning in Afghanistan", *Jihad Watch* (blog), February 24, 2012, http://www.jihadwatch.org/2012/02/senior-pentagon-official-apologizes-to-muslims-in-washington-area-for-quran-burning-in-afghanistan.html.

35.   Todd Starnes, "The Day the U.S. Military Burned the Bible in Afghanistan", Fox News, March 2, 2012, http://www.foxnews.com/opinion/2012/03/02/day-us-military-burned-bible-in-afghanistan/.

36.   Theodore Dalrymple, "The Gelded Age", *Claremont Review of Books*, April 9, 2007, http://www.claremont.org/.

37.   Steyn, *America Alone*, p. 193.

38.   Harris, *The Suicide of Reason*, pp. 198–99.

39.   Ibid., p. 19.

CHAPTER FOURTEEN: Is Islam Too Big to Fail?

1.   Quoted in Spencer, *Religion of Peace?*, pp. 40–41.

2.   Ibid., p. 42.

3.   Ibid.

4.   Gregory M. Davis, *Religion of Peace? Islam's War against the World* (Los Angeles: World Ahead Publishing, 2006), p. 123.

5. Bernard Lewis, *The Crisis of Islam: Holy War and Unholy Terror* (New York: Random House, 2004), p. 8.

6. Samir, *111 Questions on Islam*, p. 167.

7. Ibid., p. 168.

8. Robert Spencer, "Most U.S. Mosques Teach Violence", *Human Events*, June 14, 2011, http://www.humanevents.com/article.php?id=44147.

9. "Study Shows U.S. Mosques Repositories of Sharia, Jihad, and Muslim Brotherhood Literature and Preachers", *Jihad Watch* (blog), December 11, 2011, http://www.jihadwatch.org/2011/12/study-shows-us-mosques-repositories-of-sharia-jihad-and-muslim-brotherhood-literature-and-preachers.html.

10. Ahmad ibn Naqib al-Misri, *Reliance of the Traveller*, p. 602.

11. Robert Spencer, *Stealth Jihad: How Radical Islam Is Subverting America without Guns or Bombs* (Washington, DC: Regnery Publishing, 2008), p. 43.

12. Quoted in ibid., p. 16.

13. Greenfield, *Muslim Hate Groups on Campus*, p. 16.

14. Quoted in Spencer, *Stealth Jihad*, p. 195.

15. "Penn Judge: Muslims Allowed to Attack People for Insulting Muhammad", Yahoo! News, February 24, 2012, http://news.yahoo.com/penn-judge-muslims-allowed-attack-people-insulting-mohammad-210000330.html.

16. Pamela Geller, "New Docs Reveal How DOJ Kowtows to Muslim Brotherhood", *American Thinker*, January 23, 2012, http://www.americanthinker.com/2012/01/new_docs_reveal_how_doj_kowtows_to_muslim_brotherhood.html. The article contains several photocopies of correspondence between the DOJ and Muslim groups.

17. "Deputy U.S. Attorney General Orders References to Islam Pulled from Training Documents", *Jihad Watch* (blog), October 22, 2011, http://www.jihadwatch.org/2011/10/deputy-us-attorney-general-orders-references-to-islam-pulled-from-training-documents.html.

18. Robert Spencer, "New York Officials Apologize for Telling the Truth", *Human Events*, January 31, 2012, http://www.humanevents.com/article.php?id=49203.

19. Jerry Markon, "Justice Department Sues on Behalf of Muslim Teacher, Triggering Debate", *Washington Post*, March 22, 2011, http://www.washingtonpost.com/.

20. Joseph Klein, "The Obama Administration's Islamist White-Washing Campaign", *FrontPage*, December 21, 2011, http://frontpagemag.com.

21. Bruce Thornton, "Diplomatic Supping with Jihadist Devils", *FrontPage*, December 27, 2011, http://frontpagemag.com/2011/12/27/diplomatic-supping-with-jihadist-devils-2/.

22. The Venona Project was a US/UK intelligence program aimed at tracking communications prior to and during the Cold War. The release of the project papers in 1995 showed that several US agencies had been compromised by Soviet infiltration.

23. Spencer, *Stealth Jihad*, pp. 174–76.

24. Carol Glatz, "Pope Benedict's Remarks during Visit to the Dome of the Rock", *Catholic News Service* (blog), May 12, 2009, cnsblog.wordpress.com/2009/05/12.

25. Moorthy S. Muthuswamy, *Defeating Political Islam: The New Cold War* (Amherst, NY: Prometheus Books, 2009).

26. Winston S. Churchill, *The River War*, quoted in Mark Steyn, *Lights Out* (Woodville, New Hampshire: Stockade Books, 2009), p. 200.

27. Ali A. Allawi, "Islamic Civilization in Peril", *Chronicle of Higher Education*, June 29, 2009, http://chronicle.com/.

28. Geert Wilders, interview with Greg Palkot, Fox News, January 29, 2008, http://www.foxnews.com.

CHAPTER FIFTEEN: The War of Ideas

1. John F. Cullinan, "Basic Divisions Emerge", *National Review Online*, November 26, 2008, http://www.nationalreview.com.

2. James Hitchcock, "The Dynamics of Popular Intellectual Change", *The American Scholar*, October 1976. In James Hitchcock, *Years of Crisis: Collected Essays 1970–1983* (San Francisco: Ignatius Press, 1985), p. 230.

3. Ibid., p. 236.

4. Ibid., p. 238.

5. Ibid., pp. 237–38.

6. Al-Ghazali, quoted in Andrew Bostom, *The Legacy of Jihad: Islamic Holy War and the Fate of Non-Muslims* (Amherst, NY: Prometheus Books, 2005), p. 199.

7.   Father Zakaria Botros on "The Perverse Sexual Habits of the Prophet", reported by Raymond Ibrahim in *Jihad Watch* (blog), January 12, 14, 28 of 2009, http://www.jihadwatch.org/.

8.   Raymond Ibrahim, "What Did You Say about Muhammad?" PJ Media, May 12, 2010, http://pjmedia.com/.

9.   Kirk and Madsen, quoted in William F. Jasper, "GOProud and CPAC: 'After the Ball'", *New American*, February 12, 2011, http://www.thenewamerican.com/.

10.   Steyn, *America Alone*, p. 96.

11.   Ibn Warraq, *Why the West Is Best* (New York: Encounter Books, 2011), p. 90.

12.   Rebecca Bynum, *Allah Is Dead: Why Islam Is Not a Religion* (Nashville: New English Review Press, 2011), p. 52.

CHAPTER SIXTEEN: What Christians Should Do

1.   Steyn, *America Alone*, p. xv.

2.   Bawer, *While Europe Slept*, p. 34.

3.   Thornton, *Decline and Fall*, p. 134.

4.   Michael McManus interviewed by Kathryn Jean Lopez, "No Way to Live", *National Review Online*, April 14, 2008, http://www.nationalreview.com/.

5.   Amnesty International, *Annual Report 2011*, http://www.amnesty.org/en/annual-report/2011/middle-east-north-africa.

6.   Rachel Elbaum, "Abuse Plagues Muslim Women in Germany", MSNBC, May 25, 2006, http://www.msnbc.msn.com/.

7.   Soeren Kern, "Germans Stunned by Report on Forced Marriages", Gatestone Institute, November 10, 2011, http://www.gatestoneinstitute.org/2575/german-forced-marriages.

8.   "100,000 British Women Mutilated", *Telegraph*, April 22, 2012, http://www.telegraph.co.uk/news/uknews/crime/9219217/100000-British-women-mutilated.html.

9.   Katherine Kersten, "Radical Islam Gets the Better of Free Speech", Minneapolis *StarTribune*, September 25, 2010, http://www.startribune.com/.

10.   Bruce Bawer, "Unfit to Print", *FrontPage*, December 29, 2011, http://frontpagemag.com/.

11.   George Weigel, *Faith, Reason, and the War against Jihadism* (New York: Doubleday, 2007), p. 17.

12. "An Explanatory Memorandum on the General Strategic Goal for the Group in North America—5/22/1991", cited in William J. Boykin et al., *Shariah: The Threat to America*, Report of Team B II (Washington, DC: Center for Security Policy Press, 2010), appendix 2, pp. 281–82.

13. Ibid., pp. 290–94.

14. Ibid., pp. 33–35.

15. Ibid., p. 30.

16. Feisal Abdul Rauf, "What Shariah Law Is All About", *Huffington Post*, April 24, 2009, http://www.huffingtonpost.com/.

17. "Geert Wilders's 10 Points Plan to Save the West", the *European Union Times*, August 14, 2009, http://www.eutimes.net/.

18. Davis, *Religion of Peace?*, p. 123.

19. Bynum, *Allah Is Dead*, pp. vii–ix, p. 147.

20. Pew Research Center, "Pakistan: Growing Concerns about Extremism, Continuing Discontent with US", Pew Research Center website, August 13, 2009, http://www.pewglobal.org/.

21. Steve Chapman, "Repeal Religious Freedom at Ground Zero?" *Human Events*, July 22, 2010, http://www.humanevents.com/.

22. Lawrence Auster, "Answering Critical Questions about My Islam Proposals and the First Amendment", *View from the Right*, April 23, 2009, http://www.amnation.com/vfr/.

23. Kevin Myers, "Muslim Girls Are Covertly Prepared for Forced Marriage. Yet the Feminists Stay Silent", *Independent*, January 6, 2011, http://www.independent.ie/.

24. Quoted in Roland Shirk, "The New Conquistadors", *FrontPage*, December 31, 2010, http://frontpagemag.com.

25. Ibid.

26. Geert Wilders "The Lights Are Going Out All over Europe," quoted in *Jihad Watch* (blog), February 7, 2011, http://www.jihadwatch.org/.

27. John Derbyshire, "Christianity Good, Islam Bad?" PJ Media, August 21, 2007, http://pjmedia.com/.

28. Cardinal Tauran quoted in "Vatican Cardinal Decries Fear of Muslims, Says Saudi Arabia Should Permit Churches", CatholicCulture.org, January 6, 2010, http://www.catholicculture.org/.

29. "Christians Can't Vote for Wilders, Say Vicars," *DutchNews.nl*, February 25, 2010, http://www.dutchnews.nl/.

CHAPTER SEVENTEEN: A Fast-Approaching Future

1. Spengler, "The Mustard Seed in Global Strategy", *Asia Times*, March 26, 2008, http://www.atimes.com/.
2. Quoted in ibid.
3. Ibid.
4. Raymond Ibrahim, "Islam's Public Enemy #1", *National Review Online*, March 25, 2008, http://www.nationalreview.com/.
5. Ibid.
6. Pope Benedict XVI, Christmas message to Roman Curia, quoted in *Catholic World Report*, February 2008, p. 6.
7. Robert Louis Wilken, "Christianity Face to Face with Islam", *First Things*, January 2009, p. 26.
8. Ibid., p. 19.

CHAPTER EIGHTEEN: Fellow Travelers

1. Janet I. Tu, "Nonbelievers Sign at Capitol Counters Nativity", *Seattle* Times, December 2, 2008, http://seattletimes.nwsource.com/.
2. Meacham, "The End of Christian America"; Stone, "One Nation Under God?"
3. Jamie Glazov, *United in Hate: The Left's Romance with Tyranny and Terror* (Los Angeles: WND Books, 2009).
4. Reilly, *The Closing of the Muslim Mind*, pp. 179–180.
5. Claire Berlinski, "How the Term 'Islamophobia' Got Shoved down Your Throat", *Ricochet*, November 24, 2010, http://ricochet.com/. See also "Moderate Muslims Speak Out on Capitol Hill", Investigative Project on Terrorism, October 1, 2010, http://www.investigativeproject.org/.
6. Peter Sewald, *Light of the World: The Pope, the Church, and the Signs of the Times*, trans. Michael J. Miller and Adrian J. Walker (San Francisco: Ignatius Press, 2010), p. 100.
7. Soeren Kern, "Italy's Mosque Wars", Gatestone Institute, February 3, 2012, http://www.gatestoneinstitute.org/.
8. Quoted in Glazov, *United in Hate*, p. 163.
9. Quoted in ibid.
10. Ibid.

11. David Horowitz and Robert Spencer, *Islamophobia: Thought Crime of the Totalitarian Future* (Sherman Oaks, CA: David Horowitz Freedom Center, 2011), pp. 64–66.

12. Robert Spencer, "The Islamic Supremacist Propaganda Machine Cranks Out Another 'Islamophobia' Report", FrontPage, August 26, 2011, http://frontpagemag.com.

13. Glazov, *United in Hate*, p. 8.

14. Joel Richardson, *The Islamic Antichrist* (Los Angeles: WND Books, 2009), p. 164.

15. Schoeman, *Salvation Is from the Jews*, p. 31.

16. Ali Sina, *Understanding Muhammad: A Psychobiography* (LaVergne, TN: Felibri Publications, 2008), p. 265.

17. David Bentley Hart, *Atheist Delusions* (New Haven, CT: Yale University Press, 2009), p. 169.

BIBLIOGRAPHY

Bawer, Bruce. *While Europe Slept: How Radical Islam is Destroying the West from Within.* New York: Broadway Books, 2006.

Blomberg, Craig L. *The Historical Reliability of the Gospels.* 2nd ed. Downers Grove, IL: InterVarsity Press, 2007.

Bostom, Andrew, ed. *The Legacy of Islamic Antisemitism: From Sacred Texts to Solemn History.* Amherst, NY: Prometheus Books, 2008.

————. *The Legacy of Jihad: Islamic Holy War and the Fate of Non-Muslims.* Amherst, NY: Prometheus Books, 2005.

Boyd, Gregory A., and Paul Rhodes Eddy. *Lord or Legend?: Wrestling with the Jesus Dilemma.* Grand Rapids, MI: Baker Books, 2007.

Boykin, William G., Harry Edward Soyster, Christine Brim, Henry Cooper, Stephen C. Coughlin, Michael Del Rosso, Frank J. Gaffney, Jr., et al. *Shariah: The Threat to America.* Washington, DC: Center for Security Policy Press, 2010.

Caldwell, Christopher. *Reflections on the Revolution in Europe: Immigration, Islam, and the West.* New York: Doubleday, 2009.

Dalin, David G., and John F. Rothman. *Icon of Evil: Hitler's Mufti and the Rise of Radical Islam.* New York: Random House, 2008.

Dalin, David G. *The Myth of Hitler's Pope: Pope Pius XII and His Secret War against Nazi Germany.* Washington, DC: Regnery Publishing, 2005.

Darwish, Nonie. *Now They Call Me Infidel: Why I Renounced Jihad for America, Israel, and the War on Terror.* New York: Sentinel, 2006.

D'Souza, Dinesh. *What's So Great about Christianity.* Washington, DC: Regnery Publishing, 2007.

Gabriel, Brigitte. *Because They Hate: A Survivor of Islamic Terror Warns America.* New York: St. Martin's Press, 2006.

Glazov, Jamie. *United in Hate: The Left's Romance with Tyranny and Terror.* Los Angeles: WND Books, 2009.

Guillaume, Alfred, trans. *The Life of Muhammad: A Translation of Ibn Ishaq's Sirat Rasul Allah.* New York: Oxford University Press, 2004.

Harris, Lee. *The Suicide of Reason: Radical Islam's Threat to the West.* New York: Basic Books, 2007.

Hart, David Bentley. *Atheist Delusions: The Christian Revolution and Its Fashionable Enemies.* New Haven, CT: Yale University Press, 2009.

Hirsi Ali, Ayaan. *Infidel.* New York: Free Press, 2007.

Ibrahim, Raymond. *The Al-Qaeda Reader.* New York: Broadway Books, 2007.

Lewis, Bernard. *The Crisis of Islam: Holy War and Unholy Terror.* New York: Random House, 2004.

McCarthy, Andrew C. *The Grand Jihad: How Islam and the Left Sabotage America.* New York: Encounter Books, 2010.

McDowell, Josh. *The New Evidence That Demands a Verdict.* Nashville: Thomas Nelson Publishers, 1999.

Muthuswamy, Moorthy S. *Defeating Political Islam: The New Cold War.* Amherst, NY: Prometheus Books, 2009.

Patai, Raphael. *The Arab Mind.* New York: Hatherleigh Press, 2002.

Phillips, Melanie. *Londonistan.* New York: Encounter Books, 2006.

Reilly, Robert R. *The Closing of the Muslim Mind: How Intellectual Suicide Created the Modern Islamist.* Wilmington, DE: ISI Books, 2010.

Richardson, Joel. *The Islamic Antichrist: The Shocking Truth about the Real Nature of the Beast.* Los Angeles: WND Books, 2009.

Samir, Samir Khalil, Jr., with Giorgio Paolucci and Camille Eid. *111 Questions on Islam.* San Francisco: Ignatius Press, 2008.

Schoeman, Roy H. *Salvation Is from the Jews: The Role of Judaism in Salvation History from Abraham to the Second Coming.* San Francisco: Ignatius Press, 2003.

Spencer, Robert. *Religion of Peace?: Why Christianity Is and Islam Isn't.* Washington, DC: Regnery Publishing, 2007.

———. *Stealth Jihad: How Radical Islam Is Subverting America Without Guns or Bombs.* Washington, DC: Regnery Publishing, 2008.

———. *The Truth about Muhammad: Founder of the World's Most Intolerant Religion.* Washington, DC: Regnery Publishing, 2006.

Stakelbeck, Erick. *The Terrorist Next Door: How the Government Is Deceiving You about the Islamist Threat.* Washington, DC: Regnery Publishing, 2011.

Steyn, Mark. *America Alone: The End of the World as We Know It.* Washington, DC: Regnery Publishing, 2008.

Thornton, Bruce. *Decline and Fall: Europe's Slow Motion Suicide.* New York: Encounter Books, 2007.

Warraq, Ibn. *Why I Am Not a Muslim.* Amherst, NY: Prometheus Books, 2003.

Weigel, George. *The Cube and the Cathedral: Europe, America, and Politics without God.* New York: Basic Books, 2005.

Wilders, Geert. *Marked for Death: Islam's War against the West and Me.* Washington, DC: Regnery Publishing, 2012.

INDEX

Abbas, Mahmoud, 185
Abdulmutallab, Umar, 42, 215–16
Abedin, Huma, 31
Abraham, 102, 118, 120, 139–40, 172, 236
ACT! for America, 95, 199, 235
Adams, John, 242–43
Afghanistan, 20, 198
Ahmad, Omar, 32
Ahmadinejad, Mahmoud, 19, 65, 211, 259
Ahmadiyya community, 184
Aisha (wife of Muhammad), 47, 221–22
Akram, Mohamed, 205
Alamoudi, Abdurahman, 31
Alberta Human Rights Commission, 61
Alexiev, Alex, 18
Algeria, 20
Ali, Ahmed Omar Abu, 95
Alikhan, Arif, 31
Allah: and fatherhood, 172; inconsistency and unreasonableness of, 145; of the Koran, 141, 144, 217; and the Muslim conception of heaven, 147–49
Allam, Magdi, 186, 248–50
Allawi, Ali A., 212
Alms for Jihad: Charity and Terrorism in the Islamic World, 60
American-Arab Anti-Discrimination Committee, 206
American Bar Association, 239
American Civil Liberties Union (ACLU), 259
American Enterprise Institute, 55, 67
American Freedom Defense Initiative, 206

American Society of News Editors, 233
American Textbook Council, 85, 205
Amnesty International, 231–32
anti-blasphemy campaigns, 184, 232–34
anti-Semitism, 65, 188, 205, 259
Arabic language, 192
Arab spring (2011), vii, xi, 20, 204, 212
Arafat, Yasser, 188
Arnold, Matthew, 27
Arnold, Patrick, 164–65
Asia Times, 248
atheism, 3, 13, 70–76, 254; and common-ground arguments, 104; and Communist regimes, 57–58; and Darwinism, 70–76; Dawkins, 70, 72–73, 104; Fallaci, 55; Hirsi Ali, 54, 186; Hitchens, 70, 71–75, 104; John Paul II's battle against, 257. *See also* multiculturalism/ multicultural relativism; secularism
Auerbach, Erich, 115; *Mimesis*, 115
Augustine, Saint, 148
Auster, Lawrence, 244–45
Al-Awlaki, Anwar, 95, 233
Al-Azhar University (Cairo), 97, 204

Bagram Air Base (Afghanistan), 198
Bahrain, 20
Bardot, Brigitte, 49, 59, 209
Barna Group, 10–11
Bary, Rifqa, viii–x
Battle of Tours (732), 261
Bawer, Bruce, 226–27, 234, 256; *While Europe Slept*, 226–27
Benedict XVI, Pope, 49, 257; baptism of Muslim convert Allam, 248–50;